*To The Larkins —
Erin, Paige, Shea,
Tim & Helen —
It was a "WACKO!" suns
world, but a lot of fun.
Enjoy the read!
Uncle Tom*

2 WACKO!
Echoes from the Purple Palace

Tom Ambrose

2 WACKO! Echoes from the Purple Palace

Copyright © 2012 Ambrose & Company LLC

All rights reserved. No part of this book may be used or reproduced by any means, graphic, electronic, or mechanical, including photocopying, recording, taping, or by any information storage retrieval system without the written permission of the publisher except in the case of brief quotations embodied in critical articles and reviews.

ISBN- 13: 978-1466386143
Printed in the United States of America
This book is also available in Kindle format.

Front cover art by Ronald Lee Thomas
Back cover art by Tony Bustos

DEDICATION

To Tim Whitney, whose stories and actions always showed us the very best of life.

JERRY COLANGELO, A.K.A. "J.C." (LEFT) AND TOM AMBROSE

INTRODUCTION

Well, here we go again.

In **2 WACKO!** Tom has done a masterful job of relating some of the previously untold, back-stories that unfolded as the Suns organization not only moved into a new arena, but into a new era in team history.

The opening of America West Arena in 1992 was important to our franchise and our fans, but it was absolutely critical to the rebirth of a long-dormant downtown Phoenix.

Tom delves into the history and the personalities that shaped these exciting decades.

As much as we might like to go back and relive those remarkable times, regrettably, we can't. But reading **2 WACKO!** might be the next best thing.

Jerry Colangelo

Jerry Colangelo

Notes from the WACKO! File

Beginning in 1968 and spanning more than forty years, Jerry Colangelo served the Phoenix Suns franchise as general manager, head coach, president, CEO and chairman. Colangelo is chairman of USA Basketball and the managing director of the Men's Senior USA Basketball Team. The USA Basketball team won Olympic gold at the Beijing games in 2008 and at the London games in 2012.

AUTHOR'S NOTES

The WACKO! File was born out of frustration. Somewhere, somehow, I lost a classic, lunacy-laced letter sent to the Suns in 1976 by a certifiable nut-job who signed his work, "LOVE 22."

Pledging that I would never again lose a gem like LOVE 22's manifesto, I subsequently created and, over many years, carefully maintained, a collection of letters and communiqués that ranged from the amusing to the bizarre. I called it simply the "WACKO! File" For more than 30 years, the file expanded, page by page, letter by letter.

With Suns employees constantly feeding it the many strange requests they'd receive, the file, and its reputation, grew. Often, people would stop by my office and ask if they could take a look at the WACKO! File. Their reactions and laughter made me think that there might be a book lurking somewhere inside of that manila folder.

The late astronomer, scientist and author, Carl Sagan, kept his own WACKO! File. He called his collection "F/C," an abbreviation for "fissured ceramics," and code for the many letters he received from "crackpots." Dare I say that "great minds think alike?" No. I'd better not say that.

So, my WACKO! File begat the book, **Notes From the WACKO! File and Tales From the Madhouse on McDowell**. It wasn't long before **Notes** begat **2 WACKO! Echoes From the Purple Palace**. The whole thing was becoming downright biblical!

2 WACKO! picks up where **Notes From the WACKO! File** left off. I've included more of the baffling and bizarre from the WACKO! File, as well as stories featuring a new generation of Suns players. But there will still be some flashbacks to the early days of the Suns franchise.

2 WACKO! will also wander through some of downtown Phoenix's back alleys, so critical to understanding the history and vision of the city. Much of the book's focus will be on the Suns' top executive, Jerry Colangelo, and the many decisions that went into the new Suns arena.

As was the case with **Notes**, many names and dates have been changed, altered or redacted, as needed. Once again, I'll try to avoid tales already told in other books about the Suns. At the very least, those stories will be approached from a different perspective.

The chronology of ***2 WACKO!*** will clang off the rim, carom off the backboard, crash into the press table and sometimes ricochet off the scoreboard, but, no worries, each story will essentially stand on its own.

In retelling these stories, I was as precise and detailed as my memory, or the memory of others, would allow. **Notes** elicited much positive feedback from Suns fans, as well as many ideas for tales to include in this sequel. I deeply appreciate everyone's suggestions and contributions.

Imagine this narrative being like a couple of old friends, sitting at the end of the bar and swapping stories from their lives and careers. Most of the conversation is true, while some of it might be a bit embellished.

So, pull up a barstool, crack open a cold beverage, and enjoy!

– Tom Ambrose

TABLE OF CONTENTS

PROLOGUE xvii

CHAPTERS

1 – MAKING THE MOVE 1

2 – THE MAKING OF A PR GUY 19

3 – THE NEW ARENIAN ERA 39

4 – THE BARKLEY ERA BEGINS 99

5 – OBSERVATIONS 141

6 – DON'T BLINK 219

7 – SHAQ ATTACK 231

8 – LIVIN' LIFE IN THE NBA 251

EPILOGUE 313

INDEX OF NAMES 327

ALL ABOUT STORIES

"Some people think we're made of flesh and blood and bone. Scientists say we're made of atoms. But I think we're made of stories! When we die, that's what people remember, the stories of our lives and the stories we told."

– Ruth Stotter, Folklorist and Storyteller

"Remember only this one thing. The stories people tell have a way of taking care of them. If stories come to you, care for them. And learn to give them away where needed. Sometimes a person needs a story more than food to stay alive. That is why we put these stories in each other's memory. This is how people care for themselves."

– Barry Lopez, *Crow and Weasel*

"I like a good story well told. That is the reason I am sometimes forced to tell them myself."

– Mark Twain, Watermelon speech, 1907

PROLOGUE

This story's only connection to basketball was the fact that I was proudly wearing a Suns T-shirt when it happened. The Fijian Islands may seem to be an odd place to begin, but this tale relates to the importance of storytelling.

The story unfolded as I sat on a large mat of woven palm fronds, inside a native Fijian hut on the tiny island of Beqa (pronounced: "ben-ga"). I'm terrible at sitting yoga style, but I squirmed around and did the best I could.

Between basketball seasons, I was visiting Beqa for its amazing scuba diving. Several of the folks from our dive group had brought along some school supplies to donate to the island children. Subsequently, we were invited to one of the island's villages to take part in a kava ceremony. I wasn't exactly sure what that was, but we were told it was a great honor to be invited.

We were also assured that the native population's penchant for cannibalism had been curbed many years before. However, the fact that our host thought it was important enough to mention those old traditions did leave some residual doubt about local appetites.

I guessed that our little kava ceremony was the Fijian version of inviting visitors over to the house for morning coffee or afternoon tea. And it was like that, sort of.

Our small group was warmly welcomed to the hut, invited to sit down and then joined on the grass mat by several of the villagers. Six of us, sitting in a semi-circle facing the village chief, began to learn the story of kava, also known as Fiji yaqona.

2 WACKO!

Kava is Fiji's national drink and an important part of the culture in the South Pacific. A token of goodwill and respect, kava plays an integral role in virtually all Fijian ceremonies.

We watched closely as the yaqona beverage was prepared. One of the villagers used a cloth to strain into a large bowl of water, a powder-paste made from the pounded dry roots and dried base stems of the yaqona plant. The result was a milky liquid that, to me, looked like dirty dishwater. But don't let the appearance fool you, I was told, this is good, natural stuff, straight from Mother Earth.

In fact, kava has been proven to contain many positive pharmacological qualities. Along with its well-known numbing effect, it also manifests pain deadening, anti-convulsive, anti-fungal and sleep prolonging properties.

As I looked around the hut, I was heartened by the fact that I did not see a black cauldron large enough to hold a man, or any stew vegetables being chopped up. I ignored the fact that the cloth used for straining the yaqona looked like one of my old basketball tube socks. The kava was now ready.

Served at room temperature, a cup of the cloudy liquid was first consumed by the village chief. The kava was then passed around to others in a shallow, communal, coconut bowl called a *bilo*. Before accepting the bowl, you clap your hands once and say *Bula!* The word has multiple uses, but in this situation, *Bula* means "thank you."

As each person drank the kava, they would return the bowl, clap three times and say *Bula!* once more. We then found out, as part of the ceremony, it was traditional for each visitor to tell a story.

My mind was racing. Tell a story? Which one should I tell? Maybe I could do the joke about little Freddie? No, too crude. What about the priest and the rabbi who walk into a bar? God no, not that one!

In desperation, I glanced out the window of the hut and saw the steeple of a church in the middle of the little village. On top of the steeple was a cross. Thanks to Christian missionaries, these were people of Christian faith! I was inspired.

I gulped down the kava, which, not surprisingly, had an odd, dirt-like flavor. I handed the *bilo* back to one of our hosts and clapped three times. *Bula!* Then, I began my story:

"Once there was a travelling preacher, who went from village to village, spreading the word of God. He would visit churches just like yours," I said, pointing out the window at the church steeple.

"He was a preacher who believed in fire, brimstone and the wrath of God. During his sermons he would become very loud and animated. In response, the congregation would often stand, clap their hands, sing and shout for the glory of God.

"It was during one of those revivals, when the preacher held his hands high, looked up toward God and implored his flock, 'WHO WANTS TO GO TO HEAVEN? IF YOU WANT TO GO TO HEAVEN, STAND UP! COME ON! STAND UP!!!'

"Everyone in the tiny church was quickly on their feet, singing, cheering and screaming.

"Everyone, that is, except for one little old man who sat quietly in the front row. The preacher spotted the man, pointed at him and shouted, 'AND WHAT ABOUT YOU? YOU, SIR! DON'T YOU WANT TO GO TO HEAVEN?'

"The once raucous congregation suddenly quieted.

"The old man looked up at the preacher and said quietly, 'Yes. I want to go to heaven. But I think I'm gonna' wait until I die. It sounds to me like you're fixin' to take a load up there right now!'"

Bula!

***

> **Five minutes after drinking the kava, my lips went completely numb.**

Early the next morning, we were out on the dive boat and our two native dive guides were talking about the kava ceremony from the day before. They laughed and told me how much they enjoyed the story about the preacher. I was surprised they knew the story so well, because they weren't actually there for the kava ceremony. It seems that overnight, my preacher story had been told and retold in native huts throughout the island's three villages.

I was proud. My story had been entertaining enough for others to retell and it didn't ignite an international incident.

In retrospect, I was happy just to be able to finish the story, because about five minutes after drinking the kava, my lips went completely numb.

The lesson I learned on Beqa is that it's always a good idea to have a couple of stories tucked away in the back of your mind. You never know when one might come in handy.

Bula!

–Tom Ambrose

CHAPTER 1

MAKING THE MOVE

SIGNS OF THE TIME

Once the Suns were bounced out of the 1992 NBA Playoffs by the Portland Trail Blazers, the focus of the organization settled on two objectives. The first was to move our offices and entire operation from their location at Central Avenue and Thomas Road, into the new America West Arena downtown. The second, and more important goal, was to make a deal for Charles Barkley.

But there was the matter of clearing out our things from the Arizona Veterans Memorial Coliseum. So, on a hot day, late in the spring of 1992, I headed over to the Coliseum to pick up some of our stuff.

The Suns PR and marketing departments shared a tiny storage room, hidden deep in the catacombs of the Coliseum. Packed inside that room were the accumulated memories of 24 Suns seasons.

2 WACKO!

THE SUNS PLAYED THEIR FINAL GAME AT THE COLISEUM IN 1992

Even though, late in the Suns' tenure there, the Coliseum had installed a remarkable new electronic scoreboard including a massive television replay screen, the bulk of the team's Coliseum years were remarkably low-tech. Since the Coliseum didn't permit permanent advertising signage inside the building, sponsor signs were hand-embroidered on 4'x8' cloth banners and hung horizontally on wooden dowels. Every game night, a small army of Suns ball boys and ball girls would march dozens of banners, one-by-one, out of the storage room and up onto open wall space displays inside the arena. After the game, the banners would be taken down and returned to their racks in the storage room.

For most of the Suns' first two decades spent at the Coliseum, there were no electronic signs for sponsors or advertisers. All that would change dramatically in the new downtown arena.

Counted among those early Suns sponsors were many large, well-branded companies like Armour-Dial, Carnation Fresh Milk and Ice Cream, and Coca-Cola. But, reflective of the Suns' humble, grass roots origins, a good number of Suns sponsors were small, but enthusiastic, local businesses like the Weiss Guys Car Wash and the Spaghetti Company Restaurant.

CHEER FOR THE RED, WHITE AND BLUE

Boxed-up in a corner of the storage room were some red, white and blue banners and decorative bunting. Those brought back some great Suns memories for me, all of them playoff memories. Early in Suns history, Suns marketing mastermind, Ted Podleski, came up with the idea of decorating the Coliseum in a special way when the Suns were in the playoffs.

Somewhere, he made a great buy on patriotic red, white and blue decorations. Ted must have made a smokin' deal because we had a ton of the stuff. The fact that the Suns' official colors were purple and orange didn't seem to matter. However long or short the Suns playoff run would be, the entire Coliseum would be festooned in red, white and blue.

Some years the patriotic theme was so over-the-top that fans who arrived early to home playoff games thought they had walked into a Fourth of July picnic or perhaps inadvertently stepped through a time warp and into a 1930s political convention. Hey look! Is that Huey Long over there?

All kidding aside, the patriotic bunting was of immeasurable help to me later, when I was trying to identify photos for PR purposes. If I saw the bunting in the background of a picture, I knew immediately it was a playoff game and not a regular season contest.

SIFTING THROUGH THE MEMORIES

High on another shelf, above the banners, I noticed a battered, old cardboard box. Once I wrestled it down to floor level, I realized that I had uncovered a treasure trove of Suns promotional items from days gone by.

There were gift certificates for the Spaghetti Company offering two-for-one dinners. My mind drifted back to the night when the owner of the Spaghetti Company, Mike Pulos, blew out his Achilles tendon while participating in a promotional 3-on-3 basketball game at halftime. Ouch! They just don't make involved and committed sponsors like that anymore.

***

What's an autographed picture of Bill Cosby doing in here? Wait. I remember hearing about this one. It was early in the Coliseum days, the late 1960s or early '70s. Comedian-actor Bill Cosby was at the zenith of his popularity and was arguably, the funniest man in America. He was in Phoenix making a movie and stopped by the Coliseum one night to take in a Suns game. At halftime, he was asked if he would like to say a few words to the crowd.

Never one to walk away from an audience, Cosby took the microphone, walked to center court and proceeded to regale Suns fans with some of his classic comedy routines. They loved it.

When Cosby finished, he calmly walked back to the press table, handed back the microphone and then suddenly grabbed the game ball that was sitting there. Standing on the mid-court line, Cosby turned and launched a sweeping hook shot toward the basket. SWISH! The crowd went absolutely nuts. That guy knew how to entertain… and shoot! The Suns' official scorer, John Olson, only remembered that when Cosby grabbed the ball, he knocked a full cup of Coca-Cola all over the scorebook. The scoring stats from the first half of the game were literally washed away.

***

Time out! Here's another batch of coupons good for Baskin-Robbins ice cream cones. As I recall, they were the coveted prizes for the men's free-throw contest during many a half-time intermission. Unfortunately, they expired years ago. There was also an old gift box of Armour-Dial products, the usual prize for the ladies free-throw contest. I knew that it had been a few years, but I couldn't help but wonder if that Dial stick deodorant was still good. There was nobody around, so I tried it. It wasn't.

***

There was a blue surgical cap and mask from the night we honored Julius "Dr. J" Erving, on his farewell tour around the NBA. I remember a sellout crowd of Suns fans wearing the surgical masks and caps that we had distributed, Erving addressed the audience as "ladies and gentlemen… and fellow doctors."

***

Echoes From the Purple Palace

Digging down a couple of layers, I found an old sales brochure for the Suns' KPHO-TV television broadcasts during the 1974-75 season. The piece heralded the arrival of new Suns TV play-by-play man, Ray Scott. He might have been new to the Suns, but Scott was already a national broadcasting legend. He had been the CBS voice for the Green Bay Packers during "The Pack's" glory years in the 1960s. Scott's minimalist, staccato style was absolutely perfect for football on TV, but that didn't mean that Suns fans had to like it.

Unquestionably, Scott was a class act, but his debut marked a distinct change in Suns broadcasting philosophy. Suns fans had grown comfortable with the radio-TV, simul-cast style of their play-by-play man, Al McCoy. This new separation of radio and television broadcasts elicited a quick, and overwhelmingly negative, reaction from the Suns faithful.

I remember the situation fondly as one of my first big public relations challenges. I also recall Ray Scott going on the air just prior to the Suns' second televised game that season. He patiently explained to Suns fans the elementary differences between broadcasting styles for radio and television. They didn't buy it. From that day forward, most Suns fans simply turned off the sound on their televisions and cranked up the volume on their radios. They wanted "The Real McCoy." Scott left the Suns broadcasting team at the end of that season, and the Suns returned to a simul-cast format.

Many years later, a veteran director of NBA television broadcasts, George Wasch, told me that Al McCoy, "was an absolute master of the simul-cast."

When I asked him why, George told me, "Because Al will never insult his radio audience by referring directly to the television replays."

***

Hey, speaking of "The Real McCoy," here's the vinyl record album featuring Al's incredible play-by-play from those playoff series with Seattle, Golden State and then the NBA Finals against the Celtics in 1976. Wait! Are you kidding me? Here's an 8-track version of the album, still in its original wrapper. If only I had an 8-track player. Alas, they were buried long ago in technology's graveyard.

***

OMG! There's the old Gestetner mimeo stencil printer. What a beast! That old machine brought back memories of NBA Draft day and one of the annual rituals I performed as the Suns' public relations director.

The night before the draft, I would beg our basketball brain trust to give me the names of four players that we realistically might select with our first-round pick.

Then, I'd prepare four separate press releases, which, except for the draft pick's names, stats and schools, were all remarkably similar.

All four press releases would contain identical quotes from our coaches and scouts, who would enthuse, "We couldn't believe he was still available," or "He is exactly the player we wanted all along," or "We couldn't be happier, he's going to fit right in." My all-time favorite, overused phrase might have been, "This guy was born to be a Sun!"

Ultimately, when our pick was named the following day, his press release was immediately run off on the old Gestetner and distributed to the waiting media. The other three press releases were quickly, and surreptitiously, shredded.

I didn't feel the least bit guilty about it. An understaffed PR guy, given the limited technological resources of the time, had to stay ahead of the game.

THE POWER OF SUGGESTION

Rummaging through yet another box, what do my wondering eyes behold but a spare referee's shirt and a couple of whistles. These were items that each NBA team was required to have on hand in the unlikely event of a referee emergency. A typical "emergency" would be lost or stolen luggage, as the referees crisscrossed the country on commercial airlines.

It made me think however, that referee stories from the Suns' Coliseum days are too numerous to count. Engage an old Suns fan in conversation and, within minutes, he'll tell you about a game he remembers when the referees, unquestionably part of some elaborate conspiracy, would commit nefarious deeds of ill will and bad judgment, for the sole purpose of dashing the hopes of the Suns and their fans, whatever those hopes might have been at the time.

That spare officiating gear reminded me of the night that long-time Suns fan, Bill Howard, decided to call it as he saw it.

The Suns were in the middle of a knock-down, drag-out Coliseum battle with the Milwaukee Bucks and their massive center, Bob Lanier. As they often did, the Bucks, and Lanier in particular, were simply getting away with murder. And, as he often didn't, referee Manny Sokol was not blowing his whistle.

A time-out was called and Sokol came over to the scorer's table for a sip of water and a brief conference with the official scorer. That was when, from his seat in the first row behind the press table, Howard calmly and eloquently expressed his opinion on the way the game had been refereed so far.

> **"Lanier has you completely intimidated!"**
> – Bill Howard

"Hey, Manny," Howard said, "I think Lanier has you completely intimidated!"

Sokol shot Howard a somewhat crazed look and shook his head.

"No he doesn't!" Sokol exclaimed.

The horn blew, the game resumed and, within sixty seconds, Sokol ejected Lanier from the game. Proving, as NBA referees frequently do, that not only was he not intimidated, Sokol was large and in charge.

Nevertheless, the fans sitting around Howard, cheered, patted him on the back and gave him full credit for the ejection.

The Suns won the game and Bill Howard chalked up a win to the power of suggestion.

FROM THE WACKO! FILE: TOP SECRET

الاخبار و الاحداث => أخبار العراق => الموضوع المبدوء بواسطة: . في بناير

العنوان: وثيقة سرية تثبت تورط النظام البعثي البائد بقصف حلبجة بالكيماوي

وثيقة سرية تثبت تورط النظام البعثي البائد بقصف حلبجة بالكيماوي

تطلب هيئة الدفاع عن المتهمين في قضية حلبجة الشهيدة, من الشهود الذين يحضرون جلسات المحكمة الجنائية العليا, بتقديم أدلة حول قصف مدينة حلبجة من قبل النظام البعثي البائد بالأسلحة الكيماوية..

ردا على ذلك, هناك عدد كبير من الأدلة تثبت تورط نظام صدام المقبور, وذلك وفقا لبيانات وكتب صادرة عن النظام البعثي.. ففي 27 حزيران عام 1984 صدر الكتاب المرقم 5 أ\2\9871 والذي يحمل توقيع امين السر العام للقيادة العامة للقوات المسلحة العميد الركن طالع خليل ارحيم يحمل عنوان (دراسة استخدام العتاد الخاص في قاطع الفيلق الثالث), موجه الى وزارة الدفاع العراقية آنذاك.

وجاء في هذا البيان السري بان القائد العام للقوات المسلحة (صدام حسين) --في حينها- أمر بإستخدام المواد الكيماوية ضد العدو (وفق ما جاء في البيان) الذي يتجاوز الحدود.. وكان العراق في حينها داخل حرب مع الجارة ايران.

ويعتبر هذا الكتاب الصادر عن مكتب امانة السر للقيادة العامة للقوات المسلحة احد الادلة التي تثبت تورط النظام البعثي بقصف مدينة حلبجة في وبعض القرى بالأسلحة الكيماوية, كما وسيكون هذا الكتاب ردا لطلب هيئة الدفاع عن المتهمين في قضية حلبجة والتي يمثل فيها المتهم على حسن المجيد (على الكيماوي).

ما يلي نص البيان..

Author's Note: Yeah, I know. I have no idea what it says either and, I have no idea why it was sent to the Phoenix Suns. Since my Farsi is a little rusty, I had the document translated. Certain sections of the Farsi letter were redacted for national security reasons but I don't think you'll notice the difference.
Imagine my surprise when the following translation of the memo was returned to me from the Acme School of Baffling, Non-Native Languages. By golly, we may have found Iraq's "smoking gun!"

TOP SECRET AND PERSONAL

TO: MINISTRY OF DEFENSE

SUBJECT: DIRECTIONS ON HOW TO USE THE SPECIAL WEAPONS IN THE THIRD CORP SECTOR.

HIS EXCELLENCY (SADDAM HUSSEIN) HAS ORDERED THE FOLLOWING:

(This directive is written from the office of the Commander-in-Chief of the Armed Forces Command to the Minister of Defense and signed by Gen. Talia el Duri, The General Secretary of the Armed Forces Command. General Talia reports directly to the Supreme Commander, Saddam Hussein and shows him all documents before he signs them.)

  I. Don't use all the chemicals (chemical weapons) unless there is a personal command from him (Saddam Hussein).

  II. Use these weapons on the enemy when he crosses the borders (the borders of Iraq) and on his administrative forces supporting those operations.

Additional note written by hand by General Secretary of the Armed Forces Command, General Talia el Duri... "Dear Sir Minister of Defense, Please note the directives by his Excellency, Mr. President, the Commander-in-Chief, God keep him.")

Saddam Hussein in his own hand added the following directives:

  I. Be careful to remove all containers (where ever they may be) which are used for storing the special weapons.

  II. A special commission must assess the tactical situation of the enemy at the front.

I don't know if it is for our benefit and for the calculations of history that we handle this issue with written directive. I want to show that everything till now has been accomplished at the conventional weapon for use.

Signed by Saddam Hussein (in his own hand)

TOP SECRET AND PERSONAL

THE HIGHLIGHT ZONE

In that storage room box, I found a stack of blank forms which we'd use to set up and record details of all of our speaking engagements. Buried under those forms were a couple of the old 16mm highlight films I used to carry around to show to Rotary Clubs, Boys and Girls Clubs and other organizations.

The Suns no longer produce an annual highlight film, but back in the early days of the franchise it was a vital promotional tool that we used often during community appearances by the Suns front office. Now, there are endless Suns televisions "specials," including pre-season preview shows and season-ending retrospectives.

Most of the current shows are done, and done well, by the team's in-house video company, Suns Productions. In addition, local television stations, cable networks and even NBA Entertainment all get into the act. With every game of every NBA team now televised with multiple cameras and digitally recorded, there is virtually no limit on the highlights or feature footage available. It is remarkable how much the system and the industry has changed.

I thought there was room for improvement in those Suns highlight films from the early '70s. I used to joke that not only were the Suns always undefeated in their highlight films, they never missed a shot! Technically the films were fine, high quality, full-color, 16mm, covering our Suns stars and team promotions. The expense of shooting a game on film was a limitation, to be sure, but the films were long, predictable and lacked any type of story line.

Remember, back in those days, very few games were televised and video tape didn't come along until the mid-1970s. Even then, it took a while for both the film and basketball industries to adapt.

We had a great, game-action cinematographer named Sonny Stires who we would hire to shoot about four games per season on 16mm. That was all we could afford. But on a one-camera shoot, you never knew if the game would produce any memorable highlights and even if it did, you had to hope you were in the right spot to capture them. If you guessed wrong on where to set up, you could miss some potentially great shots.

Think of how many of the great, historical highlights from the early years of the NBA were lost because games weren't televised or shot on 16mm. The saddest and perhaps the most egregious example of this is that there is not one scintilla of footage from the night Philadelphia's Wilt Chamberlain scored 100 points vs. the New York Knicks in Hershey, Pennsylvania in 1962.

Much of the artful grace displayed by the Suns' high-flying Connie Hawkins, especially from his early years in the American Basketball Association, was never recorded. But sometimes Hawkins would make great highlights coincide with the games the Suns were shooting on film.

Stires remembered one game when Hawk, during a stop in play, was standing near the baseline corner and the Suns basket where Sonny was set up to shoot.

"How's it goin'?" Hawk asked.

"Terrible," Sonny responded. "I'm not getting anything good."

Hawk said, "Get ready. Next time down!"

So Sonny got ready and on the Suns' next trip down the floor, Hawkins did not disappoint. Making sure he started his move right in front of Stires' lens, Hawk made a cross-over move off the dribble, then, went behind his back as he slashed toward the front of the rim. Upward he soared, gently flipping the ball off the backboard and into the basket. It was one of Connie's classic "swoops to the hoop."

As Hawkins turned to sprint up-court, he ran by Stires' position and asked, "OK?"

Stires gave Hawkins a big grin, a "thumbs up" and shouted after him, "Got it! Thanks, Connie!"

PUTTING ON A GOOD FACE

Will ya' look at this? Here's the first mask worn by our mascot, the Suns Gorilla. I remembered that after we signed him to his first contract, I had to fly over to Los Angeles to find a proper, full-head, gorilla mask. I discovered a rubber "King Kong" mask in an old costume shop in Hollywood.

Many years, and many masks, later, the Gorilla confessed to me that the original, costume shop mask I found was probably the best and most durable of the assorted masks he wore. The others were more fragile and simply weren't made to last.

I remember one day when the Gorilla showed up at the office to show off one of his new, expensive, custom-fitted masks. The face of the mask looked great but the hair looked more like a teased out lion's mane. I thought it made the Gorilla look a little like the entertainer, James Brown, who was known for his pumped-up hairdos. "Go" did everything he could to tamp down his wild 'do and with some subtle surgery on the mask, finally got his unruly mane under control.

HOLD IT

Ryan Taggatz was a sharp young man who was applying for a spot with the Suns sales team. Although there were no openings for him in sales, he was asked if he might consider a job as one of the Gorilla's assistants.

"That sounds kind of interesting. What does a Gorilla's assistant do?" Ryan asked.

"Basically," the interviewer said, "you get to hold the comb."

NOT A GOOD HIRE

Ryan decided not to take that position as the Gorilla's comb-holder, but a few months later I had the opportunity to sit down with the young man who was selected as the Gorilla's new assistant.

"What a great job," I said to him. "You get to see all the games and then travel with the Gorilla all over the Valley for school appearances. You guys are like visiting rock-stars wherever you go. The kids love you!"

"Well, that's true," he responded, "And I do like the job, with one exception."

"What's that?" I asked.

He looked at me seriously and said, "I really hate kids."

NO PANTS

There was one thing I could never quite figure out about the Gorilla, but it never failed to crack me up.

The Gorilla's game night "uniform" was simply a Suns warm-up top. He never wore basketball shorts or warm-up pants over his fur suit.

Yet, whenever a skit called for "Go" to take off his jacket, he instantly reacted and covered his private parts as though he was suddenly completely naked.

But he never wore any pants in the first place!

INSIDER KNOWLEDGE

A million more Gorilla stories flashed through my mind, but there were a couple that still made me chuckle.

Henry Rojas, the original Suns Gorilla, was attending a pre-season Suns party at my home. He wasn't in costume and it was company policy to keep the identity of the Gorilla's alter ego a closely guarded secret.

Somehow, my five-year-old daughter, Casey, found out who this guest, Mr. Rojas, really was. She was so excited to have gained this "insider knowledge" that she just couldn't hold back. She quickly sought out our family friend and Coliseum announcer, Stan Richards, to share her secret.

Casey asked Stan, "Do you know who that is?" pointing toward Henry.

Stan played along and said, "No. Who is it?"

"He's the Gorilla!" she said excitedly.

"Well, s-h-h-h," Stan said quietly. "Don't tell anybody."

Casey quickly glanced over her shoulder to be certain that no one else was listening, and then whispered her reply in Stan's ear, "It's OK, he knows!"

FROSTY

During the late 1970s, the Suns participated in an annual celebrity waiters' night at the Spaghetti Company. Suns players, coaches and the Gorilla, all went to work as restaurant wait staff to raise money for local charities.

The Gorilla's antics were always a big hit with the many Suns fans in attendance, but there were issues. The Gorilla's costume was made of rubber, about a quarter of an inch thick, with the fur simply glued to the outside. Consequently, it didn't take very long for the man inside the Gorilla suit to work up a healthy sweat and start overheating.

During Suns games, timeouts and quarter breaks are just a few minutes long. That allows the Gorilla to perform a skit or do his high-energy dunks and then retreat to his dressing room, peel off his mask and cool off.

But the Spaghetti Company didn't have a dressing room, so the Gorilla improvised by taking his breaks inside the restaurant's walk-in freezer. He'd watch the hustle and bustle in the kitchen through the freezer door's little glass porthole. When he thought he was needed, the Gorilla would emerge from the freezer, grab a couple of the entrees that were ready to serve and hit the dining area on the run, refreshed and ready to have some fun with the fans.

No one complained about gorilla hair floating in their *pasta fagioli*, but some of the customers wondered how the food could be so hot while the Gorilla's fur was so cold.

A SUGGESTION TO CBS

Whoa! This is cool. It's one of those blue-on-gold CBS SPORTS banners that the network used to give us to hang around the Coliseum, usually to cover up the local sponsor advertising which they didn't want to be seen on national TV broadcasts.

I thought back to my first season in the NBA, 1973-74, which, coincidentally, was the beginning of a long-term CBS television contract with the league.

My first NBA league meetings were in Seattle during the winter of 1974. At those meetings, the NBA PR directors met with the on-air talent and the full support team from CBS Sports.

> **I know how you could improve your broadcasts about two hundred percent!**
> – Rudy Martzke

In the words of the CBS staff, the team PR people were "the grass roots guys who make everything happen." They wanted to develop a good working relationship with the NBA and they felt that the PR directors would be a key place to start. They not only asked for our help in developing story ideas, but they also asked for our opinions on how they could improve the quality of their telecasts.

Well, it didn't take long for Rudy Martzke, PR director for the Buffalo Braves, to raise his hand and say, "Yeah, I know how you could improve your broadcasts about two hundred percent!"

"Really? How's that, Rudy?" asked the CBS representative.

"Get rid of Elgin Baylor over there!" was Rudy's rather blunt response.

Baylor, a new commentator for CBS, was standing near the front of the room with a few other CBS folks from the broadcast team. He was slouched down a bit with his back leaning against a wall and his arms folded across his chest. With Martzke's stinging critique, Baylor seemed to suddenly inflate to his full 6-5 height and was absolutely speechless. Apparently this was the same problem Baylor was having when he was on the air. But the insensitivity of the remark stunned everyone in the room.

Martzke, however, was unfazed. He had just insulted former NBA superstar and Basketball Hall of Famer, Elgin Baylor, in front of a room full of people, but he wasn't quite done. Rudy wanted to be sure that his suggestion to CBS was not misinterpreted, so he held up his left palm toward Baylor, as a kind of "STOP" sign and added, "Elgin, don't get me wrong. I thought you were a hell of a player, but frankly, as a broadcaster, YOU STINK!"

I remember thinking, "A-h-h-h-h, so this is 'tact,' NBA style. Apparently I have much to learn."

Rudy Martzke later became much better known as the sports TV critic for *USA Today*, where, for years, he continued to rail against the TV networks, broadcasters and all of the major sports leagues.

I've often speculated that the PR directors' meeting with CBS that day in Seattle might have been the moment of awakening for Rudy, his epiphany, the day when he first visualized his future as a professional TV critic.

Even though I personally did not hear a heavenly chorus or see any sort of glowing light, I believe that I was there when it happened for Rudy.

CHAPTER 2

MAKING OF A PR GUY

SUM TOTAL

I fully believe in the theory that individually, we are the sum total of our experiences. That is, we are shaped by our families, our education, the risks we take, the choices we make, the books we read, the people we meet and the lessons we learn from our successes or failures. Of course, don't forget the stories we hear, the adventures we experience and the tales we tell.

I offer the stories in this chapter as core elements of my "sum total" and part of what went into the formation of this PR guy.

THE GAME

Growing up in New Rochelle, New York, had its advantages. Sometimes, through the Madison Square Garden connections of NBA referee Sid Borgia and our grade school basketball coach, Fire Chief Harold McAvoy, our entire team would get tickets for college basketball tournaments at the Garden. These games would always feature some of the better New York area teams like St. John's, NYU, and Manhattan College, but they would also showcase some of the top out-of-market teams like Utah, New Mexico, North Carolina and Duquesne. Without a doubt, the "big game" atmosphere at the Garden was a catalyst for the "big time" dreams for many young athletes. Count me in that group.

A few years later, when my friend, Johnny "J-Bo" Borgia, and I were in high school, his father, Sid, secured a couple of tickets for the December 30, 1964 Holiday Festival college basketball double-header at the Garden. One of the games would feature a showdown game between two of the top players in college basketball at the time, Princeton's Bill Bradley and Cazzie Russell of the top-ranked Michigan Wolverines.

The game was a sellout of 18,499 and tickets were being scalped on the street for ungodly amounts of money. Even though we had a few stressful moments proving to the ushers that our tickets were genuine and the interlopers who were sitting in our seats actually were the ones with counterfeit tickets, we ultimately were rewarded with a chance to witness one of the greatest college basketball games ever played.

Bradley was absolutely sensational that night, scoring 41 points and giving underdog Princeton a 12-point lead (75-63) before he fouled out with 4:37 to go in the fourth quarter. As he walked to the Tigers' bench, the Garden crowd gave Bradley one of the longest, sustained ovations I have ever heard for any athlete, in any sport, in any era. It was so out of control that the referees actually suspended play for several minutes without assigning a time-out to either team.

Until that point in the game, Russell had been completely overshadowed by Bradley's performance. But then, with Bradley gone, Russell went to work. In those final minutes, he led a furious 17-3 Wolverine rally, hitting a jump shot at the buzzer, to give Michigan an absolutely incredible 80-78 win.

It was a fabulous game, played out on the stage of "The World's Most Famous Arena," with talented athletes performing at the highest level. It was a never-to-be-forgotten life experience.

Some say that the game might have had a subliminal influence on me; a subtle nudge toward a future career in public relations. The only problem was, at the time, I didn't know the first thing about public relations. Like most kids, I wanted to be a player.

SPARE CHANGE

You often hear sports fans say, "I'd pay to see that guy play!" Well, there have been times, in spite of my fiscal conservatism (also called "lack of funds"), when I've stepped up and actually purchased a ticket to a concert or a sporting event. When I was in high school, the gangly, schoolboy superstar, Lewis Ferdinand Alcindor (later known as Kareem Abdul-Jabbar) and his Power Memorial Academy teammates were coming to White Plains, NY to play Archbishop Stepinac High School.

So, along with my Iona Prep buddies, J-Bo and Bill "Bonzo" Birns, I made the trip up to Stepinac, another Catholic high school in Westchester County. Admission for students was something like 75 cents, which we paid, grudgingly.

The doors leading into the Stepinac gym were about ten feet from the baseline and right under one of the baskets. Just as we walked in, Alcindor and his long, lean, teammates were going through their layup drill and dunking the ball with an almost laughable ease. The three of us looked at each other, chuckled and just shook our heads in awe.

This Power Memorial team was truly in a league of its own. In fact, back then, a lot of New York basketball fans could probably tell you the starters for Power Memorial, but I'm not so sure they could have told you the starters for the NBA's struggling New York Knickerbockers.

That 1963-64 Power Memorial team would later be declared "High School Team of the Century," by a vote of the National Sportswriters Association. During Alcindor's time there, they would forge a 79-2 record, a 71-game winning streak and three straight New York City Catholic Championships. They were just high school athletes, but they were the unquestioned rock stars of the time.

The thing I remember best about that particular game is that Stepinac "took the air out of the ball." They knew they couldn't compete straight up with this powerhouse that was virtually a pro team in size and stature. So their strategy was to freeze the ball on offense and zone up on defense. With no shot clock in high school basketball, all we could do was sit there and suffer on those hard bleacher seats as Stepinac passed the ball around in a "four corners" style offense. I remember thinking, "What a waste of 75 cents. I could've bought three or four gallons of gas with that money!"

But the game did offer some drama, because the Stepinac "Crusaders" kept it close for a while and had a shot at pulling off a huge upset. At times, Power Memorial seemed a little frustrated and impatient. It was ridiculously low-scoring and the game was very close at halftime, something like 10-6. Ultimately, Power Memorial settled down and came up with enough to win, but I think the combined scoring total for that game was close to Alcindor's 29-point scoring average a few years later, during his rookie season with the Milwaukee Bucks.

IT'S J-BO TIME

It seemed like Sid Borgia had been a referee his entire life. He blew the whistle for 19 seasons in the NBA, served as the supervisor of officials from 1964-66 and ended his career as supervisor of officials for the upstart American Basketball Association. Sid Borgia was a role model and big influence on a number of kids from Holy Family School.

Sid's oldest son, and my best pal, John, made his dad proud by earning an academic scholarship to Princeton, a roster spot on the Tigers' basketball squad and eventually, an engineering degree from that Ivy League university. But John was always hearing the sirens' call of distant whistles.

Even though he was successfully climbing the corporate ladder at Clairol and refereeing some local college games, J-Bo just had to try his hand at NBA officiating. He worked himself into position for a summer league tryout. When the NBA decided to try a three official system during the 1978-79 season, that was J-Bo's opportunity and he did not disappoint. He quickly impressed many veteran officials with his knowledge and skill level. With Sid constantly mentoring his young protégé, John proved himself to be a more than capable NBA official.

John did have one memorable moment that he once described for *Fastbreak* Magazine.

"Dick Vitale was coaching the Pistons and I had them against the Cavs in the Silverdome," John related. "As you might imagine, he was a pretty vocal guy on the bench and in the first half he already got one 'T.'

"In the second half, on a foul call that wasn't even close, he comes flying off the bench, up in my face. There we were... Italian nose to Italian nose. I gave him his second 'T,' which automatically meant ejection.

"He went completely off. He threw his coat and just went wild. A big, burly security guard ended up carrying him bodily off the court.

"You could tell even then that he had Emmy potential."

The best part was watching John trying to avoid a direct confrontation with Vitale. When they got nose-to-nose, J-Bo would just turn on his heel and walk away in the opposite direction. That seemed to further enrage Vitale, who would scramble around to once again get in front of John, who would then spin and walk the other way with the dogged Vitale in hot pursuit.

When it all unfolded on the video highlights that night, the whole scene had an amusing *Keystone Cops* quality to it. It was an unforgettable moment for J-Bo, but just another crazy night in the NBA.

HE SAID WHAT?

Back in the mid-1960s, a couple of NBA stars, Willie Naulls and Willis Reed teamed up to put on a summer basketball clinic at

Camp Kee-Wah in Pauling, New York. The camp was for boys between 8 and 15. About 200 campers and counselors were sitting on the floor of a multi-purpose room that doubled as a gym.

The youngsters were giving their undivided attention to these imposing professional players. As Naulls dribbled the basketball, demonstrating proper balance, posture and form, Reed offered some insightful commentary.

"Notice that when he dribbles the ball," Reed observed, "his fingers never leave his hand!"

WHAT WHAT

At the University of Notre Dame, I started out as a business major, but within a semester, I realized that business wasn't the best fit for me. Eventually, I would switch over to the College of Arts and Letters and change my major to English.

Nevertheless, I still learned a great deal during my brief time in ND's College of Business. I remember one accounting professor, Bernie Finnan. He was known to ND students as Bernie "What What" Finnan. It seemed that as he unraveled the mysteries of accounting for his students, he would constantly rely on a peculiar, rapid-fire speech pattern.

"So," he would say, "As we try to justify this item on the balance sheet, we would debit the WHAT? Credit the WHAT? Debit the WHAT, WHAT?"

During the first class or two, students would begin to raise their hands to answer the dizzying number of Bernie's WHATS, but we quickly came to realize that his WHATS were largely rhetorical. It was both amusing and confusing.

But it was also a means of separating the future accountants from the soon-to-be English majors, like me.

Those destined for a corner office at one of the big accounting firms would spend their class time physically counting the number of WHATS uttered by Professor Finnan. I think the record was over

100 WHATS and 16 double WHATS during a single 50-minute class session.

I didn't realize it at the time, but I was moving another step closer to a career in public relations.

EXCEPTIONALLY GIFTED

A few years later, armed with my Bachelor of Arts degree from Notre Dame, along with the accumulated knowledge of 22 years on planet Earth, I moved to Arizona and began my public relations career with *The Arizona Republic* and *The Phoenix Gazette* newspapers.

In a large company, with a big manufacturing component, the duty of taking people on facility tours usually falls to an entry-level PR person. In the early 1970s at Phoenix Newspapers Inc, publishers of Arizona's two largest daily newspapers, that person was me.

The newspapers were the largest printers in the state of Arizona and their mammoth presses were running virtually around the clock. The creation of your daily newspaper is quite a spectacular show and it was even more so in the 1970s when typewriters and teletype machines were constantly chattering, each line of type was cast in hot lead, and printing presses, three-stories high, would put out an absolutely deafening roar as they produced the final product.

As often as five days a week, the newspapers' PR department would host school groups on tours of the newspaper. It was company policy that these groups had to be at least sixth graders to participate. But there was one fifth grade teacher who called, insisting that her fifth grade class should be allowed to go on the tour.

"I'm really sorry," I said, "but they have to be at least sixth graders."

"But you don't understand," she objected, "these are 'gifted' children. They are 'exceptional' fifth grade students!"

2 WACKO!

"I'm sure they are," I responded, "but it's against company policy."

I thought that would be the end of it, but she called back at least twice a week for several weeks. After checking with management to discover that there were no real liability issues, I finally caved-in to her relentless pressure, deciding that it would probably be easier to just take these kids on the tour, rather than continue to battle over the phone. We booked a date.

Tours were scheduled for mid-morning, just as the afternoon newspaper, *The Phoenix Gazette*, was getting ready to print its first edition of the day. That edition was printed on green paper and was known as the "Green Streak." Timing on these tours was critical. If the tour ran just a minute late in some of the back shop areas, instead of seeing the exciting, last-minute, frantic activity to put the first edition "to bed," a tour might instead see everyone in that department on a "smoke break" or eating lunch.

But the timing of this tour for these "exceptionally gifted" fifth graders would go perfectly. As their guide, I must (with great humility) admit that I was simply outstanding that day in telling the story of what it takes to produce your daily newspaper.

I guided this special tour through the newsroom, the offices of the Associated Press, classified advertising, display advertising, typesetting and stereotype (where the printing plates are made) and the mailroom (where the papers are sent for bundling and distribution). Explanations were made. Questions were asked and answered. The timing was flawless.

Up and down multiple flights of stairs we walked, covering every department in Phoenix Newspapers' three-story building. Then, we headed for the basement and the press room.

The grand finale on the tour was always the press room where rows of mammoth Goss presses, each at least 30 feet high, would stand silently, waiting for the final printing plate of that morning's edition to be locked into position, before they could rumble to life.

And, smack-dab in the middle of that cavernous press room is exactly where I stood that day with this group of 30 "exceptionally gifted" fifth graders.

"Do you see that track in the floor?" I said, "In just a minute, the final plate that you saw being made upstairs in the stereotype department is going to roll down that track. The pressman that you see right here is going to pick up that plate, lock it into position and then he is going to hit a button and start the presses. Once he does that, and the presses start to roll, it will be so loud in here that you will not be able to hear me, so watch for my signal and then follow me out. OK?"

The gifted ones nodded their understanding.

> **The gifted ones nodded their understanding.**

Right on schedule, the final plate rumbled down the track and stopped at the pressman's feet. He lifted the heavy, curved, metal plate and locked it into position. He closed the safety cover on the press and then rang a warning bell so that all hands were clear. The heavy-duty electric motors began winding up and the presses started to roll.

They turned rhythmically, slowly at first, but then quickly picked up speed and sound. You could see the giant rolls of newsprint, each five feet wide, feeding a continuous sheet into this beast of a press. And the noise, like low, rumbling thunder, began to rise. It built to a crescendo until the sound and vibration from these giant printing presses reverberated through your bones. We watched with amazement as the newly cut, folded and completed newspapers literally flew up a vertical conveyor belt to the mail room for bundling and distribution.

Most of the kids began to cover their ears from the noise. That's when I knew it was time to "head 'em up and move 'em out." I began waving for everyone to follow me and we walked out of the press room. From experience I knew that the concept of the "power of the press" was nothing when compared to the thunderous power of the presses. This was something that these kids would be talking about for a long time.

With the ear-numbing noise from the presses fading away behind us, we walked down a long hallway, past a storage room where ink was stored in 50-gallon drums. Then, we passed through a heavily insulated door and, finally, into the absolute silence of a stairwell leading up to the lobby and the end of our tour.

I was feeling pretty good about how well the tour had gone and that I would no longer have to deal with this pesky teacher. Just then, after an intense, 50 minute lesson on every aspect of what it takes to produce your daily newspaper, one of the "exceptionally gifted" fifth-graders, in a delayed reaction to the overwhelming noise and excitement of the press room, exclaimed, "Holy cow, mister! What were they makin' in there?"

That's when I began to think that it might be time to move on to the next phase of my public relations career, whatever that might be.

NO HAT

When the students returned to their schools after one of my tours, invariably the teachers would ask each child to write me a thank you note or draw a picture. They would then be bundled up and mailed to me (the notes and drawings, not the kids). It was always interesting to see how they processed what they observed on their tour of the newspaper.

I once brought a batch of letters and drawings home to look at overnight, but my wife started reading them first.

"Do you wear a hat when you're at work?" Alice asked.

"A hat? No. Why?" I responded.

"In every one of these drawings it shows you and the kids standing on stairs, but they always draw you with a hat." Alice explained.

Sure enough, in every drawing I was wearing something that looked like a cross between a French Foreign Legionnaire's *kepi* and a conductor's hat from the New Haven Railroad. I guess that was the kids' way of depicting and differentiating their tour guide from their teacher.

I suppose the railroad conductor thing could be a fall-back career for me.

"Tickets please! Tickets! Next stop, New Rochelle! New Rochelle next!"

VARIATION ON A THEME

Longtime Philadelphia 76ers public address announcer, Dave Zinkoff had a distinctive style...or styles. When he introduced 76ers super-star Julius Erving, it went something like:

"The Dak-t-a-a... J-u-u-u-u-u-u-u-u-u-u-u-u-u-lee-us...

E-r-r-r-r-r-r-r-r-r-r-r-r-r-r-ving!"

But when forward, Garfield Heard of the Buffalo Braves scored a basket in Philly, "Zink's" call was a very flat, very monotone, yet still creative, "Heard... Buffalo."

FROM THE WACKO! FILE: ALL IN THE FAMILY

Author's Note: I am very proud of my youngest brother, Dick. As I was revving up my PR career in Phoenix in the early 1970s, my brother was a sophomore football player at the University of Virginia. When I read this August 19, 1973 column about him, I thought perhaps that Dick was destined to become the family "spin doctor," not me.

The following column appeared in the Richmond Times-Dispatch, written by Executive Sports Editor, Bill Millsaps, and is reprinted here with permission. It was saved in the WACKO! File for nearly 40 years for just "the right time." That time is now.

A PLATE OF GLASS

CHARLOTTESVILLE –

When Dick Ambrose wants a special culinary treat, he doesn't go down to the ice cream store and order a double hot fudge sundae. The University of Virginia football player likes to chow down on glass.

You read it right. Glass.

"I started out with just ordinary drinking glass," said Ambrose, "about two years ago. Then I went on to those thin beer glasses, the kind that flare out from the bottom. This summer, I tried eating a beer bottle but it was too thick and I chipped a tooth."

Damage to his smile worried Ambrose more than any possible havoc that might have been wrought in his gastrointestinal tract, so he had a dentist check out his teeth.

"He said the teeth look OK.

"It's not that I eat glass all the time. Sometimes I go for weeks without it. But then I get the feeling that I want some, and I'll get me a glass and eat it."

It isn't that Ambrose, an educational research major, is crazy. He's just a linebacker. One must be indulgent with linebackers, especially with a fellow like Ambrose.

"Naw, Dick isn't nuts," said U. Va. safetyman Gerard Mullins. "He keeps it under control. When he's playing, he turns it on and off between plays. He's a madman only when the ball is in play."

On the football field, this ferocity is one of Ambrose's trademarks. As a sophomore last season, he was one of the Atlantic Coast Conference's best defensive tackles, and when he was moved to strong side linebacker this spring, he immediately began looking like an all-star at his new position.

U. Va. Coach Don Lawrence laughed when asked if Ambrose had any difficulty adjusting to his new position. "In our first scrimmage this spring," said Lawrence, "we played him at defensive tackle and he looked great. In our second scrimmage, he was a linebacker and he still looked great. Dick is a born hitter, a terrific player. He could be a good fullback, but he can hurt our opponents a lot worse as a linebacker."

Ambrose did not come to U. Va. with a great reputation. In fact, it's a wonder that he came to U. Va. at all.

At Iona Prep in New Rochelle, N.Y., he was a 6-0, 190-pound fullback who received very little recruiting rush. He wanted to hear from Southern Cal, but about the best he could do was Yale, Dartmouth, Princeton, South Carolina and Virginia.

Yale, Dartmouth and Princeton would not give him a scholarship because their grants are based on need. And Ambrose's father is treasurer of the National Association of Manufacturers; which hardly makes him a candidate for financial assistance.

Virginia did, however, promise a scholarship and Ambrose signed with the Cavaliers. It was a near thing, however, for Ambrose was the last freshman signed during the recruiting season of 1971. "We held out to the last before offering him a scholarship," said one U. Va. coach, "because we were worried about his size. We almost didn't offer it to him."

When Ambrose got to Charlottesville, he quickly began making the coaches forget about their earlier worries. He was bullish fullback for the freshman team, but when spring drills rolled around, U. Va. coaches decided that Ambrose could help fill the huge hole left at defensive tackle when Andy Selfridge graduated.

Ambrose bulked up to 230 pounds and began throwing his newfound weight around. He has an instinct, the kind a coach cannot teach, for the whereabouts of the football. It was natural, then, that Ambrose would figure in the defensive changes that took place last spring.

Ambrose enjoys his new position better than his old one. "At tackle," he said Saturday (two days before the start of the Cav's fall practice). You just get lost in a mass of grunting, groaning bodies. You can't see things develop, you can't see the ball as quickly and where it's going, like you can at linebacker.

"The big thing I have to learn now is to adjust to the passing game."

Like nearly every other college linebacker extant, Ambrose admires Dick Butkus "for his hitting ability," but he doesn't think much of the way the Bears' bruiser defends against the pass. "I kind of like Mike Curtis, too, and I've been a big fan of Les Richter (a long-retired LA Ram) since I was a kid."

Ambrose has heard and read some very nice things about his performance as a football player, and he is looking toward a career in the pros.

Many pro scouts wonder if Ambrose is fast enough to play corner linebacker in the NFL. "To gain the speed," said Ambrose, "I'd have to lose 20 pounds, and then I'd wonder about my strength.

"I ran a 4.9 (in the 40-yard dash) this spring. A few weeks ago back in New Rochelle, a guy with a crummy watch times me in 5.05. If I don't run a 4.9 the first day of practice here, the coaches are gonna kill me."

Ambrose does not believe he is tall enough to play middle linebacker in the pros.

"You know," he sighed, "If I was 6'3" I'd be just about perfect." Laughing, he added, "Do you know of any company that makes high heel cleats?"

Author's Postscript: A few years later, Dick Ambrose would be drafted by the National Football League's Cleveland Browns, where he would enjoy an outstanding, nine-year career as their middle linebacker. Today, my youngest brother is a respected judge in Cleveland's Cuyahoga County Court of Common Pleas and he has given up eating glass in favor of more traditional snacks.

The real lesson here is that you shouldn't, believe everything you read in your daily newspaper. My suggestion is that you take all things with a dash of skepticism or perhaps with a grain of salt, but never, ever, with a shard of glass.

DICK AMBROSE AT THE UNIVERSITY OF VIRGINIA

NO GOOD DEED

Another brother, Michael Francis Aloysius Ambrose, is the consummate storyteller. He once told me about a bitterly cold winter when he was working at a convention in Philadelphia. His hotel was only about five blocks from the convention center, so each morning Mike would get up early, stop by a little shop for coffee and a muffin and then walk the short distance to the convention hall. On the first day, as he made his way along the snowy street, he walked passed a man who was curled up on the sidewalk, wrapped in multiple layers of blankets and clothing. All that day, Mike just couldn't shake from his mind the image of that poor soul on the sidewalk.

So, on the second day, he once again stopped by the coffee shop, but this time he bought an extra coffee and a blueberry muffin. As he walked toward the convention center, the same man was wrapped up in his cocoon in the same spot on the sidewalk. Mike walked over and gently placed the coffee and muffin near the sleeping man. The raggedy pile never moved.

On the third day, Mike tried to repeat his act of kindness, but when he placed the items on the sidewalk near the sleeping vagrant, the man quickly sat up.

"Are you the guy who left me the coffee and blueberry muffin yesterday?" the man asked Mike.

"Yeah, that was me," Mike said, anticipating a word of thanks.

"Well," the man said with a bit of an attitude, "I don't like blueberries!"

FLASHBACK

When I was in high school back in New Rochelle, I had a small reel-to-reel tape recorder that I often used to record radio broadcasts of some of my favorite New York teams – the NHL's Rangers, the NFL's Giants and the NBA's Knickerbockers.

It was a very low-tech operation. When a game broadcast started, I just parked the microphone in front of the radio's

Echoes From the Purple Palace

speaker and let the tape roll. When the game was over, I would go back and edit all of the high-energy, play-by-play highlights from those game tapes and splice them onto a special reel.

Some athletes listen to rock music to get "amped up," but on a night before I played in a big game, I would always listen to that play-by-play highlight tape over and over, in order to "get psyched."

Back then, a New York sportscaster named Win Elliot called the action for the Rangers and he became a frequent contributor to my "best of" tape. I still get goose bumps when I remember his passionate call over the thunderous roar of a Madison Square Garden hockey crowd, "...the puck goes over to Goyette. He shoots! SCORE! SCORE! SCORE!"

Many years had gone by and I was in my courtside seat at the Coliseum as the Suns battled Julius Erving and the Philadelphia 76ers in a nationally-televised game. It was about midway through the first quarter and everything seemed to be going smoothly. Just then, my courtside phone rang.

"Press table!"

"Hello. This is CBS radio in New York and I'd like to arrange for a stringer to call in some post-game reports."

PR people do this kind of thing all the time and it is generally not a problem, but it's really nice when all these things are arranged before the game, not during it. So I got a little huffy with this guy.

"Look, we are in the middle of the game and I'm not sure that I can find someone for you right away," I said curtly. "It would have been nice if you had called earlier."

"I know and I'm sorry," he responded. "This is Win Elliot and I..."

"Win Elliot!?" I all but shouted. "THEE Win Elliot?"

"Why, yes..."

"Mr. Elliot, don't worry about it." I said breathlessly. "Give me the phone numbers and I will personally take care of it. If I can't find someone to do it for you, I will do it myself!"

I had gone from "offended tough guy" to "wimpy hero worshiper" in the span of about three seconds.

I thought about engaging "Mr. Elliot" in conversation and telling him about the tapes I used to make, but then I quickly came to my senses, took down his numbers and respectfully ended the call.

It was a strange moment because I had never actually met the man. I only knew his play-by-play voice and now, his voice over the phone. But like an old favorite song, it took me back to those youthful days when I listened to those tapes and his exciting words-eye-view, over and over and over.

Win Elliot, a New York broadcasting legend, passed away in 1998.

A CLASSIC INTRO

The long-time voice of New York's Madison Square Garden was the venerable John Condon, a true gentleman and a professional of the highest order. One night he made his typically eloquent introduction of the National Anthem.

"And now, ladies and gentlemen, the New York Knickerbockers are pleased to present our National Anthem, played for you tonight on the Madison Square Garden organ by Miss Gladys Gooding."

As the crowd slowly rose to its feet, a respectful silence hushed the Garden, until some leather-lung New Yorker shouted out for all to hear, "Gladys Gooding SUCKS!"

Condon, unfazed, didn't miss a beat as he smoothly followed with, "Nevertheless… Miss Gladys Gooding!"

A QUESTIONABLE QUESTIONNAIRE

College sports information directors and their professional sports cousins, the PR directors, usually ask all new players to fill out some type of personal information questionnaire.

The questionnaires are designed to provide information that can later be turned into story lines for the media. Questions range from information about the population of their hometown, to the coach or person who had the greatest influence on their lives, their favorite music, their biggest sports hero or what they might want to do when their sports careers are over.

Then there are the questionnaires that take some twisted turns, like those that ask, "If you were a tree, what kind of tree would you be?"

I was explaining this to a local radio reporter, Bob Huhn, who seemed very interested. So, I couldn't resist spinning him a tale about a questionnaire the Suns PR department asked players to fill out during the early days of the franchise.

In addition to the usual questions, there were a few queries on this document that could be categorized as being "a little different."

> **"Why is the thermos bottle the greatest invention of all time?"**

One in particular was, "In your opinion, what is has been the world's greatest invention?"

The question was not as puzzling as the response the PR staff got back from one rookie player who answered, "the thermos bottle."

"OK, rook, we'll bite," said a PR staffer. "Why is the thermos bottle the greatest invention of all time?"

"Well," the rookie began, "it keeps cold drinks cold when it's hot out. Right? And it keeps hot soup hot when it's cold out. Right?"

"Yeah," the staffer agreed, "but how does that make it the greatest invention ever?"

The rookie's face lit up as he said with amazement, "How do it know?"

My tale thus told, Huhn looked at me skeptically, one eyebrow raised.

"Hey," I said defensively, "it happened before I got here!"

CHAPTER 3

THE NEW ARENIAN ERA

LOCATION, LOCATION, LOCATION

Jerry Colangelo was born and raised in Chicago. Even though, by 1988, he'd lived and worked in Phoenix for more than 20 years, he remained, unquestionably, an "urban" guy. That fact would play mightily in the location of the Suns' new arena.

Looking around the Valley at the time, there were several possible sites for a new Suns facility. Along with a lot of other folks, I thought that a suburban arena was the answer, since many businesses and most people had already fled downtown Phoenix. On weekdays, the main business district in the city's center was a ghost town by 6 p.m. The East Valley was where most Suns fans now resided, so why not put the new arena in a convenient spot for them?

I personally thought that a large, open and available tract of land near the intersection of Interstate 10 and US 60 on the border of Phoenix and Tempe would be ideal, but I was just the PR guy, what did I know? That location was quickly dismissed as a possible arena site, but soon afterward, it would be developed as the Arizona Mills shopping mall.

Suns CFO, Rich Dozer, thought that another huge tract of vacant land, just off AZ 202 at 40th Street in Phoenix, was not only available, but also offered considerable financial advantages. That site was also rejected.

Both of these outlying locations were close to freeways, but probably a little too close. Traffic studies for game night access and egress predicted major congestion and long waits at both sites.

Colangelo told Dozer, "Rich, you're just a bean counter. You'll never have a great city until you have a great downtown."

And downtown Phoenix was exactly where the new arena would go, because, after all, J.C. was an "urban" guy. Turns out, he was absolutely right.

THE HEART OF A CITY

Author's note: Some people said that the Suns were more focused on building a shiny new place to play basketball than they were trying to help revitalize downtown Phoenix. The fact is that city leaders felt that the arena project was an absolutely critical piece of their plan to bring people back to downtown.

Many other investors and developers, including a forward-thinking Arizona State University, have been involved with the growth and development of downtown, before and since the arena opened in 1992. It will always be a work in progress, but one could conclude that the original strategy for a downtown comeback was "spot on."

The following article first ran in Phoenix Suns Fastbreak Magazine in 1990 and was later expanded to run in The Arizona Republic. The piece reflects the shared vision of the Suns and their full partner in the arena project and in downtown, the City of Phoenix, now the sixth largest city in the United States.

When you think about it, cities are living, breathing, and constantly evolving entities. And a city's downtown is its beating heart, providing community spirit, focus, and an identity.

A city that lacks a vibrant downtown is either dead or dying. Although Phoenix's downtown area was once on the critical list, it is staging a remarkable comeback.

A hundred years ago, the entire City of Phoenix existed within the boundaries of what we now call "downtown." There were theaters, hotels, saloons, retail stores and restaurants. Life in Phoenix revolved around the central city. It's ironic that after a century of growth and outward expansion, we are now refocusing on downtown and, in effect, returning to our roots.

It wasn't very long ago, about the time that the Suns franchise came to be in 1968, that Phoenix was regarded as a quiet retirement community known principally for its great weather. During the hot summer months, the local resorts and many businesses would close for a month or more because there simply was not enough business to justify staying open. On any workday, downtown became a virtual ghost town after six o'clock. Needless to say, things have changed dramatically for the better.

> **On any workday, downtown became a virtual ghost town after six o'clock.**

Now the sixth largest city in the United States, Phoenix has sprawled geographically, but the central city has begun to reclaim a position of prominence in the lives of Phoenicians.

Realizing past mistakes in zoning and urban planning, Phoenix has begun to breathe new life into its downtown. Trends that once led the citizenry away from downtown are now shifting. People are being drawn back to downtown for sports, cultural activities, restaurants and shopping.

Because Phoenix is a relatively "young" city, even by American standards, the timing is good. Unlike many, older, Eastern cities facing huge problems with decaying infrastructures, Phoenix will emerge as one of the bright, new cities of the 21st century.

If a city is truly a living, breathing thing, then we must ensure that its downtown, its heart, continues to beat strongly.

KEEP DIGGING

The prehistoric Hohokam Indian tribe populated the Salt River Valley beginning around 200 A.D. Mysteriously, they disappeared from the region around 1400 A.D. The location eventually selected for the Suns new arena was near the historic center of downtown Phoenix and early civilization in the Valley of the Sun.

The Hohokam had no written history, but the tribe is credited with the development of an extensive system of irrigation canals for agriculture. Centuries after the Hohokam departed, Phoenix area settlers would use the ancient Hohokam canal system as an archeological blueprint for new water systems.

Interestingly, the Hohokam are reputed to have built ball courts in Arizona similar to those found at the center of the Mayan culture, far to the south in Mexico and Central America.

As the architects and excavation teams got ready to begin construction of the Suns' new, downtown "ball court," Jerry Colangelo received a caution. If ancient artifacts were unearthed during arena construction, Colangelo would be informed immediately, the project would have to be stopped and, a methodical, archeological dig would begin.

When he heard that, J.C. jokingly issued instructions to the excavation crew, "Dig at night... and don't call me."

ANCIENT BALL COURTS

Although archeologists have yet to unearth an ancient, Mayan-style ball court in downtown Phoenix, there is evidence that these courts existed throughout pre-historic Arizona and New Mexico. There is also the strong likelihood of links between the ancient Mayan and Hohokam cultures.

According to finds unearthed in Mexico and Central America, Mayan sport courts measured 49 to 115 feet in length and 10 to 39 feet in width. By comparison, standard NBA courts today are 94 feet long and 50 feet wide.

Echoes From the Purple Palace

Archeologists tell us that the ancient Mayan game also featured two stone rings set high on the arena walls, the forerunners of our modern hoops. Depending on the court, the rings were positioned six to ten feet off the ground. Similar to today's game, the object was to get the ball through one of the stone rings. In order to accomplish that, just about anything was permitted.

In a way, I guess every Mayan match was a lot like the NBA Playoffs.

THE SUNS NEW 'HOOD

The Suns were moving from the Arizona Veterans Memorial Coliseum on the westside of Phoenix, into a downtown neighborhood with a rich history, some of it noble and some of it, well, let's call it "colorful."

THE ST. JAMES HOTEL ON MADISON

Phoenix old-timers will remember that the area was dotted with dozens of transient, single-room occupancy hotels. Many were built in the 1920s and '30s, but some dated back to Arizona's territorial days.

The Madison Hotel and Bar, one of the few remaining examples of those old hotels, finally fell to the wrecking ball in 2012. Although they'd been closed for many years, the St. James Hotel along with the Madison, stood just west of the Suns' arena, near the corner of Madison and 1st Street,

> **During Prohibition... The Deuce was well-known for its speakeasies.**

Many of those old hotels started out at the turn of the 20th Century, as housing for workers who were building sections of the Union Pacific Railroad. Later in life, those establishments would be adapted to serve other purposes.

The area designated for the Suns' new facility had long been referred to as "The Deuce." It ran along Second Street from Van Buren south to the Union Pacific tracks. There is confusion and debate over the borders of The Deuce, which seem to expand or contract depending on which old-time Phoenician is doing the talking.

There is even disagreement on how the name Deuce came to be. Some say it is actually, "Duce," sliced off the word "produce," because of the many fruit and vegetable warehouses that once lined the railroad tracks in the area. Others think it was "Deuce" because 2nd Street was the area's main thoroughfare. Phoenix police veterans usually define The Deuce as the downtown area between 2nd Avenue and 2nd Street.

Beginning in the late 1890s and running into the 1930s, the area was the hub of Phoenix's bustling, prosperous and, at times, nefarious, Chinatown.

During the years of Prohibition in the United States, The Deuce was well-known for its speakeasies. Another part of the neighborhood, "Paris Alley," was home to several brothels and gambling establishments.

Echoes From the Purple Palace

World War II effectively turned the entire state of Arizona into a giant military training base. With a collective wink from city officials, the local police and the military, the many hotels and bars in The Deuce formed a convenient "red-light" district for the thousands of armed forces personnel training in and around the Phoenix area.

A DENIZEN OF THE DEUCE

After the war was over, many of those flop houses and bars closed down, but the area's warehouse district remained a big part of Phoenix commerce, as a shipping and processing hub for agricultural products. The nearby railroad tracks filled warehouses with onions, lettuce and citrus produced in Arizona.

The building that now houses Majerle's Grill on 2nd Street once did business as Skomer's Clothing Store, selling work clothes and boots to the migrant workers who labored in the produce warehouses. Many of the remaining transient hotels offered guests a place to sleep at reasonable weekly, daily, or sometimes, even hourly rates.

By the 1960s, The Deuce had deteriorated into Phoenix's version of skid row. A misguided tourist or a cautious visitor to The Deuce would walk past pawnshops, blood banks, bars, greasy spoon cafes and second-hand stores.

For those looking to clean up their act, there was a barber college. For those seeking escape, there were package liquor stores that sold whiskey by the pint. For those seeking redemption, they had a choice of gospel missions.

The local population was largely comprised of the forgotten wreckage of society… homeless drunks and vagrants. They, and their neighborhood, The Deuce, had definitely seen better days.

In the 1970s however, many of the Deuce's seedy shops, bars and hotels were reduced to empty lots in the name of urban renewal. This historic neighborhood became, perhaps for the first time since the ancient days of the Hohokam tribe, a largely barren landscape. But it was only getting ready to become the catalyst for a new, exciting chapter for downtown Phoenix.

THE CHINA CONNECTION

If there is a history buried in the ground beneath the Suns arena, one that Colangelo's excavation crews somehow missed, that record is probably written in Chinese.

As the city expanded during the final decade of the 1800s, Phoenix leaders decided to move the city's growing Chinese population from an area around 1st Street and Adams to one further south. The new site was between Madison and Jackson on the North and South, running from 1st to 3rd streets on the west and east. Walk to the center point formed by those four streets today, and you'll find yourself standing on the Suns basketball court at US Airways Center.

The history of the Chinese in Arizona was a realization of the "American Dream." Virtually all of the Chinese immigrants to the American West came from Guangdong Province to work on the Southern Pacific Railroad. When the railroad work was mostly finished, thousands of Chinese migrated to Arizona where they found a much more tolerant atmosphere than they did in California, where there was an aggressive, anti-Chinese sentiment.

The hard-working Chinese arrived in Arizona and quickly established grocery stores, restaurants, laundries and vegetable stands. They became domestic cooks, gardeners and servants to Phoenix families. They worked long hours for little wages, but they saved, invested carefully, helped each other and became successful.

Phoenix's Chinatown had its own Chinese language school, so that Chinese children would not forget their roots, or their language. There was also a temple and a community hall, all within the borders of what became the US Airways Center.

In the early decades of the 20th Century it was well known, even to the leading citizens and landed gentry of Phoenix, that if a person wanted to engage in illegal activities, like gambling or smoking opium, they could find anything they desired down in Chinatown.

Law enforcement records and newspaper reports of the day spoke of underground tunnels and subterranean chambers, used by the Chinese, to conceal these illegal activities. As workers excavated for the Suns' arena, digging down some 20 to 25 feet below street level, they found a few, old, secret "hidey-holes." However, an underground network of interconnecting tunnels, honeycombing the area under Chinatown, proved to be more urban myth than fact.

Interestingly, when preliminary archeological digs unearthed old Chinese artifacts, they usually came from areas that were once used as latrines. Archeologists found broken china, children's dolls, even old wedding bands. In addition, the old privies were great places to ditch drug paraphernalia, weapons and other evidence.

PRESERVATION

During the first part of the 20th Century, as Phoenix and Arizona grew, Chinese grocery stores flourished throughout the state. A successful Phoenix grocer for some 20 years, Tang Shing, invested $80,000 to build a red brick warehouse in Chinatown, on the corner of Jackson and 3rd Street. It opened in 1929, as the Sun Mercantile Company. It became the largest wholesale grocery business in Phoenix.

SUN MERCANTILE, 230 S. THIRD STREET

Flash forward to 1989 when the "irresistible force" of Jerry Colangelo was finalizing the architectural plans for the Suns' new arena. Margaret Mullen, of the Downtown Phoenix Partnership, was playing the role of "immovable object," when it came to preserving old, historic structures.

As the arena plans unfolded, there were protracted discussions on the fate of the Sun Mercantile warehouse. The old building was one of the last remnants of the glory days of the city's Chinese community and was considered by Mullen to be an essential part of the history of downtown Phoenix. In her mind, its preservation should not have even come into question.

Colangelo however, knowing that the arena project had limited space for its architectural footprint, realized that the old warehouse building might have to go.

> **"They will knock that building down over my dead body!"**
>
> – Margaret Mullen

Sniffing a potential controversy, reporters would frequently go back and forth between Colangelo and Mullen for their perspectives on the issue. A minor war of words, a classic "he said, she said," in daily installments, flared between the two. A reasonable summary of their comments follows:

She said, "I hope that, in their planning, they will be able to preserve this wonderful, old, historic structure."

He said, "I don't see any way we can keep that building and still have a viable arena project."

She said, "They will knock that building down over my dead body!"

He said, "Whatever it takes!"

In the end, the Sun Mercantile warehouse was spared and gained a new lease on life. It first served as the construction office for the arena project. Then, in the years following the opening of America West Arena, it became home to the Suns' in-house advertising and public relations agency, the Phoenix Suns Athletic Club, a medical office and rehabilitation facility, as well as a travel office and the general headquarters of *Phoenix Suns Fastbreak Magazine*.

The building won several architectural awards as well as recognition for historical preservation. It was even considered as a possible site for a satellite museum of the Rock and Roll Hall of Fame.

At last report, Margaret Mullen is alive and well, and Tang Shing's beautiful old building is still in use by the Suns, ironically, as a warehouse.

MIRANDA

There is no question that Ernesto Miranda was a bad guy with a long rap sheet. Unintentionally, he became an interesting sidebar in Suns, and arena, history.

A grade school dropout who later was dishonorably discharged from the military, Miranda was arrested in 1963 in Phoenix and charged with rape and kidnapping. Both the victim and the cops knew that he did it. And, if that wasn't enough, Ernesto offered a written confession to his crimes. He was subsequently tried, convicted and sent to prison.

But just three years later, a June 13, 1966 ruling by the United States Supreme Court threw out his confession and overturned his conviction.

The court claimed that, upon his arrest, Miranda was not properly informed of his Constitutional rights, specifically, his Fifth Amendment right to remain silent and, his Sixth Amendment right to counsel.

The result of this Supreme Court case was the establishment of the so-called "Miranda Rights."

Because of the popularity of TV police dramas, virtually everyone in America now knows at least the first part of the Miranda warning, "You have the right to remain silent."

Police officers nationwide soon carried special, pocket-sized "Miranda cards" to remind them of the new arrest rules.

Prosecutors retried and convicted Miranda without his "tainted" confession and he was sent back to prison on a 20-year sentence. But by the early 1970s, he was paroled and returned to the streets of Phoenix. He would hang out in The Deuce, and occasionally find some work in the produce warehouses there.

Because of the Supreme Court decision, Ernesto became somewhat of a local celebrity. He would often ask cops who patrolled the downtown beat, for a few of their Miranda cards. He would then autograph the cards and sell them to raise a few dollars to feed his gambling, drinking and drug habits. Sometimes police officers would ask him to sign one of the cards so they could keep it as a souvenir. When he could, Miranda sold the cards for $1.50 each.

Ten years after the Supreme Court ruling, on January 31, 1976, his lifestyle caught up with him and Ernesto Miranda was stabbed to death in a dispute over a card game at La Amapola Bar in downtown Phoenix. He was 34.

In his pocket were a few of the Miranda warning cards. One police official reported that a few weeks before his death, Miranda had raised the price of his autographed "Miranda Cards" to $2.00. Apparently, inflation had reached The Deuce.

Miranda's best customers for his autographed cards had been the young lawyers and police officers who frequented the downtown Superior Court Building.

It was ironic that the man who inflicted Miranda's fatal wounds with a lettuce-cutting blade, a Mexican national named Ezequiel Moreno, was, upon his arrest, read his Miranda rights. He elected to remain silent.

> YOU HAVE THE RIGHT TO REMAIN SILENT
> ANYTHING YOU SAY CAN BE USED AGAINST YOU IN A COURT OF LAW
> YOU HAVE THE RIGHT TO THE PRESENCE OF AN ATTORNEY TO ASSIST YOU PRIOR TO QUESTIONING, AND TO BE WITH YOU DURING QUESTIONING, IF YOU SO DESIRE.
> IF YOU CANNOT AFFORD AN ATTORNEY YOU HAVE THE RIGHT TO HAVE AN ATTORNEY APPOINTED FOR YOU PRIOR TO QUESTIONING.
> DO YOU UNDERSTAND THESE RIGHTS?
> WILL YOU VOLUNTARILY ANSWER MY QUESTIONS?

A MIRANDA RIGHTS CARD SIGNED BY ERNESTO

Because authorities lacked sufficient evidence and credible witnesses, Moreno was released. He quickly disappeared from Phoenix and headed to Mexico. Miranda's murder remains on the Phoenix Police Department books as "unsolved."

La Amapola Bar, where Miranda met his demise, was located in the heart of The Deuce, 233 South Second Street, just south of Jefferson and, precisely where the US Airways Center now stands.

So, if you are fortunate enough to be able to afford Suns tickets, and you happen to be sitting toward the south end of the arena, be aware. Should you suddenly feel a cold chill, it could be the arena's ever-efficient air conditioning system, or maybe, just maybe, it might be the unsettled, malevolent spirit of Ernesto Miranda.

Echoes From the Purple Palace

WHERE MIRANDA MET HIS DEMISE

A PHOENIX RISING

There is absolutely no evidence that Ernesto Miranda was ever a Suns fan. But on the very night that Miranda was pronounced "dead on arrival" at Good Samaritan Hospital, just two miles west of the hospital, on McDowell Road, the Suns were beating up on the Philadelphia 76ers, 119-105, in front of 8,314 fans at the Coliseum. It marked the first game of a 24-13 season-ending run that would propel the Suns into the NBA Playoffs for the first time in six seasons.

The next day, February 1st, the Suns acquired Garfield Heard and a second-round draft pick from the Buffalo Braves in a trade for Phoenix rookie, John Shumate. It was a move that would help carry the team all the way to an NBA Championship match-up against the storied Boston Celtics.

WRECKING BALL

By the 1980s some of the old warehouses in the neighborhood had found a new purpose as artists' studios. Spaces were large, rents were cheap and the small arts community that had taken root there really didn't want to move.

As plans for the arena were being finalized, Colangelo and city officials found themselves going to work to find new spaces for these soon-to-be-displaced artists.

Many of the artists were grumbling about being evicted to make way for a basketball arena, of all things. But muralist Mark Switlik didn't mind. He was already a big fan of the Suns and the NBA. Switlik's studio was located at 201 E. Madison, which would be roughly, inside the lower bowl of today's US Airways Center.

After the city officially informed the artists that their buildings were scheduled for demolition, Switlik playfully painted a mural of a shadowy Suns Gorilla falling backwards while kicking a basketball through the wall of his warehouse. He titled his work *Wrecking Ball*. He did his work quickly one night so he wouldn't offend those artists who were not too thrilled about moving.

Switlik's mural appeared three-dimensional. The oversized, bright orange basketball looked like it had crashed through the wall and was now imbedded inside the dark warehouse. To add to the realism, Switlik took a few pieces of stucco and brick that matched the wall and scattered them on the sidewalk in front of the mural.

Before the sun came up the next morning, the day shift was reporting to work at the fire station just across the street. In the dim street lights, one of the early-arriving firefighters noticed what appeared to be a giant hole in the warehouse wall and something round and orange buried on the inside. His first thought was that an orange Volkswagen "bug" had crashed into the building during the night. His immediate reaction was to race across the street to see if anyone was hurt.

THE SUNS GORILLA CHECKS OUT "WRECKING BALL"

For our heroic firefighter, what followed was one of those moments when illumination, clarity and embarrassment collide. It was a moment that his fellow firefighters will never let him forget. In his defense, the scene looked very real, even in broad daylight.

The City of Phoenix provided some funds for the artists' relocation and that eased much of their pain. Switlik and

> **...what followed was one of those moments when illumination, clarity and embarrassment collide.**

another artist moved to a warehouse down the street a few blocks on West Jackson, while the majority of the artist community found a very nice home nearby, on the upper floor of the Phoenix O.I.C. building on the southwest corner of Jackson and 1st Street.

A REAL HOCKEY PUCK

The new arena's public-private partnership deal called for the Suns to manage the America West Arena (AWA) as its primary tenant. Virtually every arena in the country needs to fill a minimum of 200 event-dates per year to have a viable and sustainable economic model.

With pre-season games and playoffs, the Suns would fill a few more than 50 of those dates. That was a good start, but way short of what would be needed. Even as the building was in its early planning stages, contracts were being drawn up with the circus, ice-shows and all manner of touring concerts, not to mention a lineup of new sports teams that would soon call America West Arena "home."

The new teams included indoor soccer's Arizona Sand Sharks, Team Tennis' Phoenix Smash and, of course, Arena Football's Arizona Rattlers. The WNBA's Phoenix Mercury would join that list in 1997, as one of the league's original franchises.

A National Hockey League (NHL) team would have been nice, but when the AWA was in its early planning stages, the NHL soundly dashed that hope.

It was an enthusiastic Jerry Colangelo who called several NHL franchise owners as well as the then-commissioner of the NHL, John Ziegler. Colangelo told Ziegler that he would love to have an expansion NHL team as part of the Phoenix sports line-up at what would be the newest and glitziest arena in the country.

Ziegler seemed neither excited nor impressed, telling Colangelo that the NHL was not interested in putting an expansion team in Phoenix. He added that he couldn't see the NHL even considering such a possibility before the year 2015, a mere 27 years in the future. Ziegler also added that if the NHL was to expand, it probably wouldn't be to the Southwest, when there were many U.S. cities, like Portland and Seattle that were much closer to the Canadian border and might be a better fit for an NHL team.

When Colangelo asked if perhaps there was an existing NHL team looking to relocate, Ziegler indicated that all of the franchises in his league were in great financial shape and nobody was seeking to move. Even though Ziegler may have overstated the financial health of his league, for Colangelo, it was a very disappointing discussion.

But it was a critical conversation when it came to the final design of the arena. Without even the remote prospect of an NHL franchise coming to Phoenix, AWA could (and would) be designed with basketball sightlines as the top priority. Sure, AWA could bring in a minor league hockey franchise to fill some dates, but with their smaller crowds, hockey sightlines would not be critical to the arena design.

If Ziegler and the NHL had said "yes" to Colangelo in 1988, AWA would have been designed differently. Basketball's half-court line and hockey's center-line would have been in approximately the same location in the arena. But that would have also mandated that seats at both ends of the arena be pushed farther back to fit the larger hockey layout. The building's architectural footprint would have been significantly larger, making the arena far less intimate for basketball. Colangelo wanted "the most intimate basketball venue" in the league. Without the realistic prospect of NHL hockey, that would now be possible.

With the benefit of 20/20 hindsight, if Ziegler had said "yes" to Colangelo, almost certainly, there would not be a Jobing.com Arena in Glendale competing directly with the US Airways Center in Phoenix. There would be no taxpayer issues related to hockey and, most likely, there would be no controversy over the Coyotes staying or leaving the Valley of the Sun.

2 WACKO!

AWA WAS BUILT WITH PERFECT SIGHTLINES... FOR BASKETBALL

OUT OF THE BOX

Before the early rejection came from the NHL, the arena's architectural design team was brainstorming some ideas that were nothing short of extraordinary. Creating an arena with excellent sightlines for both basketball and hockey is both difficult and expensive. But the design team floated an innovative idea that had been tried once at the Target Center in Minneapolis.

The concept called for an arena floor and ice sheet that could be raised and lowered on multiple hydraulic jacks. To prepare the floor to be raised for hockey, the first five rows of the basketball seats would be retracted. Then, the hockey rink would be raised and the sixth row of the basketball configuration would become the first row of hockey seats. It was a potentially costly idea that was never fully developed for AWA, but it was clear that lead architect, Michael Hallmark and his team understood sports sightlines and they were willing to go to great lengths to create a venue that worked for both basketball and hockey.

Understandably, Colangelo did not want to design an arena based on a hockey team that might never come to town. Just a few years later, however, with Ziegler replaced as NHL commissioner by the former deputy commissioner of the NBA, Gary Bettman, the Winnipeg Jets came knocking on the arena door. At that point, however, a redesign and rebuild of AWA's inner bowl was not architecturally or financially feasible.

It was Bettman who introduced the new owners of the Jets, Steven Gluckstern and Richard Burke, to Colangelo. Prior to committing their team to the Valley of the Sun, the two owners visited America West Arena. They saw the arena in a Rattlers' Arena Football configuration, which would be exactly the same as the set-up for NHL hockey. Gluckstern and Burke sat in every section and carefully evaluated those seats with blocked sightlines. They felt comfortable that they could sell those seats at a discount and still make their economic model work.

So, the Jets came to Phoenix. They changed the team's name to the Phoenix Coyotes and then skated the first of their seven seasons at AWA in 1996-97. During their entire stay at the arena, Coyotes ownership and management never stopped complaining about the bad ice, poor sightlines, small locker rooms and a design that was not the best for hockey fans.

But, from the outset, their ownership had been fully aware of the arena's sightline issues for hockey. Revisionist hockey history claims that these poor owners were "sold a bill of goods." But that is simply not true. If it is your wont to blame somebody for the hockey sightline problems at AWA, blame the myopic, former commissioner of the NHL, John Zeigler. The Coyotes eventually left AWA for a newly-built Jobing.com arena in Glendale, AZ in time for the 2003-04 season.

Whatever its shortcomings as a hockey venue, America West Arena's fan amenities were a vast improvement over the old Coliseum. AWA boasted 88 luxury suites on two levels, upgraded concession, more restrooms, better acoustics and, absolutely perfect basketball sightlines for 19,000 Suns fans.

THE GROUNDBREAKING

It was Aug.1, 1990 and, as frequently is the case in summer, a monsoon storm was building over Phoenix. Groundbreaking ceremonies for America West Arena would go forward, regardless of the weather.

All we could do is pray that we could get through the opening remarks, indoors, at the Phoenix Civic Plaza, before crossing Jefferson Street to the site of the groundbreaking. Hopefully we could put shovels in the ground, take the necessary ceremonial photos and get out of there before we were drenched by a downpour or blown away by the wind and dust of a fast-moving desert haboob.

GROUNDBREAKING SITE ON 2nd STREET

We had blocked off a major piece of 2nd Street, just south of Jefferson Street and painted a full-sized NBA basketball court on the pavement. The location was just a little north of where the Suns court would be positioned once the facility was opened, a little less than two years later. Inside the center-court jump circle of that faux court, the pavement was removed and the space filled with sand. Workers then applied a thin shell of concrete over the space.

Once the concrete was dry, we called in our "artist-practically-in-residence," Mark Switlik, to paint a Suns logo over the center spot. The ceremonial shovels would easily break through the thin crust of concrete. But that would come later.

First, inside the cozy confines of the Phoenix Civic Plaza, special guests heard a string of speeches from the mayor, sponsors, dignitaries and, of course, Jerry Colangelo, who said, "In spite of all the impressive statistics and financial figures, the America West Arena is more than just an economic instrument. It's a partnership of people and ideas, of hearts and minds, dedicated to moving Phoenix forward."

To back up the remarks, there was a big screen with rear projection of artist renderings and important arena facts.

When that portion of the program was completed, we threw open the outer doors and escorted the crowd of several hundred people, across the street to the site prepared for the groundbreaking.

After most of the crowd had moved through the open doors, wind from the brewing storm literally sucked the air out of the convention center and the huge, 16-foot screen we'd used for the presentation began to topple over. A couple of alert Suns employees saw what was happening and immediately grabbed onto the base of the screen to keep it upright. If it had gone down when the room was filled with people, it would have taken out the first three rows of our VIP guests.

Outside, on our ceremonial basketball court, the winds were swirling, keeping the remarks mercifully brief. Naturally, all of the Phoenix media outlets were there and the one-and-only casualty of the night was a TV light blown over by the wind.

AMERICA WEST ARENA FACTS

- The entire arena site is 11 acres
- 34,000 cubic yards of concrete were used in its construction
- The roof consists of 2,000 tons of steel
- There are 8,000 light fixtures in the arena
- The ice floor is kept between 16 and 20 degrees
- To smooth the ice, the Zamboni uses 140-degree water
- There are 88 private suites
- Capacity for basketball was 19,023 in 1992-93
- There are 175 full-time and 275 part-time employees
- The facility averages over 220 events per year
- The original America West Airlines advertising contract was for $15 million over 30 years
- The original cost to construct the arena was $89 million

(L TO R) PHOENIX MAYOR PAUL JOHNSON, JERRY COLANGELO OF THE SUNS AND ED BEAUVAIS OF AMERICA WEST AIRLINES BREAK GROUND FOR THE ARENA

THE ARENA DEAL

The arena was developed as a public-private partnership between the Suns and the City of Phoenix. The agreement, and the arena design, quickly became the prototype for a new generation of facilities around the country.

The City of Phoenix contributed the land, plus a portion of the construction costs. In return, the city owns the facility. Phoenix Arena Limited Partnership (a division of the Phoenix Suns) covered the majority of the construction costs and holds a long-term managing and operating agreement. Revenues are split between the partners.

DECISIONS, DECISIONS

Figuring out the official "sellout number" for a new arena can be a moving target. Elements going into the equation include permanent and temporary seating, suite seats, standing room, plus areas for the media and the handicapped. And, of course, don't forget the "fudge factor." On any given night, the announced attendance can vary considerably from the actual number of derrieres in seats.

As the arena prepared to open, Jerry Colanglelo and CFO Rich Dozer huddled, trying to settle on a comfortable number for the 19,000-seat arena. They came up with a sellout number of 19,023. Why that odd number? The answer is that Jerry Colangelo's uniform number in high school and college was 23. It didn't take long to decide that one.

But when it came to selecting the color scheme and seat fabric for the arena, Colangelo's thought process was a little more deliberate.

Arena manager Bob Machen and designers showed Jerry a wide array of colors and fabrics, but Jerry's only hesitation seemed to be over which shade of purple would be "just right."

Before making his final decision, Jerry consulted with a design expert of impeccable taste and reputation, a person with a discerning eye for color, his wife, Joan.

When the arena's color scheme was finally decided, what else could you possibly call the joint but, "The Purple Palace"? As the arena was readied for opening ceremonies, the city offered the Suns the opportunity to create a street name for the area directly in front of the arena. Although it would never gain popular acceptance, we dubbed it "Purple Palace Way."

THE TUNNEL

For decades, Arizona schoolchildren heard stories of mysterious tunnels running underneath Phoenix's Chinatown. When asked for clarification, their parents would usually dismiss the talk as "just stories." But there actually is a tunnel underneath what used to be Chinatown and it's big enough to drive a dump truck through, maybe even a locomotive.

Designers and architects working on the Suns' new arena had to figure out how to construct their building over the existing infrastructure that ran underground through the middle of the city. Water, gas, sewer and power lines all had to be rerouted in order to continue to serve the surrounding community. Then, new infrastructure had to be designed and built to service the considerable demands created by a 19,000-seat arena.

One of the unexpected obstacles builders faced was a giant, storm drain tunnel that was directly under the AWA site, running north to south and eventually emptying into the Salt River.

Starting at Interstate 10 and running south along 2nd Street, the monstrous drain pipe is more than 20 feet in diameter and runs approximately 50 feet below street level. Additional support pylons, buried some 90 feet deep, had to be drilled and poured to protect the tunnel and support the massive arena structure that would be built directly above it.

OPEN HOUSE

The grand opening of the America West Arena (AWA) wasn't just a single event, but a month-long string of activities and celebrations that touched every part of the community and, in the end, left our staff extraordinarily proud, exhilarated and exhausted. The grand opening activities drew over 200,000 people in less than a month's time.

The building's certificate of occupancy was granted on June 1st and the first event at AWA followed the next day. It was a luncheon to thank and recognize the staff and all those who were instrumental in the creation of the arena.

On the following night, June 3rd, the arena hosted an open house for Phoenix's disability community, showing off the arena's many accessible features, from parking spaces to restrooms and countertop heights.

On the evening of June 4th, a benefit, black-tie dinner for 1,500 people, was followed by a concert featuring Huey Lewis and the News. The event raised over $300,000 for Phoenix Suns Charities and Valley Boys and Girls Clubs.

The grand opening extravaganza continued the following night with Colangelo, Phoenix Mayor Paul Johnson and Ed Beauvais of America West Airlines, dedicating the new arena. The trio smashed champagne bottles on the balcony overlooking Phoenix Suns Plaza and what was once an area of blighted warehouses and run-down businesses. Phoenix's old Chinatown and its Deuce had, at last, been transformed.

One veteran observer thought that, given the neighborhood's somewhat checkered history, it might have been more appropriate to perform the christening ceremony by smashing pint bottles of cheap whiskey, rice wine, and muscatel. But the champagne worked just fine.

Each of the arena's opening events featured back-of-the-house tours that included a peek at the Suns' locker room. The snazzy, new basketball facilities actually rendered the term, "locker room," obsolete. The space now included cherry wood finishes, expanded medical treatment facilities, a full laundry, a team-sized Jacuzzi and sauna, a steam room, along with a weight training facility. There wasn't a traditional "locker" anywhere in sight. The new layout would be called, the "Phoenix Suns Clubhouse." Just a few steps away, a full-sized, basketball practice court awaited the Suns first workouts.

The arena's first, ticketed, public event was a sold-out, Saturday night, George Strait concert. That was followed by Family Circus Sunday which opened up the arena to everyone in the community. More than 15,000 families, approximately 45,000 people, flooded the new facility, far exceeding the expectations of the event organizers.

The arena then hosted and somehow survived, back-to-back sold-out concerts by Metallica.

The set-up crew then readied AWA for its first-ever Arena Football game, featuring the brand-new Arizona Rattlers. AWA's first sporting event resulted in another sellout of 15,500 and, a 51-36 win over Sacramento.

Many local organizations booked meetings and functions into the new facility and there were community benefits like Linda Ronstadt's, "Fiesta Mexicana," and concerts with The Cure and MC Hammer. In late June, the Suns staged their NBA Draft Party in the arena bowl, drawing a record draft day crowd as they selected Oliver Miller, of Arkansas, with a late first-round pick.

When everyone caught their breath, they realized that a new chapter for the Suns and, a new era for downtown Phoenix, were officially underway.

I remember Jerry Colangelo telling an exhilarated, but absolutely exhausted, executive staff, "You can all sleep in the off-season."

We suddenly realized that, with the arena's year-long schedule of events, there would never again be an "off-season."

IMPACT

During the spring of 1992, as Colangelo looked out the expansive windows of his new, fourth-floor office, he had a panoramic view of the high-rises of downtown Phoenix. But when he glanced down and across Jefferson Street, all he could see was the big, brick, ugly backside of the old J.C. Penney's building, replete with a large loading-dock door and ventilation grates. It was a totally uninteresting eyesore.

But there wasn't much Colangelo could do about it. The City of Phoenix was housing several of its departments in that huge, old building while the new Phoenix City Hall was under construction a few blocks to the west. As soon as that construction project was completed, those city departments would move out and, the old building would be demolished. But that was still several years away. In addition, the Suns organization was still moving into the arena, the Suns were getting ready for the coming season and, J.C. had lots of other things to worry about.

During an arena open house, artist-muralist Mark Switlik took a tour and soon found himself in Colangelo's office, looking out the window at the old J.C. Penney's building. But he didn't see a dilapidated old building waiting for the wrecking ball. What he saw was a giant canvas and an opportunity to make a statement.

Switlik raced the few blocks back to his Jackson Street studio and prepared a proposal for Colangelo. It was a proposal that would not only take care of Colangelo's view, but it would also dress up the city for people attending arena events or just visiting the newly revamped downtown.

Switlik called his mural concept, *Impact*. He believed that the new arena and the NBA would have a tremendous, positive impact on the downtown area. His idea was to paint a mirror image of the America West Arena as the background of the mural with the focal point being a huge, 45-foot high, NBA basketball.

Colangelo was not an easy man to pin down. But when Switlik finally met with him to discuss the concept of a new mural, the first thing J.C. said to him flashed back to the *Wrecking Ball* artwork.

2 WACKO!

THE J.C PENNEY'S BUILDING – BEFORE "IMPACT"

"Nice basketball!" Jerry kidded. A deal was struck. The Suns would pay for the artwork and then gift it to the owner of the building, the City of Phoenix. Switlik started painting on his 45' by 152' "canvas" in October of 1992 and finished the mural four months later.

Switlik worked from a 50' Swing Stage scaffold, which had to be moved three times before the project was finished. To cover the 6,750 square feet of space, the mural consumed somewhere between 55 and 60 gallons of paint.

The signature feature of the mural was the giant basketball, which also created the project's biggest challenges. Switlik admitted that it wasn't easy to outline the ball, using just a compass, some charcoal and a string. Once that was done, Switlik used a flexible, 16-foot piece of aluminum to create the design curves demanded by the basketball's seams. Other special requirements included spray equipment to airbrush the basketball, and, of course, duct tape for masking the seams. It was, perhaps, the 1,002nd practical use of duct tape.

The mural was dedicated on the day that the Suns and the NBA came together to announce that the 1995 All-Star Game would be played in Phoenix. On hand for the dedication were top Suns executives, Mayor Johnson, Arizona Governor Fife Symington and the Commissioner of the NBA, David Stern.

When the mural was dedicated, everyone knew that it was only a temporary exhibit. Even the most optimistic among us thought it would be no more than five years before the mural, and the building, would come down. However, thanks to assorted real estate maneuvers by the city, Impact would grace downtown Phoenix for the next 14 years. The wrecking ball finally knocked it down in 2007.

THE VIEW AFTER "IMPACT"

EARLY CONCERTS AND SHOWS

Colangelo was as proud as any man could be of his new, state-of-the-art arena. But he was used to marketing and promoting basketball. The concert world was new to him.

On the night of the arena's first public event, a country music concert featuring George Strait, Colangelo looked out his fourth-floor office window and beamed with pride at the rivers of people, many wearing white cowboy hats, streaming into the arena from all over downtown. He was both moved at the sight and grateful for their support. Later, when the concert got underway and he saw hundreds of those concert-goers standing on his brand-new, purple arena seats, he wanted to strangle them.

Down on the floor level of the arena, there is a security office that features two, jail-like holding cells for fans or concert goers who might get a little rowdy. Security staff that worked that first concert, remember that the very first guest detained in one of the arena's jail cells was a woman. Nobody remembers her name, but they all remember that she was wearing "really tight jeans."

A week or so later, another concert came to the AWA, bringing with it a whole different breed of music fans. The group was Metallica. Before the doors opened that night, the line of concert-goers snaked around the building. It was an interesting group with lots of leather outfits, multiple piercings, wild hair-dos, tattoo body art, chains, boots, net stockings and spiked dog collars. An absolutely mystified J.C. said, "Who are these people? Where do they live? What do they do during the day?"

HOW QUICKLY THEY FORGET

When his sterling NBA playing days were over, Suns center Alvan Adams enthusiastically went to work on the arena project. Among other things, he drew on his 12 years of traveling through NBA arenas and locker rooms to help design the new Suns Clubhouse and the basketball-related facilities that went into AWA.

When Metallica came to town, Adams was pitching in to help arena staff with crowd control. The concert was over and the band was moving off-stage. Alvan was standing near the side of the stage when a fan leaned over a rail and handed him an autograph book and a pen. Without thinking, Alvan grabbed it, scribbled his signature and handed it back to the fan, who was clearly annoyed.

"Not YOU!" the fan snapped at the one-time Suns star, "THE BAND! THE BAND!"

JUST A LITTLE CRAZY

As previously mentioned, the first sporting event played at the new arena was not a Suns game but an Arizona Rattlers, Arena Football League game. The game was a complete sell-out. Not only was AWA new, but so was the certifiably insane sport of indoor football. It was promoted as "The Fifty-Yard Indoor War" and for good reason. Players in full pads, on a compressed football field, smashed into each other, banged into sideline dasher boards and often flew into the first row of seats. It was a pass-oriented, high scoring game that offered non-stop, wickedly hard-hitting action.

The excitement and craziness of it all energized the fans, the players and even our game-night promotional staff. Suddenly, all the conservative rules, harnesses and shackles of the NBA were removed and game operations could do just about anything they wanted. Our game-ops guys didn't waste the opportunity.

There were lights-out introductions featuring indoor pyrotechnic displays. There was a dance team that unofficially became known as the "Rat-Chicks." The Rattlers' mascot was a bad-ass biker named "Fang" who rode his custom "chopper" up and down the indoor field whipping fans into frenzy. Fang had long hair, tattoos and the maximum amount of leather and chain. When compared to the more conservative Suns game night operations, everything had just a bit of an "edge" to it.

One night, Andy Coviello, a Rattlers player, wearing his full game uniform and gear, executed a successful swan dive, bungee jump, from the arena rafters.

We cross-promoted the Suns at every opportunity; building towards the opening of the 1992-93 season. New Suns acquisition, Danny Ainge, was introduced to Phoenix fans at a Rattlers game by taking a rumblin' spin around the field on the back of Fang's motorcycle.

At one Rattlers game, against the Portland Forest Dragons, Suns guard Dan Majerle begged to ride Fang's motorcycle, solo, around the field. He hopped on and took off through the tunnel and onto the field. Almost in control, "Thunder Dan" careened toward Portland's sideline huddle, narrowly missing the Forest Dragons' quarterback.

2 WACKO!

As Majerle roared toward the end zone, he tried to slow down. He thought he was applying the brakes, but instead, he got confused, accelerated, and smashed the bike into the wall at the back of the end zone. Somehow, he hopped off at the last possible second and avoided any permanent damage. The motorcycle wasn't so lucky. Fang was not a happy biker.

But in early Rattlers lore, perhaps the best story was Harvey Wallbanger. He clomped into town during the Rattlers second season in 1993. Nope, Harvey wasn't a player; he was a giant, 2,000-pound American Bison whose massive back was close to seven feet off the ground. Already a legend at western cowboy shows, this bison had a trainer, T.C. Thornstenson, who rode on the beast's wooly back.

> **Harvey wasn't a player, he was a giant, 2,000-pound American Bison.**

Harvey's arena debut was to be a surprise. He would be sequestered behind a curtain in the end-zone until the Rattlers scored. Then the curtain would fly open and Harvey would come charging out onto the field for a "victory" lap.

Everything went according to plan but, unfortunately, that plan was never shared with any of the players.

So, when the Rattlers scored, indoor fireworks started going off, the curtain was pulled back and Harvey charged onto the field, bucking and snorting. Perhaps it was the fireworks, but even with Thornstenson clinging to a tiny strap, Harvey seemed a bit out of control.

A Rattlers lineman, Richard Ashe, was walking toward his bench when he noticed all the other players frantically racing for the sideline boards, their eyes wide with terror. Still wearing his helmet, a puzzled Ashe turned around to see what was going on and was promptly hit full-on by the charging bison.

Witnesses say that Harvey knocked Ashe "into next week." Miraculously, both the bison and Ashe survived the hit-and-gallop collision without serious injury.

Unfortunately, the game was not televised and there is no photographic or video tape evidence of the incident. That's too bad. Harvey's one-buffalo stampede would still be setting records on YouTube.

B.C.

Bryan Colangelo grew up in Phoenix as his father, Jerry, was growing the Phoenix Suns into one of the most respected franchises in professional basketball.

"B.C." grew up in the basketball business, sharing his father's love of the game as well as his insights and indefatigable work ethic. Bryan attended Central High School in Phoenix, and then it was off to Cornell University in upstate New York. After graduation, Bryan went to work in New York City in commercial real estate. He had several successful years invested in the Big Apple, when his dad called him and said, "It's time to come home."

Bryan returned to Phoenix and joined the Suns organization as an assistant to Cotton Fitzsimmons who was then director of player personnel. In addition to his dad, Bryan had a host of experienced mentors around him. No silver spoon here. Bryan was a fast learner and flat-out, the hardest working Suns employee in the building. I'd arrive at 8:30 in the morning and Bryan had already been there for an hour or two. I'd leave at 6:30 and Bryan would be deeply engrossed in a project for Cotton.

Bryan took over the management of the Arizona Rattlers in 1994 and they promptly won the Arena Football League (AFL) title. It was the first championship for any professional team, in any sport, in the State of Arizona.

Some will say that Bryan was lucky to have the last name that he did. But B.C. always wanted to break out of his dad's shadow in Phoenix and prove himself. Now, with the Toronto Raptors, he has. He was one of the top GMs in the NBA with the Suns and it was no surprise when the Raptors heavily recruited him.

B.C. has already won the NBA Executive of the Year Award twice, first in 2005 with the Suns and then again in 2007 with the Raptors. His dad won the award four times.

LOOKS LIKE A LOGO

Sometimes the daily work of a franchise takes place in fancy, high-tech conference rooms, with cad-cam computers and big screen televisions but, at other times, the work is done in humble, back offices that were once storage rooms.

It was in a one-time storage room, where Bryan Colangelo, designer Greg Fisher and I gathered frequently to conceptualize the design of the new Rattlers' logo for Phoenix's AFL team. We'd meet in that back office, usually at the end of the day to go over Fisher's design ideas.

We all liked the Rattlers' color scheme of black with turquoise and gold trim, so our focus was on making the logo design one of the best in pro sports. Our biggest problem was that a snake can often be interpreted as a phallic symbol. Obviously, we had to avoid that.

Usually a little punchy at the end of the day, we'd reject one design after another because they just didn't seem right. And when Fisher would ask, "what don't you guys like about that one?" Our bleary-eyed response was usually, "It looks like a @#$%!"

But the time spent was worth it, since the result was, in my humble opinion, one of the best logos in sports.

TRIBAL ELDER

Not long after the Rattlers had come to be, our in-house advertising agency, SRO Communications, went to work on a campaign to introduce the new Arena Football League team to the Phoenix market.

One day, the agency's creative director, Eric Labas, came into my office to show me some ad concepts. Labas, like many creative people, had his eccentricities. While working in his office he would never wear shoes or socks. I made it a rule that if he visited my office, I didn't care about the socks, but I asked him to please wear shoes.

He was appropriately shod one day when he stopped by my office.

"Tell me what you think about these," he said.

I looked at four or five different ideas for campaign graphic designs for the Rattlers, before I said to him, "You realize of course that I'm not directly involved with the Rattlers and I'm not going to have any input on the final decision."

"Oh, I know that," Eric said before adding, "But you've been around the organization a long time and you know how people think. You have a sense of what they like and don't like. You're kind of a, well, a tribal elder!"

I laughed and said with feigned outrage, "Wait a minute! I think I've just been insulted!"

"No. No." he responded, shaking his head. "That's not what I meant. You just have a lot of experience and I really respect your opinion on things."

Overnight, I thought about what Eric had said... a tribal elder... h-m-m-m.

The next day, when I was asked to help a Phoenix Suns Charities committee by picking up some heavy, bulky items for a special event, my response was clear, "I'm sorry, I don't do that anymore. I'm a tribal elder!"

Honestly, it felt pretty good.

A NEW LOGO AND NEW UNIFORMS

It was the beginning of the Suns' third decade. J.C. had purchased the team from its original ownership group and plans

Echoes From the Purple Palace

for a new arena in downtown Phoenix were proceeding nicely. But Colangelo wanted more than just a new arena. He wanted a new approach, a modern style to match the new home of the Suns. He wanted to see a new attitude and a new look for the "Purple Gang."

I don't remember exactly how responsibility for the new uniforms and warm-ups fell under my purview as a newly-minted vice president, but I was honored that it did. Interestingly, the Charlotte Hornets had just joined the NBA and their uniforms had been created by award-winning designer, Alexander Julian. It is said that Julian once boldly proclaimed, "I own teal!" At about that time, another new NBA team, the Orlando Magic, created a uniform design that seemed to be influenced by Disney's nearby Magic Kingdom.

That certainly was competition at uniform design's highest levels, but it also signaled a loosening of traditional NBA styles which had seen only minor changes for many years. Oh sure, there were exceptions like the Knicks' experiment with a "Big Apple" design on their uniform shorts, but generally speaking, teams like the Suns and Celtics stayed very close to their original, conservative, uniform designs.

I'd like to say that we had a budget for research to determine what designs would resonate with our fans and key stakeholders, but we didn't. I'd like to say that we invested in a world-renown design house to help create our new look, but we couldn't afford that either.

The only resources we had were me, a very creative local firm called Campbell-Fisher Design, a big, rubber chicken skewered onto the end of a pointer and a good relationship with the NBA's in-house design team. Somehow, we would make it work.

RESEARCH

Without a budget, I did my own informal survey of fans, Suns executives, former Suns players and pretty much, anybody who would listen to me. I asked them what they would like to see in a new Suns logo, new uniforms and warm-ups. Interestingly, Jerry

Colangelo's desire to go "new and modern," was not universally shared.

Many, including the "Original Sun," Dick Van Arsdale, wanted to keep the long-standing traditional design. They liked the lettering. They liked the colors. They liked the sunburst on the side of the shorts. After 24 years, they didn't see the need to change. Uniforms should be straightforward and simple.

I also did some research on colors. I found out that the original Suns colors, purple and orange, were considered to be "festival colors," not to be taken seriously. Conversely, colors like navy blue and black are considered "sincere" and "professional."

We always thought that the Suns primary colors were unique. How unique? Well, for one thing, purple and orange are two words in the English language that rhyme with no other words.

Let's take a moment to examine "sincere" and "festival" colors. Imagine that you've just boarded a jetliner and the pilot, wearing a dark blue uniform and military-style captain's hat, steps into the cabin. Just from his professional appearance, you feel confident about his abilities and assured that the flight will go well. Now imagine the same pilot steps into the cabin, but his uniform and hat are orange, or maybe a light purple! Break out the margaritas, it's party time! But first, get me off this flight!

Having done this research, I proposed a Suns' color change to a very sincere, dark blue uniform trimmed with silver (another English word that rhymes with no other). But that idea was quickly shot down. The original selection of the team's colors in 1968 was based on the purple and orange hues of those sensational Arizona sunsets. Symbolically, you can't argue with that. But after two years with our new uniforms, the NBA allowed us to add an alternative road uniform and we selected black as the base color, with purple and orange trim. It was a very sincere choice.

We worked simultaneously with Campbell-Fisher Design and the NBA's artists. We were open to ideas and we allowed the creative process to flow. The design ideas ranged from medieval to modern and just about every conceivable style in between.

By a process of elimination, we gradually reduced a dozen concepts down to five possibilities.

That's when the rubber chicken came into play.

Understanding that change can be difficult, at the final meeting with Colangelo and key executives, I used my unique, rubber chicken pointer to encourage everyone "not to be chicken."

Ultimately, we chose one of the NBA design concepts. So, the 24-year-old, straight-up Suns logo morphed into a right-leaning parallelogram. The uniforms went from western style lettering to a clean, modern font and the team's famous sunburst moved off the shorts to become an integral part of the jersey design.

ORIGINAL SUNS LOGO (TOP LEFT), SOME CONCPTUAL DRAWINGS AND THE NEW SUNS LOGO (LOWER RIGHT)

NO JOKE

We tried to keep the new uniform design under wraps, with the idea that they would be unveiled on opening night in the new arena. We almost blew it though, when we decided to play a joke on Suns CFO, Rich Dozer.

During one of our executive staff meetings, we had just received a prototype uniform from the manufacturer and we wanted to show it off at the meeting. J.C. asked Rich if he would go put on the uniform so we could get a better idea of what the uniform and the warm-ups would look like with someone actually wearing them.

Rich left the meeting and came back a few minutes later wearing the prototype. Rich is about 6'2" but a very slender guy. Some cruel people might even refer to him as "skinny," but I would never say such a thing!

The sample uniform was cut for an NBA athlete, so the uniform literally hung on Dozer. We all had a good laugh, took a couple of pictures, did a final critique of the design and colors and Dozer went back to his office to change.

When we were looking at the photos a few days later, we chuckled at how comical Dozer looked in the over-sized uniform and we decided the timing was right to play a practical joke on our CFO.

The America West Arena had been open for just a few weeks and throughout the building there were large, back-lit advertising posters, each about four feet wide by eight feet high. The vendor who handled that piece of our advertising business agreed to play along and we took one of the photos and created a huge poster of Dozer modeling the new uniform. We then positioned the poster in a spot where we knew Dozer would see it as he walked from the parking garage to the lobby of the Suns' office.

Echoes From the Purple Palace

AN EARLY UNIFORM CONCEPT

2 WACKO!

Our plan went off without a hitch. Dozer was surprised, amused and a bit embarrassed as he walked into work the next morning and saw his image up in lights. But before we could take down the poster, an *Arizona Republic* reporter came to the arena for a previously scheduled interview with Colangelo.

As he walked from the parking garage to the Suns' offices, the reporter noticed the poster and adroitly figuring that it was the new, super-secret, Suns' uniform design. He called one of the *Republic's* photographers to come over and take a picture of it.

There were still a couple of days before the regular season would open and we would "officially" unveil the uniforms, so when we found out that our big fashion secret was about to be revealed, I called the reporter and his editor and begged them not to run the Dozer photo.

Not only would it not give an accurate picture of the uniform, which was being changed slightly, but the quality of the photo was not the best and running it would really be embarrassing for Dozer, not to mention the rest of the organization.

I agreed to give *The Republic* the final design drawings of the home uniforms, road uniforms and the warm-ups. I also gave them the exclusive to run all of them just ahead of opening night. We gave the poster to Dozer as a memento, but I think he wasted little time in destroying it.

THE FINAL WARM-UP DESIGN

Echoes From the Purple Palace

I wondered if Alexander Julian ever have to deal with these sort of issues?

Nevertheless, there were still some anxious moments with the arrival of the new uniforms. The team wore their old, western-style uniforms for all of the pre-season games, even those games played at America West Arena. But as the pre-season came to a close, the new threads still had not arrived from the manufacturer. Some uniforms arrived the day before the first game, but many were sized incorrectly. The rest showed up on the day of the season opener. Suns athletic trainer Joe Proski had to scramble to have many of the uniforms custom tailored before they could be worn.

In spite of the anxiety, the first regular season game at AWA went off to rave reviews. The Suns had a new power forward in Charles Barkley, a new, sold-out arena in downtown Phoenix and a new, modern look for their uniforms.

When the final buzzer sounded and Barkley celebrated the Suns' win by punting the basketball high up into the seats, a new era in Suns history had begun.

After waiting 24 years to make their first major uniform change, it took only eight more seasons for the Suns to make another one. For the 2000-01 season the Suns adopted a basic uniform design that I thought was very similar to that of a number of other NBA clubs. It seemed like the manufacturers just changed the colors and the name on the jersey. There was nothing particularly unique about the style. I think those designs were dictated more by the uniform manufacturers, rather than by the league or the teams.

The push was on for greater world-wide marketing of NBA products and I had no problem with that, but all of the new, cookie-cutter styles made a traditionalist like me, long for the old-school, home-grown and classically unique, team-created styles.

2 WACKO!

JOE PROSKI, "MAGIC FINGERS"

COVER UP

The new America West Arena was created as a public-private partnership. The City of Phoenix owns the bricks, mortar

Echoes From the Purple Palace

and steel of the arena, as well as the land upon which it stands. The Suns organization agreed to manage the new facility and the franchise agreed to play at AWA for 40 years.

As the new arena took shape in downtown Phoenix there was another design element that came into play, the public arts requirement for all new buildings in Phoenix. The Suns organization had already implemented plans for two different, high-tech art displays inside the building, but they were still deliberating on what artwork would go onto the new plaza in front of the arena on the corner of Jefferson and First Street. A piece of sculpture seemed most likely.

At the invitation of the Phoenix Arts Commission, several artists brought samples of their work in for Jerry Colangelo and the Suns management team to evaluate.

I remember one piece in particular. It was a bronze statue, contemporary in style; an elongated, nude, male figure reaching toward the sky with a globe or ball at his fingertips. We were looking at an 18" high scale model of the statue, which would be at least 12 feet tall in its final form. Even in this smaller scale, it was an impressive work.

> **"Is it going to be, you know, unclothed?"**
> *– Jerry Colangelo*

Jerry examined the model for a minute or two and then asked, "Is this the way it's going to be?"

"I'm sorry," the artist said, "I don't understand."

"Is this the way it is going to look when it's finished?" Colangelo tried to clarify.

"It will be much larger, but I'm still not sure exactly what you mean," the artist said.

Colangelo stammered a bit before he said, "Is it going to be, you know, *unclothed*?"

Next, please!

The sculpture eventually selected was a bronze of a small boy (fully clothed, by the way), holding a basketball and looking up in awe, contemplating what it will take to "make the goal." The piece,

2 WACKO!

created by sculptor Rosalind Cook, was titled "Great Expectations" and was illustrative of what it takes to accomplish any goal in life.

It was a winning concept. However, a few years ago, during the arena remodeling, the bronze piece was removed from the plaza and now stands in an area not open to the public, in a fourth floor corner of the Suns' executive offices at US Airways Center.

In my opinion, the Suns should let this kid go outside to play. It's where he belongs.

ROSALIND COOK'S BRONZE SCULPTURE, "GREAT EXPECTATIONS"

PRESS CHECK

During the summer of 1992, the America West Arena had debuted and the Suns were getting ready to open, not only their first season in their new home, but also their 25th season in the Valley of the Sun. To salute the past and look toward the future, we launched an ambitious book project that was published as *A Silver Anniversary Celebration, Phoenix Suns Basketball 1968-1992*.

As co-authors, Jim Brewer and I engaged a team of writers, editors, photographers, designers, binders and printers and we pulled together the 232-page, full-color, coffee table book in just three months. The book was published by the Suns and its first and only print run of 10,000 copies, sold out in six months.

Naturally, the 1975-76 season, and the Suns' remarkable run to the NBA Finals, received plenty of attention in the book. One of the great moments from the 1976 playoffs was the team's triumphant return to Phoenix following their victory over the defending champion, Golden State Warriors, in Game Seven at Oakland. It was almost incomprehensible...THE SUNS WERE GOING TO THE NBA FINALS!

Suns fans jammed the airport's Terminal 2 to welcome their conquering heroes. On pages 64 and 65 of the *Suns Silver Anniversary* book there is a two-page spread of that insane night at Sky Harbor. As that section of the book went to press, one of the printers, on a routine press check, noticed in the foreground of the photo, a young boy holding up a single finger. Was he saying that "the Suns are number one!" or was it something else less tasteful?

The section was immediately taken off the press and "Doctor" Thom Meaker of Meaker the Printer deftly performed some graphic arts surgery that not only amputated the kid's taunting digit, but turned it into an enthusiastic Suns "fist-pump."

2 WACKO!

1976 AIRPORT MOB WITH OFFENDING FINGER REMOVED

FROM THE WACKO! FILE: SUCCOR? OR WHAT?

Author's Note: When perusing contributions to the WACKO! File, my curiosity about these letters and e-mails always leads me back to one question, "Why?"

Why the Suns? Why professional basketball? Why me?

Money, of course, is the usual answer, but in this case, the writer wanted to give the money to us. Nevertheless, it had a certain scam-like feel. Its total irrelevance to basketball made it a perfect submission for the WACKO! File.

Dear Brethren,

I am the above named person but now undergoing medical treatment in London, England. I was married to Dr. Walter Smyth-Wilson who worked with British railway commission in Chelsea, England for over a decade before he died on 5th of July in 2006. We were married for 15 years without a child. He died after a brief illness that lasted for two weeks.

Before his death he made a vow to use his wealth for the downtrodden and the less privileged in society. Since his death I decided not to remarry or get a child outside my matrimonial home. When my late husband was alive he deposited the sum of 10 million pounds sterling in a vault with a Security/Finance house in the UK. Presently, this money is still there.

Recently, my doctor told me that I would not last for the next 150 days due to a cancer problem. Though what disturbs me most is my stroke. Having known my condition, I decided to donate this fund to an individual, or better still, a God-fearing person who will utilize this money the way I am going to instruct herein. I want an individual that will use this fund and provide succor to poor and indigent persons, orphanages, and above all those affected in the tsunami in far Asia. I understand that blessed is the hand that giveth.

I took this decision because I do not have any child that will inherit this money and my husband's relatives are not inclined to helping poor persons. I do not want my husband's hard-earned money to be misused or spent in a manner that my late husband did not specify. I do not want a situation where this money will be used in an ungodly manner, hence the reason for taking this bold decision.

I am not afraid of death; hence, I know where I'm going. I know that I am going to be in the bosom of the Almighty. I do not need any telephone communication in this regard because of my health and because of the presence of my husband's relatives around me always. I do not want them to know about this development. With God all things are possible. As soon as I receive your reply, I shall give you the contact at the Security/Finance house in UK. I will also, through my lawyer, issue you a letter of authority that will empower you as the original beneficiary of this fund.

> I want you to always pray for me. My happiness is that I lived a life worthy of emulation. Whosoever that wants to serve the Almighty must serve him with all his heart and mind and soul and also in truth. Please always be prayerful all through your life. Any delay in your response will give me room in sourcing for an individual for this same purpose. Please assure me that you will act accordingly to my specifications herein.
>
> Hoping to hear from you. Thank you and may the Almighty bless you. My Attorney-Barrister will contact you as soon as you reply to this e-mail.
>
> Yours sincerely,
> The widow Smyth-Wilson

BADGES

If not one of the greatest movie lines of all-time, it has certainly become one of the most frequently quoted.

"Badges? We ain't got no badges! We don't need no badges! I don't have to show you any stinking badges!"

With respect and apologies to the Mexican bandito who uttered that line in John Huston's *Treasure of Sierra Madre*, unfortunately, in the secure arena environment of the sports-entertainment world today, yeah, pal, you do need badges, and usually more than one.

When the America West Arena opened in 1992, those of us in management each received a 3"x 6" laminated, "All-Access Pass" to all events at America West Arena. This credential would get you backstage for any show, concert, game, wrestling match or religious revival. It was kind of like the "golden ticket" to Willie Wonka's chocolate factory. It wasn't so much that you would use or abuse the privilege, it was simply about the fact that you could. That was powerful.

Echoes From the Purple Palace

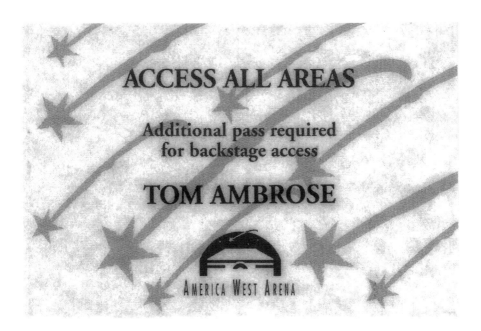

As director of security, George Bevans was "da man" when it came to these passes, so you made sure you used them judiciously and you always made sure that you stayed on the right side of George.

After a year or two all the security badges were changed in size and shape, but I continued to wear my "AWA All-Access" badge on a lanyard along with all the other required security passes.

One night, Bevans said to me, "Tom, you know that All-Access badge isn't good anymore."

"Yeah I know, George" I said, "but I like wearing it because it impresses everybody, and it's just s-o-o-o cool!"

George was a Viet Nam veteran and a "hands-on" guy who took personal responsibility for the arena's security.

The first official public event in the new building was a George Strait concert. About 10 minutes before the doors opened to the public, with the concert crowd lining up outside, I was walking along the upper concourse. I remember seeing Bevans, huffing and puffing, running up the arena staircase, struggling to climb the last few steps to the fourth floor. He'd been doing a last-minute check of the facility, but clearly, he was gassed.

"George, are you OK?" I asked.

George's exasperated and nearly breathless response was, "Do you have any idea how many doors there are in this place?"

SERIOUS STUFF

A little more than five years later, Bevans really clamped down arena security, but not because someone didn't want to display their badge. It was because of a downtown shooting and a very real threat on the life of Jerry Colangelo.

Leaving a meeting of the County Board of Supervisors on August 13, 1997, Maricopa County Supervisor Mary Rose Wilcox was accosted by a gun-toting man who had attended the meeting and followed her from the auditorium. A split second later, the assailant fired a .38 caliber round at Wilcox's back.

The gunman, Larry Marvin Naman, a 49-year-old transient with a history of mental illness, told police he was angry about the board's support of the baseball stadium sales tax. He also ranted about targeting Jerry Colangelo.

Wilcox was left with bullet fragments in her hip and thigh. It could have been much worse had not an alert security guard hit the assailant's gun-hand just as he fired his weapon. The gunman was eventually convicted on charges of attempted first-degree murder and sentenced to 15 years in prison.

In reality (a concept with which Mr. Naman rarely dealt), the stadium tax had been authorized by the state legislature several years before Jerry Colangelo became involved with the drive to bring a Major League Baseball franchise to Phoenix. Wilcox and the Maricopa County Board of Supervisors simply confirmed the implementation of the tax plan after Major League Baseball approved the new Phoenix franchise in March of 1995.

I doubt that Colangelo would have become involved with the baseball project at all, if that funding mechanism for the construction of a new stadium was not already in place.

Echoes From the Purple Palace

Since Colangelo's offices were located at America West Arena, security was immediately stepped up after the Wilcox shooting.

Within weeks, a pass card system for all employees and sign-in procedures for all visitors went into operation and construction began on multiple security doors. A bodyguard was assigned to Colangelo for all Suns games and public appearances. Even Colangelo's car was fitted with a remote starting device.

In Phoenix, the world of sports and entertainment was no longer just fun and games.

AUTOGRAPHS

Part of the planning for the new arena was to make Suns players as accessible as possible to the fans. The players' designated parking area was a surface lot at the northeast corner of the building. As Suns players exited the arena, heading for their cars, fans would have the opportunity to line up for autographs. Suns management encouraged the players to be as open and cooperative as possible.

On the first night of this new arrangement, Suns star Tom Chambers headed for the parking lot. He knew the drill and stopped to sign autographs. The fans were lined up behind those waist-high, portable, aluminum barricades.

Over the next 30 minutes Chambers chatted amicably with the fans and signed dozens of autographs. The crowd grew. But Chambers had places to go and people to meet, so he apologized to the remaining fans, "I'm really sorry, but I have to get going. I'll catch you all next time."

Upon hearing that, a "fan" standing toward the back of the crowd, proceeded to rip Chambers for being selfish and uncaring. The fan then called Chambers names which, in the interest of civility, we will not report here. Chambers displayed extraordinary self-control, by not going over the barricade and decking the guy. Instead, he just walked away.

Needless to say, Chambers was not happy about the incident and, the following day, he had a chat with Jerry Colangelo.

2 WACKO!

"I don't mind signing autographs," Chambers told him, "but I don't need to take that kind of abuse."

Colangelo agreed and immediately changed the post-game procedures. Thereafter, players parked inside the arena on the lower level, where there was no fan access and much better security.

Sorry. We really tried to make the players more accessible to our fans, but one "wacko" spoiled it for everybody.

SEEKERS

Not everyone looking for a player's autograph is a fan. Many of the people lined up near the arena's player entrances, or outside the team hotels on the road, though often dressed in appropriate team apparel, are simply doing business. They are in the business of selling autographed basketball cards and merchandise and, they will resort to just about any means to get those autographs.

Through their agents, many of the NBA's top players will enter into exclusive arrangements with apparel manufacturers or card companies. Typically, that means that the player will not sign anything unless authorized by their sponsoring company. At the very least, most NBA players are wary of signing things for people who might be trying to exploit their autographs for profit.

One day, as Charles Barkley was leaving the arena after practice, he was confronted by a young lad, about eight years old, who asked him to sign a rare and valuable Charles Barkley rookie card. Charles looked around the immediate area and spotted a well-known dealer of autographed merchandise, who, for a couple of dollars, had probably hired this cute little kid to do the asking for him.

"Would you please sign this card for me, Mr. Barkley?" the kid asked politely, handing him the card and a pen.

"Sure, kid," Barkley said, "what's your name?"

"Tommy!" was the kid's enthusiastic response.

So Charles signed the valuable rookie card, "To Tommy, Best wishes, Charles Barkley."

The "To Tommy," rendered the card nearly worthless.

Charles then looked over at the dealer, who was going to be severely disappointed when he got his card back in a few seconds.

Charles pointed at him, smiled and said, "Gotcha!"

DECIBELS

In promotional advertising that extolled the exciting, new features of America West Arena, the acoustics were described as being "like the Sydney Opera House."

Although it was true that there was some acoustical material draped from inside the arena's all-metal roof and ceiling, comparing it to an opera house, fine-tuned for sound, was just a bit of a stretch.

Actually, when the arena opened, the sound system's coverage inside the seating bowl was "spotty," at best. Some fans could hear but a whisper of the public address announcements, while other fans had their ears blown back.

Bryan Colangelo heard what was happening and led the charge to have the whole system revamped, and, if necessary, replaced. It took over a year, but after much tinkering and experimentation, the entire system was replaced. The sound was then measured as "even" throughout the seating area.

With the system well-focused and the sound "pure," fans soon began to complain that the music was too loud. The increased decibel levels were, in part, the result of the increased clarity of the new sound system, but they also reflected a league-wide trend to pump up the volume in NBA arenas.

HERE KITTY, KITTY

Once the arena was operational, with its wide-open garage entries, it was not difficult for a number of stray cats to move in and call AWA home. The arena staff was concerned that the issue of these feline interlopers had the potential to grow into greater problems.

The arena's in-house counsel, Tom O'Malley, contacted the Arizona Humane Society and told them about the issue. They agreed to come out and remove the cats. Seemingly within minutes, a woman called O'Malley to tell him that if he allowed the Humane Society to take the cats, she knew that they would most likely be immediately euthanized.

When O'Malley asked if there was an alternative, she suggested that he use a particular rescue shelter that would neuter the cats, then return them to the arena and allow them to go feral.

She explained that those neutered cats would be saved from euthanasia. The subsequent feral cat colony, or "clowder," that would form, would then drive off any new cats that might have thoughts about moving into the arena. Once the original AWA cats passed away from natural causes, the arena cat problem would be solved. Obviously, all of that wasn't going to happen overnight.

O'Malley was baffled. "What happens if we don't do as you suggest?"

"Then I will go to the media," the woman threatened, "and expose you for what you are."

Tom decided that the safe and expedient bet was to go with the Humane Society. The following day, the trespassing cats were rounded up and removed from AWA.

A short time later, O'Malley was enjoying a quiet day at home when his wife called his attention to the Pat McMahon radio program.

"They're talking about you," she said.

The woman from the cat shelter was on the air, expressing her disgust with the way the situation had been handled at the arena. Specifically, she took O'Malley to task, branding him, for all time, as "the cat murderer of America West Arena."

CHAPTER 4

THE BARKLEY ERA

DAY ONE

It is not every new player acquisition who is picked up at the airport by legendary coach-turned-front-office-guru, Cotton Fitzsimmons, but Charles Barkley was special.

It was over 110 degrees in Phoenix, but Cotton had the top down on his Mercedes convertible as they drove toward America West Arena. When Barkley made some remark about the heat, Cotton responded, "Look, Charles, everybody knows that eventually, you're goin' to hell. We're just getting you used to the heat."

It was Barkley's first day in Phoenix, following the blockbuster trade that sent Jeff Hornacek, Tim Perry and Andrew Lang to Philadelphia.

Cotton drove Barkley onto one of the upper levels of the AWA parking garage. When they walked into AWA only a few of the security lights were on, but it was enough to dimly illuminate the arena.

2 WACKO!

"Tell me Charles," Cotton asked the newest Sun, "what do you see?"

"I see seats, coach," Barkley said, "lots of seats."

"That's right Charles," Cotton said, "and every single one of them is already sold!"

"So, Charles," Cotton added, "Tell me what you do NOT see."

"I don't know, coach," Barkley said.

Cotton instructed Charles to "look up."

"I don't see any championship banners, coach," Barkley responded.

"That's right Charles," Cotton said, "You weren't brought here to sell a single seat. You were brought here to win a championship!"

"I've got goose bumps, coach," Barkley responded, "Let's go!"

A DEFINING MOMENT

It was the summer of 1992. Fitzsimmons had stepped down as the Suns' coach, America West Arena had just opened, Barkley had just been traded to Phoenix and the former governor of Arkansas, William Jefferson Clinton, was running for President of the United States.

Cotton and JoAnn Fitzsimmons were on a NIKE sponsored trip to Hawaii. Charles was there too but, because they were moving and working through some other issues, his wife Maureen was not with him.

During the course of the trip, Barkley repeatedly declared that he no longer wanted people to call him "Charles," or "Chuck." Instead, he told everyone that he wished to be referred to as a "black, multi-millionaire."

Later, as Cotton, JoAnn and Charles watched Clinton's campaign unfold on television, Charles stated, "I usually vote Republican. People think that because I'm rich, I should vote

Republican. But this time, I think I'm gonna' have to vote for Clinton."

Cotton quickly put things in perspective for Charles, the self-styled, "black, multi-millionaire."

"Charles, if you vote for Clinton," Cotton said, "when he's done taxing you, you're gonna' wind up being just a black millionaire."

Cotton paused for a few seconds before adding, "And once Maureen gets through with you... you're just gonna' be black!"

ROLE MODEL

It wasn't long after Charles Barkley joined the Suns, that NIKE released his now famous, "I'm not a role model" television spot. And it did not take long for the phones at the Suns' office to start ringing off the hook. Fans, parents and just about anyone who saw the spot had a negative opinion of it.

One father called and said he would never go to another Suns game, buy another Suns t-shirt or watch Suns games on TV because of that spot. I thanked him for offering his opinion, but before he cast his opinion in concrete, I encouraged him to listen carefully to the entire spot.

> **"Fewer things are harder to put up with than the annoyance of a good example."**
>
> **– Mark Twain**

Nobody ever seemed to listen beyond Charles' opening line, "I am not a role model." In the spot, Charles said this:

I am not a role model.

I'm not paid to be a role model.

I am paid to wreak havoc on the basketball court.

Parents should be role models.

2 WACKO!

Just because I dunk a basketball, doesn't mean I should raise your kids.

Nike's inspiration for the spot may have come from my literary hero, Mark Twain, who once said, "Fewer things are harder to put up with than the annoyance of a good example."

SIR CHARLES BARKLEY

Echoes From the Purple Palace

HE'S NOT SO BAD

When Charles Barkley and his visiting Philadephia 76ers came to Phoenix for a 1991 game, it was well known among NBA fans that visiting teams usually stayed at the Westcourt Hotel.

Roger Moore, a local coach, took a chance and brought five of his young players to the lobby of the Westcourt. He picked up the house phone and asked for Charles Barkley. To his total surprise the hotel operator connected him and the phone was ringing. Then, to his utter shock, Charles Barkley answered the phone.

Roger couldn't believe his luck! He told Charles that he had five young boys with him, down in the lobby. They were all between nine and ten years old and played on the basketball team that he coached. Would Charles consider coming downstairs to meet and talk with the boys for a few minutes?

"Sure," Charles said. "I'll be right down."

A few minutes later, Barkley came down to the lobby and spent the better part of an hour talking to the boys and signing autographs. It was a meeting that those kids, not to mention Roger Moore, will never forget.

However, I don't think Roger's good fortune could be repeated today. Most NBA players, including TNT's Charles Barkley, now check into their team hotels under assorted aliases.

OCCUPY CHARLES

One day, early in the Barkley era in Phoenix, before he had grabbed a rebound, scored a point, or intimidated a referee for his new Suns team, Charles was enjoying the morning in his new Paradise Valley home, when his cell phone rang. It was Suns PR maven, Julie Fie.

Julie explained that she had been listening to one of the local, morning radio shows. The show hosts wanted their listeners to welcome Charles to his new team and his new home, so they boldly announced his address over the air. Live reports were now coming back to the show that a large crowd was gathering in front of Barkley's house.

"What?" Barkley said in disbelief.

"Look out your front window," Julie told him.

Charles did as instructed, opening the blinds just enough to take a peek. There were well over a hundred people milling around on the street in front of his house.

"Holy _____!" he exclaimed.

Charles thanked Julie for the "heads up" and then went outside to meet his new fans. Barkley shook hands, signed autographs and posed for pictures with everybody.

Since Charles had just moved into this new, supposedly secure, gated-community, he wondered how all those people got in there. It turned out that the guard-gate was still under construction and was not operational.

Even twenty years later, Charles still had a laugh remembering that crazy morning.

HOMEWORK

When it came to the media, without question, Charles Barkley was the biggest star to ever play for the Suns. In the NBA's media world he was bigger than Shaq; bigger than Steve Nash; bigger than any other player in the Suns' Ring of Honor. In fact, the Suns' advertising campaign following the trade that brought Barkley to Phoenix, was themed simply, *THIS COULD BE BIG*.

In fact, it turned out to be *GINORMOUS*.

The media, both local and national, doted on Barkley's every word. To them, the best thing about Charles was his total unpredictability. Race relations, politics, women; nothing was off-limits and you just never knew what he was going to say next.

The Arizona Republic went as far as to create a daily sidebar column called "The Barkley Beat." Several TV stations did similar features. In order to capture material, *The Republic* assigned a second staffer to attend every Suns practice or post-game media session.

"The Barkley Beat" guy would rarely ask questions. Usually, he would just stand by the throng of reporters that always surrounded Charles and would simply take notes or record everything Barkley said, including some of the "perhaps-better-left-off-the-record" banter with reporters or other Suns players.

I was surprised that "The Barkley Beat" guy didn't follow Charles into the showers. The column made for fascinating and entertaining reading. People either hated it, or they couldn't get enough of it. With Charles, there never seemed to be any in-between.

During the four year reign of Sir Charles in Phoenix I always said that he was just like a newspaper columnist. He was compelled to say something every day, even on days when he really had nothing to say. It would be difficult to get fully inside that well-polished head of his, but I sensed that Barkley felt that he had an obligation to be "Charles." He needed to be not only a superstar on the court, but also a rock-star personality off it.

Charles had a ready and creative wit and an up-to-date knowledge of popular culture. He worked hard at maintaining his revered position with the media, who annually voted him the honor of being "The Best Interview in the NBA."

I remember traveling with the team on the outbound leg of an East Coast road trip. I was surprised to see Charles turn down several invitations to join the poker game that was a regular part of the team charters. Instead, he hunkered down to read. He read every page of USA Today, putting in extra time on the Lifestyle and Sports sections.

He then scanned several other "lifestyle" publications like People magazine for information on Hollywood, stars, politics, fashion and, of course, gossip on the hottest new super-models.

It was clear to me that he was doing his research, getting ready for the inevitable onslaught of creative media questioning that he would face during the road trip.

Like any well-researched, well-prepared, daily columnist, play-by-play announcer or TV commentator, Barkley was just doing his homework.

FULL COVERAGE

It wasn't too long after Barkley had taken hold of an overly-pesky bar patron, picked him up and sent him crashing through the saloon's plate glass window and onto the sidewalk outside, that he was asked if he had any regrets about the incident. Barkley's response was, "Yes. I regret that we weren't on a higher floor!"

> **"I got one of those raincoat policies."**
> – Charles Barkley

So it was no surprise that Suns teammates Tom Chambers and Danny Ainge were teasing Charles one day in the locker room, asking him why, with all his shenanigans, he wasn't worried about getting sued for damages.

"Na-a-a," Barkley said, "I got one of those raincoat policies."

Ainge and Chambers looked at each other incredulously and then simultaneously burst out laughing.

"Charles, do you mean an umbrella policy?" they asked.

"Yeah, whatever," was Barkley's sheepish response.

Chambers added, "Well, it better be a huge umbrella because, there isn't a raincoat big enough to cover up some of the stuff that you do!"

MR. MENTOR

From the ever-expanding list of Barkley stories, here are some of my favorites:

Echoes From the Purple Palace

Even after Sir Charles was traded from the Suns to the Houston Rockets, he was always willing to share his experience and wisdom with impressionable, young NBA players, especially rookies. So it was not really a surprise to learn that Charles once confronted Rockets' rookie Cuttino Mobley's on his sloppy attire.

"Hey, haven't I told you to dress better than that?" Barkley said.

"You're in the pros now. This ain't Rhode Island anymore. The girls have teeth here."

***

Barkley is reported to have once said to Steve Kerr, "Hey Steve, no offense, but if you couldn't shoot, there would be no reason for you to be alive."

***

Charles claimed to have been misquoted in his own autobiography: "That was my fault. I should have read it before it came out."

HOLDING COURT

Barkley loves to hold court. It could be in a locker room, on an airplane, in a restaurant, or in a bar. From his center-limelight position, he jests, insults, confronts and entertains. One of his favorite stories supposedly originated on the Oprah Winfrey Show.

Charles told the story, according to one insider, "at least a thousand times." Barkley said it all happened this way:

The topic of the show was paranormal activity. Oprah first asked her studio audience, "Does anyone here believe in ghosts? If you do, please raise your hand."

It was an impressive response, with perhaps three-quarters of the audience holding up their hands.

Oprah continued. "Has anybody here ever seen a ghost? If you think you have, please stand up."

A good number of people, approaching half of the audience, stood.

"OK," Oprah continued, "Have any of you actually talked to a ghost? If you have, please remain standing and everyone else please sit down."

The number of people standing dwindled down to maybe 10.

"Very good," Oprah said. "Now, this is a little unusual, but can any of you claim to actually have had sex with a ghost?"

Everyone sat down, except for one older man who just stood there, gazing around the studio.

Genuinely surprised, Oprah exclaimed, "Sir, are you telling me that you have actually had sex with a ghost?"

The man looked a bit confused and hesitated before he responded, "Ghost? Oh, I thought you said 'GOAT!'"

For Barkley, the story was always a sure-fire winner. I'm not sure how Oprah felt about it.

HOW 'BOUT A BEER?

It was a Sunday night at Dutch John's restaurant in Scottsdale, when Charles Barkley and his teammate, Frank Johnson, came in for dinner. There were 50 to 60 people in the restaurant and it seemed that, at one time or another, every one of them came up to Charles to talk to him and ask him for an autograph.

People asked him to sign scraps of paper, napkins or cardboard drink coasters, whatever they could find. The restaurant manager said that Barkley was very gracious and accommodating to almost everyone who came up to him that night.

But one woman walked up to Charles' table and asked for 10 autographs. Charles said he was sorry, but he could only sign one autograph per fan. He couldn't sign one for everyone she knew. She accepted the single autograph on a napkin, but five minutes later she returned to confront Charles. She said she wanted to show him what she thought of his autograph. She then tore up the autograph in front of him and threw it in his face.

Charles was sitting there with a glass of beer in his hand and, in reflex, threw the beer in her face. Her boyfriend, sitting at a nearby table, immediately leaped to his feet. Charles pointed directly at him, glared and said forcefully, "Don't even THINK about it!"

Wisely, the boyfriend sat down.

Dutch John's manager told me that the patrons there that night, could not believe the woman's totally out-of-line conduct. They described her behavior as "insulting and abusive." It was so bad that, right after the beer flew, everyone in the restaurant let out a big cheer.

The restaurant bouncer came over, ended the disturbance and asked the couple to leave. Charles and Frank remained to finish their dinner and they continued to be gracious and accommodating to all.

If the incident had involved anyone else, it would have been reported simply as a "scuffle in a local restaurant," if it was reported at all. But this was Charles Barkley and the timing was just a few days before the Suns would open the 1993 playoffs. The story went coast-to-coast and international by the next morning. That was life with Charles, never a dull moment.

HAVE A HEART

Charles was a larger than life figure and everyone wanted a piece of him. His "Dream Team" Olympic experience gave him world-wide exposure and an international reputation, on top of an already huge NBA persona. The local and national media wanted him for daily commentary, interviews, special features and guest appearances. Sponsors, both in the U.S. and overseas, wanted him to do their commercials.

The team needed him for photo sessions, marketing and community relations. Everyone wanted his autograph, while his coaches and teammates wanted him to lead them to the "promised land" of an NBA championship. It all added up to a lot of pressure, which Charles often said was "what you put in tires."

But, somehow, Barkley seemed to do it all... or most of it anyway. Among his early, off-the-court projects with the Suns, was a commercial for the Arizona Heart Institute. Actually, Charles and Suns broadcaster, Al McCoy, did voice-overs for the spot, which was done in "claymation."

BARKLEY IN CLAYMATION

In the commercial, Charles, ever the role model, encouraged youngsters not to be couch potatoes, but to get up, exercise and, "get in the game." Of course, that was right after he "clotheslined" two opponents, knocking them out cold. The innovative spot can still be seen on YouTube.

THE SIR CHARLES ROYAL ROAST

One of Barkley's oft-used nicknames was "Sir Charles." That, along with the "imperial" respect he commanded, provided sufficient inspiration for the Suns organization to create The "Sir Charles Royal Roast" to be held on the Thursday preceding the 1995 NBA All-Star Game in Phoenix.

The teammate considered to be the "anti-Charles," Suns guard Kevin Johnson, served as honorary chairman for the black-tie event which benefited Phoenix Suns Charities, the Charles Barkley Scholarship Fund, and KJ's St. Hope Academy. We borrowed the theme and many of the actors, from the local Renaissance Festival. Even the invitation was written in old English:

Attende, gentle folke, a merrie fest

To honor gamesman twiced blest:

Of skill in shooting ball to basket,

And saying all before you ask it.

A wit oft given to canard,

To hoist upon his own petard,

With friendly, teasing words of toast,

Sir Charles of Barkley, then to roast!

Following dinner, the roast began. Charles was introduced as "His Royal Immenseness!" He was positioned center-stage, sitting on a huge throne and wearing the appropriate royal robes (Suns purple, of course).

Comedian Billy Crystal served as the "jester of ceremonies" and kept up a steady stream of insults. When Crystal looked out at the audience of over 1,000 people, he confessed that he was not used to big crowds. He's a Clippers' fan. He revealed that a "triple-double" at a Clippers game, means that three couples are in attendance.

"The waiter asked me if I'd like a 'little white wine,'" Crystal said. "I said no, that's OK, Danny Ainge is right over there!"

The evening's roasters included: Jerry Colangelo teaming up with Cotton Fitzsimmons, Cavs coach Mike Fratello, Barkley's teammate Danny Ainge, comedian George Wallace, David Robinson of the Spurs, NBA Commissioner David Stern, NIKE's Phil Knight, Charles' wife Maureen and a corpse-like character named "Dead Bob" from the Renaissance Festival. Everyone took their shots.

The skeletal spirit, "Dead Bob," said he had no fear of Charles. "What's he going to do, kill me?!"

Cotton remembered the night he got a phone call from Charles, who told him that his eyes were burning. He was blinded and needed to get to a hospital. Apparently, Charles had been rubbing Vaseline Intensive Care lotion on his shaved head and got some of the lotion in his eyes. Cotton advised the "Chuckster" to use a wet towel to wipe his eyes and, the next time he was shining his noggin, use Turtle Wax!

Ainge, introduced by Crystal as "the world's funniest Mormon," got in some good shots saying that "Charles often describes himself as being 'thick-skinned,' but I think that's just his excuse for being fat!"

"Charles says, he's not a 'role model,' but we've seen him naked and we'll put his rolls up against anybody's!"

"A writer once asked me if Charles suffers from insanity. I told him, 'No, I think he actually loves it!'"

Ainge also remembered a few of Charles' classic lines, like, "Even a blind acorn finds a nut now and then!"

And..."Water always sinks to its own level!"

Ainge also reflected on the fact that no one seems to have as many nicknames as Barkley: the Round Mound of Rebound, Chuck, Chuckster, Charles, the Crisco Kid and the Good Time Blimp.

Then Ainge revealed some of the newer nicknames for Charles recently coming out of the Suns locker room. Those included: the Plump Rump of No Jump, the Lard Bard of Right Guard, the Nitwit of Kid Spit, the Great Bass of No Pass and the Emcee of No D.

Phil Knight of NIKE recalled his long relationship with Charles that went back eleven years.

"In the summer of 1984," Knight recalled, "we took all the money we had in the corporate treasury and invested it in a talented young player. Fortunately, that player was Michael Jordan. We had a little money left over so we also signed "The Round Mound of Rebound."

"I still wasn't too sure about Charles, so I wanted to visit him at his home. But when we arrived, I wasn't sure if I had the right house, so I rang the bell, opened the door and shouted, 'Is this Charles Barkley's house?' His wife shouted back, 'Yes, just drag him in and put him on the couch!'"

The Nike chief continued, "When Charles first arrived in Phoenix, he thought Taco Bell was the Mexican phone company."

Knight went on to tell the audience, "I once confided in Cotton Fitzsimmons that I was thinking about naming a shoe after Charles. Cotton said, 'He already has a shoe named after him, the loafer!'"

Comedian George Wallace said, "To come here and see a black man named George Wallace, I know is a surprise to some and a disappointment to others."

"I'm here for my good friend, Charles Barkley," Wallace said. He then paused for a long while before adding, "I don't even know Charles Barkley!"

Does anybody... really?

STARSTRUCK STAR

Phoenix sportscaster Brad Cesmat covered Tony Gwynn and the San Diego Padres for many years. One night, at the height of Barkley-mania in Phoenix, Cesmat treated his old baseball buddy to some prime, close-to-courtside seats at a Suns game. Barkley immediately recognized Gwynn and came over to say hello.

Charles proceeded to totally ignore the team warm-ups and engaged Gwynn in a long, animated conversation. The horn sounded to signal the end of warm-ups and the start of the National Anthem. Barkley and Gwynn continued yakking, pausing only briefly out of respect for the anthem.

2 WACKO!

Charles finally went back to the Suns bench to get ready for the opening tip.

Remember, at the time, Tony Gwynn was well on his way to becoming one of the greatest professional baseball players of all time. He'd spend 20 years in the major leagues, all with the Padres. He would collect a total of 3,141 hits and forge a .338 lifetime batting average, which would result in eight batting titles. He would appear in two World Series and 15 All Star Games. He'd win five outfield Gold Glove Awards and seven Silver Slugger Awards during his amazing career. Gwynn would be elected to the Baseball Hall of Fame in 2007, his first year of eligibility.

> **"Brad, Charles Barkley thinks I'm cool!"**
>
> —Tony Gwynn

But after meeting Charles, Gwynn was acting like a little kid. All he could do was grin and say excitedly, "Brad, Charles Barkley thinks I'm cool!"

BRAWLERS

During the 1992-93 season, on their way to a league-best record of 62-20, the Suns took on the Eastern Conference-leading Knicks at AWA on March 23, 1993. Some considered the game a possible preview of the NBA Finals.

The Suns win was marred by a bench-clearing brawl that led to the ejection of six players, including the future mayor of Sacramento, Suns guard, Kevin Johnson.

All in all, 21 players were fined a then league record of $292,500. But the real irony was in the fact that the normally angelic Johnson was singled out by the NBA as an "instigator," fined $60,000 and suspended for two games, while the player who usually defines "trouble," Charles Barkley, was neither fined nor disciplined and came away with his somewhat battered and twisted halo intact.

Echoes From the Purple Palace

KEVIN JOHNSON

FROM THE WACKO! FILE: MINI BRAWLERS

PRESS RELEASE

Contact: Cassie Stoneberg
E-mail: cassie@bravobsp.com
Date: October 26, 2007
FOR IMMEDIATE RELEASE

Half-Pint Brawlers...
A Night of Midget Wrestling Featuring

Puppet – The Psycho Dwarf:
Puppet stands 4 foot 4 and Totally Hardcore, there is nothing this dwarf wont do inside or outside the ring. PROOF is in the DVD - Wrestler, Stunt Man, Stand Up Comic, and Professional Drinker - he is an original. Puppet has appeared on many pay per views in the last 5 years beating the hell out of midgets and is honored to have started the Half Pint Brawlers. The one word that comes to mind to describe Puppets demeanor: XTREME!!!!

Madd Mexx – Immigration Sensation:
Mexx stands in at 4ft. 8 in. and is one of the rarest forms of midgets there is. His wrestling technique ranges from Hardcore, to High Flying Luchaa Libra, to even traditional technical wrestling. To this day (SIX MONTHS LATER) one of his ankles hasn't healed right after a balcony jump, but he continues to give it all he's got for the fans. He might not speak a word of English, but this Vato is totally LOCO!!!!

Little Kato – The Dwarf Destroyer:
Kato stands in a 4ft 6in. and is the "grandpa" of the Half Pint Brawlers with 20 years behind his black belt. Kato might not like ya, but ladies he wont tease ya....HE'll JUST PLEASE YA!!!! Kato is known all over the world as "The Master Midget of the Martial Arts"!! SOMEBODY GIVE THIS OLD GRUMPY MAN A STOGIE!!!

Little Justice – The Public Midget Prosecutor:
Justice stands in at 4ft. 4in. and looks to put all midgets in the Slammer!!! Justice doesn't fight fair and doesn't care, because he is the Law inside and outside the ring. ATTENTION LADIES, Justice is ready to put you in his cell and have his way with the 12inch tongue. OOHHH, DRINK ANYONE? Evildoers beware cause JUSTICE will prevail.

Teo – The Tattooed Midget:
"3 foot 8 and ready to mate"

He is the ultimate mini host with the most, is a true midget pimp and is always the life of any party! Teo keeps the crowd jamming, the drinks pouring and the women dancing!

Saturday, January 26, 2008
Big Easy
Boise, ID

Doors – 7:00 pm   Show – 8:00 pm

Tickets on sale now.

Tickets available at all Ticketweb outlets including Newt & Harold's, The Record Exchange, The Boise Co-op, & A New Vintage Wine Shop, or by calling 800-965-4827, 466-TIXX(8499), and online at www.ticketweb.com or www.bigeasyconcerts.com

Tickets: $15.00

Produced By Bravo Entertainment – www.bravobsp.com
"The Big Easy – Where Downtown Gets Up Close"
General Admission, All Ages, Full Bar w/ ID

ONE PROMOTER'S PITCH TO AWA

Echoes From the Purple Palace

PLEASE DON'T TELL

At the risk of mitigating Charles Barkley's carefully cultivated, "bad boy" image, let me tell you about a side of him that very few people ever saw.

The original idea was hatched over a Thanksgiving dinner at the home of Suns' CFO, Rich Dozer. The result of that discussion was that every holiday season during the four years he played for the Suns, Charles would work with Rob Harris and our community relations staff to set up a special evening for homeless kids.

Just before Christmas Eve, the Suns would secure a bus and Charles would ride it to the Salvation Army Center in Phoenix where many homeless families were trying to get back on their feet. He would pick up a busload of children from the center and would talk to them as a group.

His message was simple; he knew that times were tough for their families but the best thing the kids could do was to go to school every day, study hard, be good and help their parents in any way they could. Charles would then take them to a Toys 'R Us store, where he invited the children to pick out whatever they wanted. Charles would pay for everything.

An interesting and unexpected consequence was that many of the kids picked out gifts, not for themselves, but for brothers, sisters or friends who were not there. Charles' tab for the evening was usually around five or six thousand dollars. Barkley did this willingly and generously each year, but with one stipulation: no reporters, no cameras and no publicity of any kind, before, during or after the event. If one camera showed up, the deal was off. The Suns always honored his request.

In my opinion, Charles did not want people to think that he was doing it just for the publicity and consequently, he did not want any publicity at all. To Charles, the only people who really mattered were those kids from the Salvation Army Center.

But s-h-h-h-h-h-h. Please don't tell anybody. Charles has an image to maintain!

2 WACKO!

OFFENDED

When Paul Westphal coached the Suns, he once made a post-game reference to his sharp-shooting guard, Wesley Person, as being as accurate from long range as an Old West cowboy picking off the Indians, one by one. His comment elicited much outrage from some in the Native American community as well as many others who seem to work up outrage for anything not politically correct.

Paul penned an apology/explanation/response which he asked me to release to the media. It began, "Dear Offended People..."

NICE GIFT

It was the spring of 1993 and the night of my birthday. Where did I go to celebrate? Why, a Suns-Lakers game at my home-away-from-home, America West Arena. I really didn't have a choice.

But, I was feeling pretty good that the fourth quarter was underway and the Suns had built a 20-point lead against that hated L.A. team.

"What a thoughtful gift." I remember thinking, jokingly.

But then things began to unravel for Phoenix. The Suns lead dropped to 16... no worries. Then it was cut to 12... OK, come on, guys! Suddenly the lead was six... gulp! Then, in what seemed like the blink of an eye... the Lakers led by two with 1.6 seconds to go! Say it ain't so, Westy! For cryin' out loud! It's my birthday! This is ridiculous!

Following a time-out, the Suns inbounded the ball to Dan Majerle, who was out between the circles and well beyond the three-point line. He barely had enough time to catch the ball, spin and fire a high, arching "Hail Mary" at the basket... the ball seem to hang in the air, turning in slow motion... the buzzer sounded... SWISH! Suns win, 115-114! Pandemonium ensued!

The crowd went absolutely insane. Majerle raced over to the press table and jumped on top, right in front of me, to celebrate with the fans. His miracle, 33-foot shot had not only won the game, it meant that the Suns, for the first time ever, had swept the Lakers in a season series.

An unforgettable moment in Suns history and a very nice birthday present! Thanks, Dan.

Emotional ups and downs, that's just the everyday roller coaster ride that is life in the NBA.

ANOTHER #24

During the 1993 playoffs, actor James Garner, a friend of Suns coach Paul Westphal, was attending a game at America West Arena. At the request of Westphal, Suns staffer Kenny Glenn was escorting Garner and his guests from their seats up in the stands, down to some of the coach's personal seats close to the Suns bench. Accompanying Garner was a young man who appeared to be about 20 years old.

Garner whispered to Glenn, "Watch this kid. He's gonna' be great!"

But Kenny didn't recognize the young man. "Who is he?" K.G. asked Garner.

"His name is Jeff Gordon." Garner informed him.

Garner obviously was a good judge of NASCAR talent. That year, 1993, was when Gordon began racing with Hendrick Motorsports in the Winston Cup and won Rookie of the Year honors. By the time he was 24, he had won four Winston Cup Championships. Gordon continues to be one of NASCAR's best. He drove his #24 car into the winner's circle at Phoenix International Raceway (PIR) in 2011. Sadly, at PIR in 2012, Gordon was responsible for a four-car pile-up that could best be described as "payback" to another driver.

FROM THE WACKO FILE: FENG SHUI

Dear V.I.P.   October 21, 1999

I am writing to you about a very important Transaction in History!!!!. It is about Walt Disney Theme Park being built in one of the most important cities in the World!!!!, Hong Kong, China!!!!. Hong Kong not only represents the free trade with the World, but is World Famous for the art of Feng Shui!!!!, pronounced={Fung Schway!!!!} which means in English, Wind and Water!!!. Feng Shui is a doctrine of Philosophies, with Symbol Logic and a system of moral principles!!!!. Feng Shui dates back thousands of years!, It was only used by the Chinese elite in the Olden days, Nowadays, there are many books written in the United States of America, and throughout the World!, by Feng Shui masters, born in Hong Kong, {Feng Shui is also practiced in Beijing, the Capital city, of the Peoples Republic of China!!!! That adds up to millions of readers, throughout the World!!!!. Hong Kong, China, was built with so much influence of Feng Shui, that the ~~about~~ amount of money, Feng Shui represents

(over)

in Hong Kong is in the billions of dollars, and Trillions of dollars throughout the World!!!!.

Oct. 1, 1999, is the day the Peoples Republic of China, celebrated 50 years of Modern Day China!!!!. On Oct. 1, 1949 was when Modern Day China was born!!!!. The Feng Shui year of the OX, which is in 1949! Coincidently, Walt Disney himself, was born in the year of the OX!!!!. On Dec. 5 1901!!

What I am asking you is before time runs out in the year 1999, 1999 is the year of the Rabbit or (Cat), which is the luckiest animal sign in Feng Shui!!!!, please make some kind of effort in helping this Historical Transaction, to come to a perfect agreement!!!!

My name is _____
I live at _____

Please write to:
Board of Directors
Chairman Michael Eisner

Burbank Calif. 91521-9722
or call Ms.

ITALIANS VS. INDIANS

Members of the local Italian American Club, Jerry Colangelo included, were proud and excited about the dedication of a Christopher Columbus statue at Central and Columbus Avenues in mid-town Phoenix. If Colangelo was involved with the project, so was the entire Suns organization, even the non-Italians.

The dedication ceremony was planned for Columbus Day, October 10, 1992. That day would mark the 500th anniversary of Columbus' historic voyage to the New World. Columbus discovered that there was life and land beyond what many skeptics felt was the "edge" of a very flat world.

But Arizona's Native American community wasn't particularly happy about the scheduled Columbus Day activities. They planned to protest, largely because they felt that Columbus' voyage was the catalyst for the ultimate devastation of North America's Native American tribes. They didn't like that.

Thinking that he had discovered a new trade route to India, Columbus called the first native people he encountered, "Indians." The Native Americans didn't like that much either. The protestors objected strongly to honoring Columbus with a holiday, a parade or, on this day, the dedication of a commemorative statue.

As the crowds gathered for the dedication, Native American protesters started beating their ceremonial drums: *BOM-bom-bom-bom... BOM-bom-bom-bom.... BOM-bom-bom-bom*

The Italian American contingent, which included Ron Costello, Jack Duva and Art Consoli, did not want to see the ceremony descend into a possible confrontation, so they went to their *consigliere*, Colangelo.

Jerry advised them, "Make a deal with the Indians!"

A group from the Italian American Club reached an understanding with the tribal leaders, but as the ceremony prepared to get underway, there were still some unruly protestors and the potential for an ugly incident.

Adding to the stressful atmosphere, the drums continued to beat rhythmically in the background: *BOM-bom-bom-bom... BOM-bom-bom-bom...BOM-bom-bom-bom.*

Echoes From the Purple Palace

COLUMBUS STANDS WATCH IN PHOENIX

But, Jerry Colangelo, like Christopher Columbus 500 years before him, was resolute, "We have the permit! Let's go!"

As Colangelo and others spoke that day, there was a little jeering from the protestors at the back of the crowd. But those drums, those damnable drums, continued to thump: BOM-bom-bom-bom... BOM-bom-bom-bom...BOM-bom-bom-bom.

Even after the dedication, the controversy continued, as did Columbus' journey. The statue, created by sculptor, George-Ann Tognoni, moved several times around Phoenix before finding a welcoming and permanent home at the Arizona Italian American Club.

After surviving the statue's multiple moves and the entire Columbus experience, Costello observed, "It would have been a lot easier if Columbus had been on roller skates!"

HAPPY EASTER

The Paul Westphal coached Suns had just scored a big win on the Saturday before Easter. In the locker room after the game, "Westy" announced that practice would be cancelled and the players would have the following day off to be with their families.

Westphal told his players, "Happy Easter to each and every one of you."

Danny Schayes, the Suns' only Jewish player at the time, piped up and added, "and a happy Passover to me!"

"Oh! Right!" Westphal said, "Sorry, Danny!"

THE BIG "O"

One Suns draft pick with great promise, but ultimately unfulfilled potential, was Oliver Miller. "The Big O," as he was so aptly nicknamed, was drafted late in the first round in 1992 out of Arkansas. He was listed at 6'9" and 315 pounds, but that's being charitable since he always had difficulty controlling his weight. When he first showed up, the Suns did not have a scale big enough to weigh him properly, so the coaches and trainers took him over to an onion warehouse near the America West Arena to weigh him on a large commercial scale. The fact that Miller wasn't really embarrassed about it should have sent up a caution flag.

The Suns did everything they could to help Miller. They set him up with a nutritionist, who he ignored. They arranged for several chefs to prepare well-balanced meals at Oliver's home. Ollie either didn't pay them or he fired them. The team even took the extreme move of having Miller admitted to one of the local hospitals to control his environment and hopefully, his appetite. Incredibly, Oliver would bribe the security guards with Suns tickets and then have pizza and beer surreptitiously delivered to his hospital room. Legend had it that he actually sweated Twinkies.

When Cotton Fitzsimmons asked Oliver how come he seemed to be gaining weight, Miller responded, "I don't know coach. I'm not eatin' much."

But Cotton knew the truth, long before he asked the question.

It wasn't hard for Cotton to keep track of Miller's dietary abuses, since he lived right next door to Miller.

On trash pick-up day, when Cotton wheeled his covered container to the curb, all he had to do was look over at Oliver's. Typically, Ollie's trash container was so full that the lid couldn't close properly. Jammed every which way into it were empty boxes, buckets, and carry-out containers from Pizza Hut and Kentucky Fried Chicken to name just a couple of Ollie's favorites.

When Cotton confronted him with that evidence, Miller responded, "Oh yeah, I forgot about that."

STEAMIN' MAD

So they wouldn't have to take a trip over to the onion warehouse every time Oliver was scheduled for a weigh-in, the Suns purchased a huge scale that went up to 500 pounds and had an immense, three-foot diameter, glass face. The team even took the trouble to ship the scale by truck up to training camp, so Ollie could have his regular weigh-ins.

It was not unusual for Miller to chow down on junk food all night and then come to practice early and sit in the steam room for a couple of hours, trying to "sweat off" the pounds. Of course, that weight-control modality wasn't particularly effective. Sweating off two or three pounds in an hour, might be possible for a man of Miller's size, but not 23 pounds! When Oliver stepped on the scale for his weigh-in he was way over the poundage that the training staff had targeted for him. Demonstrating that he not only had a weight problem, but some anger management issues as well, a frustrated Miller smashed his fist through the glass face of the scale.

NULL AND VOID

NBA player contracts include clauses that prohibit players from engaging in what are termed "hazardous activities." Things like sky-diving, riding motorcycles, horseback riding, hang-gliding, skateboarding, driving racecars, skiing and snowboarding are just a few of the prohibited items.

In their player contracts, the Suns have a list of over 30 excluded activities. Should a player engage in any of these high-risk endeavors, his contract could be declared null and void. Given the size of NBA contracts today, it is only fair for teams to protect their investments in players.

Also, players prove, time and time again, that they need protection from themselves. These excluded activities are not hidden in the fine print of the contract. They are made crystal clear to the player, and the player's agent, at the time the contract is signed.

That brings us to the day, during Oliver's first season, that Suns CFO Rich Dozer got a call from a friend, who told him that Miller had just purchased a motorcycle from his dealership.

Rich immediately called Oliver.

"Oliver, is it true that you just purchased a motorcycle?" he inquired.

"A motorcycle?" Oliver said, "No, Rich, I didn't buy a motorcycle."

Rich's next call was to Oliver's agent to ask if it was true, but the agent claimed he didn't know anything about it.

Knowing that his friend in the motorcycle business had no reason to lie and knowing that Oliver wasn't always totally forthcoming, Dozer had his doubts.

Rich stopped doubting the very next day, when a report came to him that Miller had been involved in an accident, a motorcycle accident.

But wait. It gets better.

According to the police incident report, Mr. Miller was riding the motorcycle while holding his girlfriend's infant child in one arm! When he lost control of the motorcycle and fell, he used his body to cushion the fall and protect the child. Fortunately, the child was unhurt, but Miller suffered multiple contusions and abrasions.

Because Miller's injuries did not prevent him from playing basketball, the Suns did not void his contract, but only because the playoffs were about to get underway.

SUMO

Unquestionably, Miller had some basketball skills. He had great hands. He could pass, shoot and often displayed great court vision. As a rookie, he was a key player in the Suns first round playoff series win over the Lakers and helped the Suns reach the NBA Finals in 1993.

But after two years in Phoenix, he rejected a contract offer from the Suns, decided to become a free agent and signed with the Detroit Pistons. He bounced around the league for a few years, even returning to the Suns briefly for the 1999-2000 campaign. A few years later, he came back to America West Arena as a Sacramento Kings reserve.

Sometimes irreverent and not always politically correct, the Suns Gorilla picked that night to spoof "The Big O" and his well-documented weight problems.

During a time-out, the Gorilla waddled out onto the floor wearing one of those inflated "sumo suits." Stretched over the sumo suit was a mock-up of a Kings' uniform, complete with Ollie's name and number. The uniform was stretched to the fabric's absolute elastic limit.

The jumbo-sized "Milla-Gorilla" went over to the fans seated in the front row, grabbed a big bucket of popcorn and tried to "pour" it into his mouth. Popcorn flew everywhere. Acting as though he was so full that he could barely walk, the over-inflated Gorilla then staggered to center court where he flopped to the floor on his back. Kicking his feet and waving his arms, he made it apparent to all that he'd fallen and he couldn't get up!

The crowd of 19,000, players on both teams, the referees, just about everyone in the building except Oliver, howled with laughter. Finally a team of ball boys came onto the floor, picked up the helpless Gorilla by his arms and legs and lugged him off the court.

Naturally, a huge controversy erupted over the incident and there were many offended people.

Miller threatened to sue, but apologies were made and eventually the issue faded away. The incident resulted in new NBA rules restricting the in-arena "spoofing" of players and coaches.

WE ALL SCREAM

Utah coach Frank Layden was another guy who always battled weight problems. He'd often use his great sense of self-deprecating humor to deal with his weight-related ups and downs.

He once said that he only put on weight "in certain places – pizza parlors, bakeries and ice cream shops."

Speaking of ice cream, Layden once confessed, "The last time I said 'No' to ice cream, I misunderstood the question!"

Another time, Layden talked about stepping onto a scale that gave out fortune cards. The card read, "Come back in 15 minutes – alone!"

Coach Layden once observed, "It's hard to feel as fit as a fiddle, when you're shaped like a cello."

Layden also recalled a time when, "I go see the team doctor for my annual physical. When we're done, I ask him, 'How do I stand?'"

"That's what puzzles me," the doctor said.

> **"The last time I said 'No' to ice cream, I misunderstood the question!"**
> – Frank Layden

THE SHEIK

Dan Majerle had successfully launched his namesake restaurant two blocks from America West Arena in downtown Phoenix. Majerle's Sports Grill opened to standing room only crowds, rave reviews, and a menu that featured items like the "Sir Charles Chicken Sandwich" and the "Mama Majerle Burger."

Things were going so well that Jerry Colangelo thought it was the perfect time to pull off a well-orchestrated practical joke on the new restaurateur. Pulling together the many resources at his disposal, Colangelo convinced Majerle that a friend, a "sheik" from the Middle East, wanted to invest millions of dollars in the "Majerle's" concept. If Dan was interested, Jerry would set up the meeting with the sheik.

Of course, Majerle was interested.

In addition to the bogus sheik, Jerry recruited some of Dan's teammates, coaches and friends to attend the lunch meeting, so Dan would feel more comfortable. In actuality, they would be there merely to serve as "straight men" and to otherwise "bust Majerle's chops" when the time was right.

A week or so later, in an executive dining room at America West Arena that had been "wired" and set up with multiple hidden cameras, the trap was sprung.

2 WACKO!

WOULD YOU BUY A USED CAMEL FROM THIS MAN?

The sheik was a local actor who wore white robes, a tribal headdress and could fake a passable Middle Eastern accent. When Colangelo orchestrated the introductions, the sheik hugged Majerle and then kissed him on both cheeks. Majerle, a kid from Traverse City, Michigan, seemed a little uncomfortable, but not wanting to cause an international incident, he rolled with it. After all, there were millions of dollars potentially riding on this meeting!

Everyone sat down for lunch. At the request of the sheik, everyone around the table held hands and bowed their heads.

The sheik then mumbled through an incomprehensible chant-like prayer to some unidentified deity. As the prayer droned on, the "straight men" were barely holding it together. Then, taking control of the meal, the sheik told Dan that he wanted to introduce him to some of his region's cultural delicacies. He directed everyone to pass each platter of food to the left.

The sheik invited Dan to try some steak tartare, claiming that it was a traditional delicacy of his region. Although you can make a legitimate case for steak tartare as an Eastern Mediterranean staple, it was still chopped, raw hamburger meat served with a raw egg on top. The egg's raw yolk stared up at Dan, Cyclops-like. Majerle was a little wary.

The sheik then directed Dan to eat this traditional food with his fingers, but cautioned him not to use the hand that he used "for personal hygiene." At that point, Danny Ainge pretty much lost it. He was about to burst out laughing and blow the gag, but he wisely got up and left the room, biting his lip as he walked out past one of the hidden cameras. Majerle was beginning to sense that perhaps he'd "been had."

No longer able to hold onto the "con," the sheik ditched his accent and walked over to reveal the cameras. The whole episode was videotaped, edited down to a short feature that was shown at a special Suns event a few days later. Majerle, as you might expect, took it all like a man.

By the way, the next time you stop by Majerle's Grill, I highly recommend that you try the "Mama Majerle Burger." Order it medium-rare, or, if you like, try it raw with an egg yolk on top.

HOT DAY

When the 1993 NBA Finals ended in defeat for the Suns, Phoenix fans were naturally disappointed, but they were still riding the adrenaline that helped them through emotional playoff series with the Lakers, Spurs, Sonics and finally the Bulls. The fact was, even though the Bulls won the title, Suns fans just didn't want their fabulous season to end. So, on the day that had been scheduled

2 WACKO!

for a Suns victory parade, they gathered for one last time to say, "Thank you, Suns. Well played. Well done!"

Knowing that city bureaucracies move slowly, the Suns officials applied for a parade permit several weeks in advance, probably about the time the team opened the NBA Finals against the Bulls. The thought was, if the Suns didn't win the championship, the parade date could always be cancelled. But even after the Suns lost the series, fans were still looking for closure. It was decided that the parade would go on as scheduled.

> **Thank you, Suns. Well played. Well done!**

There is precedent for teams to be welcomed home by large crowds, even after losing championships or suffering difficult losses, but that day in Phoenix was something special. An estimated 300,000 people turned out to line the streets of downtown Phoenix and close to a million more watched the parade on local television.

It was mid-June in downtown Phoenix and the day was brutally hot. Temperatures quickly rose to a brain-frying 114 degrees. The Phoenix Fire Department was on hand to handle medical emergencies and occasionally, from one of their pumper trucks, they would set their hoses to "fine spray," point them skyward and douse the steaming crowd with a light, artificial rain. Nobody seemed to mind, except perhaps those fans who had painted themselves purple and orange using water-based paints.

City of Phoenix and Fiesta Bowl officials, who were used to staging plenty of parades, advised us that we would not need to put up any barricades along the parade route to hold back the crowds. We were told to just spray paint a line a few feet out from the curb on both sides of the street and the crowds will stay behind the line. They never had a problem before.

Really? We didn't think it would work, but what the heck. They're the experts. A purple line it will be!

The parade was staged inside the America West Arena garage and was designed to loop around the downtown streets. Most of the team and coaching staff had rolled out of the garage riding atop an assortment of vintage cars and special trucks. They motored slowly through the downtown streets past cheering, adoring fans. Amazingly, the purple line seemed to be working.

Charles Barkley was held back to go last. As his car, a rare Shelby Cobra, finally entered the parade route on Jefferson Street, the crowd surged forward and forced the car to a stop right in front of the arena. The purple line had worked about as well as the French Maginot Line!

The crush of the overly enthusiastic crowd was so forceful that the Cobra's windshield was cracked and security shifted their focus to Charles' immediate safety. Instantly, Suns security chief George Bevans declared the parade "OVER" and mustered about half-a-dozen burly security guards to haul Barkley off of his perch on top of the convertible. Security created a "flying wedge formation" that would have brought a smile to the face of old-time footballer, Jim Thorpe.

Pushing people aside, the wedge inexorably chugged through the crowd, heading toward one of the arena entrances. Barkley trotted along, securely ensconced in the middle of the formation. Fans risked getting plowed under, but still, they reached out to try to touch "Sir Charles." Describing things as "chaotic" would be an understatement.

The situation was fluid. Security and Suns management were definitely playing things by ear. The decision was made that we would get all the players off the parade route and up to the fourth floor arena balcony that overlooked the plaza. Security closed down the arena to everyone but players, coaches and management.

The view from the balcony was stunning. Down below, hundreds of thousands of people covered the entire America West Arena Plaza, Jefferson Street and three full city blocks to the west, north and east. The crowd kept growing as people who had been spread out along the downtown parade route made their way back towards the arena. Simply put, there were Suns fans as far as the eye could see.

Each of the players, coach Paul Westphal and CEO Jerry Colangelo addressed the cheering fans.

Barkley shouted, "We didn't come here to be runners-up. Wait 'til next year!"

Colangelo followed that with, "I just want to tell you that I LOVE YOU!"

The crowd roared back, "Jer-ry! Jer-ry! Jer-ry!"

It was truly a hot time in downtown. But I will always wonder how insane that day would have been, if the Suns had actually WON!

PAY-PER-VIEW

Just prior to the opening of the 1994-95 season, I released a Suns television schedule that featured several new developments in our TV package. But, as was the case with most of my insightful and well-written press releases, no one paid much attention.

The facts were that all 41 Suns road games would be broadcast over free commercial television and 29 Suns home games would be carried on basic cable television. The remaining 12 games on the Suns home schedule would also be televised and carried on cable TV, but on a special pay-per-view (PPV) tier. Those 12 games featured some of the NBA's best teams: the Lakers, Celtics, Knicks, Rockets... you get the picture.

Suns home games were sold out for the season, so radio and television broadcasts were the only options for many fans to hear or see their Suns.

Since pay-per-view television was a new concept to Suns fans, I was surprised when the release garnered little reaction. My initial thought was that fans must be OK with it and, with the season getting underway, I put it out of my mind for a couple of months.

The first PPV game would not come up until mid-season. The new season and the Suns regular telecasts were going along fine until January, when we began to get some push-back on the new PPV plan.

There were problems with outlying cable system operators who wanted to show Suns' games, but were being hit with new charges which they did not want to pass onto their customers. There were bar owners who wanted to show Suns games but couldn't, or didn't want to comply with the new regulations for pay-per-view games. Establishments who committed to take the pay-per-

> **"pay-per-view television was a new concept to Suns fans..."**

view feed bristled at the idea that they would be monitored, inspected and audited on game days. There were also folks who simply couldn't get cable because their part of town had not yet been wired. We heard from all of them, usually more than once and, usually in very loud voices.

Outside of a few heavyweight boxing matches, pay-per-view had not been attempted in the Phoenix cable TV market for sporting events. If you were a Suns fan, had cable television and paid a premium for the Suns pay-per-view package, you could watch all 82 regular season Suns games on TV. But if you didn't have cable, your options were limited. Fans who thought they could just shuffle on down to their favorite bar to watch the big games, quickly found out that they would not only be charged for their beer and pretzels, but they'd also have to pay an admission fee.

Then, in January, about a week before the first pay-per-view game, the "Suns Nation" finally awoke, achieved full clarity as to what was happening, and the you-know-what really hit the fan! Or perhaps, more accurately stated, it hit the fans! Many finally realized that they would not be able to watch the PPV games on their home TV and they'd have to pay an admission fee at those bars and restaurants that did carry the PPV games. The fan reaction was visceral and the situation quickly became an unmanageable public relations disaster for both the Suns and the cable company.

It had been a bold experiment, but by the end of that season the corporate enthusiasm for the plan had faded and the cable company developed a different business model that was more palatable to bars, restaurants and Suns fans. As far as Suns basketball was concerned, the basketball pay-per-view era was over before it really got started.

OPPORTUNITIES LOST

Against the Bulls, the Suns had come tantalizingly close to winning the championship, so the off-season produced just a few tweaks to a very solid roster. Optimism remained high that, behind the amazing feats of Sir Charles, the Suns could, and probably should, return to the NBA Finals in 1994.

The year unfolded and, in spite of injuries to KJ and Barkley, the Suns battled their way to a 56-26 record.

The playoffs opened in April with the Suns roster finally healthy. Phoenix swept the Golden State Warriors 3-0 in the first round. Then, taking on the Houston Rockets in the second round, Phoenix came from behind to win the first two games, but they eventually lost the series in seven frustrating games. The Rockets seized that momentum and went on to win the NBA title.

The next season, in a bid to capture that elusive NBA Championship, the Suns added free agents Danny Manning and Wayman Tisdale. They posted 59 wins and swept their first-round playoff opponent, Portland. Next up was their new favorite nemesis, the Rockets.

The Suns jumped out to a 3-1 lead in the series and Houston newspaper headlines of "CHOKE CITY" derided the Rockets.

Inspired or just plain angry, the Rockets came storming back to win three-straight games and the series. Houston would go on to win its second consecutive NBA title, prompting Houston coach Rudy Tomjanovich to declare, "Never underestimate the heart of a champion!"

In 1995-96 Barkley became only the 10th player in NBA history to reach the 20,000 point and 10,000 rebound level, but the Suns struggled to a 41-41 record and were eliminated in the first round of the playoffs by the San Antonio Spurs.

Even the most optimistic Suns fans recognized that the window of opportunity to win a championship with Barkley was rapidly closing.

END OF THE BARKLEY ERA

The trade that officially ended the Barkley era took place on August 19, 1996. Barkley and a second-round pick were traded to arch-rival Houston, in exchange for Chucky Brown, Mark Bryant, Sam Cassell and Robert Horry.

Sir Charles had been acting imperiously over the previous year or so. He didn't appreciate that Suns management seemed to be breaking up that old gang of his. Westphal had been replaced as coach and Majerle was traded to Cleveland. He was not at all happy with the way the Colangelos were managing things and he wanted out. Always outspoken, Charles sounded off in the media, including one NBC interview during the NBA Finals, when he ripped J.C. and Bryan, effectively sealing his fate as a member of the Suns.

Eventually, the Colangelos accommodated Barkley's desire to leave. The deal, unfortunately for Phoenix fans, was struck with the Rockets, the team that had twice turned back the Suns championship aspirations in the 1994 and 1995 playoffs.

The fact that the Rockets had gone on to claim two consecutive NBA titles, just added to the Suns irritation. Almost everyone in Phoenix felt that those were championships the Suns could have won. There was more than a little bad blood between the two teams.

> **For all sad words of tongue and pen, the saddest are these, 'It might have been.'**
> – John Greenleaf Whittier

Barkley might have been happy to be out of Phoenix, but the same cannot be said of the players coming from Houston. They did not want to come to Phoenix and, as we quickly learned, they sincerely acted like it.

With the exception of Bryant, who hung around for a couple seasons as a Suns reserve, in my 37 years in the NBA, I never saw a group of more uncooperative, un-coachable and unprofessional malcontents.

With Cotton Fitzsimmons serving as the team's interim head coach, the beginning of that 1996-97 season was an unmitigated disaster. Horry and Cassell played key roles as the Suns went 0-13 to open the season. Fitzsimmons, long-known for getting the most out of his players, could not find the motivational key to this team. Cotton always knew that this stint as coach was temporary, so he relinquished his coaching duties on November 14th and returned to the Suns front office, reclaiming his self-styled title of "Senior Executive Vice President of Nothing."

Cotton had a pragmatic view of the NBA coaching life. He always said that coaches were "hired to be fired. It wasn't a question of 'if,' only 'when.'" Although, when Cotton said it with that Missouri twang of his, it sounded like "ha-a-ar'd to be fa-a-ar'd." Danny Ainge succeeded Fitzsimmons.

The Colangelos, meanwhile, not known for their patience in these matters, were also frustrated.

Subsequently, Brown was traded away on December 4, while Cassell was dealt the day after Christmas. Horry was dispatched on January 10th just a few days after he deliberately threw a towel in the face of Ainge, who had committed the unpardonable sin of taking him out of a game.

Ironically, back during the summer, three weeks before the Barkley deal was consummated with Houston, the Suns signed their first-round draft pick, a promising point-guard named Steve Nash.

It was the 19th Century American writer, John Greenleaf Whittier, who once wrote, "For all sad words of tongue and pen, the saddest are these, 'It might have been.'"

Imagine Barkley and Nash playing together for the Suns. Even if just for a couple of seasons, it could have been something special.

THE BRAIN DOCTOR

I suppose, over the years, there were more than a few Suns players who were perceived as good candidates for pre-frontal lobotomies or brain transplants. Those options however, were not what Suns coach Danny Ainge had in mind when he brought in a consultant known as the "Brain Doctor." The guy's real name was Jon Niednagel, pronounced "Need-noggle." His name alone guaranteed him a spot in the WACKO! File, but he was not a doctor or even a psychiatrist. So what was the deal?

Niednagel had spent the better part of 20 years studying neuroscience, genetics and psychology. He figured out that humans, including the tiny sub-set of professional athletes, have 16 different brain types that can be used to explain their behaviors. Those 16 types are composed of varying combinations of eight mental preferences. Are you still with me?

Niednagel's preferences focused upon included things like: introverted, extroverted, perception, intuition, judgment, thinking, sensing and, my favorite, feelings. When Niednagel combined the brain profile with a player's basketball scouting report, he could supply Ainge with a fairly accurate prediction of future performance.

It all sounded very futuristic, but did it work?

Confidentiality prohibits us from pinpointing successes with individual players but, Ainge's overall coaching mark with the Suns was 136 wins against 90 losses, a winning percentage of .602. That ranks Ainge fourth on the Suns all-time coaching list, behind Mike D'Antoni (.650), Paul Westphal (.685) and Cotton Fitzsimmons (.621).

Not bad for Ainge, who had no prior professional head-coaching experience. So, Niednagel must have helped a little.

But I always wondered what the Brain Doctor found when he peered into the cranium of that towel-throwing thug, Robert Horry.

CHAPTER 5

OBSERVATIONS

Author's Note: It was Yogi Berra who once said, "You can observe a lot just by watching." Over 37 seasons with the Suns I couldn't help but see a few things, draw some conclusions and, here and there, collect some stories for the WACKO! File.

A LOCKER ROOM LESSON

Two Suns players, Kurt Rambis and Mark West, along with their wives, had agreed to support a local charity by serving as celebrity chefs for a major fund-raising event at one of the local resort hotels. The dinner was taking place on a Saturday night in mid-season.

On Friday night, prior to a Suns home game, I stopped by the locker room just to remind the guys about some of the details of the event coming up the next evening. I walked into the Suns Clubhouse at the AWA and the first guy I see is Kurt, sitting quietly in front of his locker. On the floor in front of him, West was stretching out. Both of them were in their warm-ups and just a few minutes away from taking the court.

"Perfect!" I said, "Both you guys are right here. I just wanted to remind you about a couple of things for tomorrow night. First, they would like you and your wives to be there by 5:30, and secondly, don't forget that it's 'black tie.'"

Mark nodded his understanding, but when I glanced at Kurt, he had a look of utter befuddlement on his face.

"What?" I said, "Don't tell me you forgot about this!"

"No, but I'm confused," Kurt said. "You just said it was 'black-tie.' I thought you told me originally that it was 'black-guy!' That's why I'm bringin' Mark!"

I looked down at Mark who just smiled, rolled his eyes back and shook his head as if to say, "You can dress him up but you really shouldn't take him out in public!"

Over the years, in a healthy NBA locker room, I've found that the only "colors" that really matter are "commitment" and "talent."

THE ROAR OF THE CROWD...THE SMELL OF...

Without question, sitting courtside at the center of an NBA press table, as I did for 17 years, has its advantages. First of all, the view is phenomenal. You simply can't get any closer without being in the game. Also, you can hear just about everything said on the court by players, coaches and referees. Even if it's not always clear what they're saying, quickly developed skills in lip-reading and body language usually fill in any blanks. Basically, you are up close and personal, sometimes a little too personal.

That brings us to the disadvantages. The referees will sometimes come over and bust you for not being "neutral" while sitting at the table. Occasionally, a hustling player will come flying over, or crashing into, the press table in pursuit of a loose ball. The result is usually, spilled beverages, sheer panic, broken technology and, during one game during the mid-1970s, a size fifteen basketball shoe belonging to Rick Barry, that turned a reporter's portable typewriter into a twisted pile of scrap metal.

There's a lot of perspiration expended during an NBA game and sitting courtside is, at times, an olfactory experience. During the game, players must report to the Official Scorer at the press table before entering the fray. If the game is underway, players will kneel and wait in front of the table until they are whistled into the game by the referees at the next time-out, or the next dead ball opportunity. That can often take several minutes. Under those circumstances, all press table personnel fully understand the meaning of the term, "the smell of fear."

The main culprit is those pesky apocrine sweat glands, of which everyone has a set. Those are the ones that become active when a person is emotionally upset, nervous, frightened, or in pain. Let's face it, the anxiety produced by a rookie or a substitute, coming into an NBA game, could throw those sweat glands into overdrive. The primary odor wafting over the press table seemed to be ammonia based, but occasionally some players would involuntarily add the elemental essence of dead-fish, garlic, sulfur spring, circus train or low tide.

Trust me, and my often-offended proboscis, it is one NBA experience you can skip.

MILLIONAIRES SQUABBLING WITH BILLIONAIRES

Philosopher, George Santayana has been credited with saying, "Those who cannot remember the past are condemned to repeat it."

That might help to explain why, in 2011, NBA owners and the NBA Players Association could not agree on a restructured collective bargaining agreement, and NBA arenas went dark for the second time in 13 years. The league's golden goose immediately ceased production of its 24-carat eggs.

However, it seemed as though the participants actually learned something from the first labor shutdown, because the

2 WACKO!

2011 NBA lockout was not nearly as entertaining as the 1998 version.

Oh sure, in 2011, the sports media and blogosphere tried to make comic fodder out of the "how u?" tweet by journeyman NBA guard, Roger Mason and don't forget Nugget's guard Ty Lawson's tweet, "I wonder if I can file for unemployment?" But overall, the rhetoric was pretty tame in 2011.

Now look back to the summer of 1998, when collective bargaining talks between NBA players and owners broke down over the issue of a hard salary cap. The players refused to agree and the owners declared a lockout. Player salaries were suspended, pre-season games were cancelled and training camps were postponed indefinitely. Then, the first part of the regular season was canceled. Still, there was no progress in the negotiations. On January 6, 1999, just one day before the league would vote to cancel the entire season, a settlement was reached and the league played a scaled-down, 50-game schedule.

> **They make a lot of money, and they also spend a lot of money.**
> – Patrick Ewing

Fortunately, owners and players also came to terms in 2011, agreeing to an abbreviated 66-game schedule for 2011-12 and a new Collective Bargaining Agreement.

During the 1998-99 lockout, team officials, under threat of a one million dollar fine by the league office, were not permitted to comment publicly on anything related to the league's labor issues. Needless to say, there was nary a peep from anyone on the owners' side. However, locked-out players had no such gag order in place and that led to some amazing comments regarding their collective "plight."

At the time, the average salary for all NBA players was well over a million dollars per year. But Knicks center Patrick Ewing, then president of the Players' Association, wanted to stage exhibition games during the lock-out to raise money for "needy" NBA players.

"If you look at people who play professional sports, not a lot of them are financially secure," Ewing said at the time, "They make a lot of money, and they also spend a lot of money."

Boston guard Kenny Anderson agreed. He had a seven-year, $49 million contract and was spending $75,000 annually just to insure and maintain his eight cars. But he came up with a painful, personal solution. "You know, just get rid of the Mercedes," Anderson said. "It's like they say, the more you make, the more you spend. I have to start getting tight."

It was probably his multi-year, multi-million dollar contract that made the lament of guard Gary Payton particularly poignant, as he sighed, "I guess we'll just have to start pinching pennies!"

FROM THE WACKO! FILE: ADOPT A PLAYER

Author's Note: It was comments like those that led to a great deal of sarcastic, public backlash over the NBA lockout. I'm not certain of the source of the following proposal, but it came to me during the lockout of 1998 and it went directly into the WACKO! File.

NBA PLAYER ADOPTION PROGRAM NEEDS YOU!

With an NBA players' strike against the team owners, now is the time for us to show the world how much we care. It's just not right. Hundreds of basketball players in our own country are living at, or just below, the seven-figure salary line. And as if that weren't bad enough, they will be deprived of pay for several weeks – possibly a whole year!

But now, you can help! For about two thousand dollars a day—that's less than the cost of a large screen projection TV – you can help keep a basketball player economically viable during his time of need.

Two thousand dollars a day may not seem like a lot of money to you, but to a basketball player it could mean the difference between a vacation spent golfing in Florida or a Mediterranean cruise. For you, two thousand dollars is nothing more than a few months rent or a mortgage payment. But to a basketball player, two thousand dollars a day will almost replace his salary.

Your commitment of two thousand dollars a day will enable a player to buy that home entertainment center, trade in that year-old Lexus for a new Ferrari, or enjoy a weekend in Rio.

"HOW WILL I KNOW I'M HELPING?"

Each month you will receive a complete financial report on the player you sponsor. Detailed information about his stocks, bonds, 401(k), real estate and other investment holdings will be mailed to your home. You'll also get information on how he plans to invest the $5 million lump sum he will receive upon retirement.

"HOW WILL HE KNOW I'M HELPING?"

Your basketball player will be told he has a SPECIAL FRIEND who just wants to help in a time of need. Although the player won't know your name, he will be able to make collect calls to your home via a special operator just in case additional funds are needed for unexplained expenses.

Simply fill out the form below.

YES, I want to help!

I would like to sponsor a striking NBA basketball player. My preference is checked below:

- o   Starter
- o   Reserve
- o   Star *
- o   Superstar **
- o   Entire Team ***

I'll sponsor a player most in need. Please select one for me.

(*) Higher cost

(**) Much higher cost

(***) Please call our 900 number to ask for the cost of a specific team. (Does not include cheerleaders.)

Please charge the account listed below $2,054.79 per day for reserve or starter for the duration of the strike.

Please send me a picture of the player I have sponsored, along with a team logo and my very own NBA Players Association badge to wear proudly on my lapel.

( ) Master Card

( ) Visa

( ) American Express

( ) Discover Card

( ) Diner's Club

Your Name: _____

Telephone Number: _____

Account Number : _____ Exp. Date: ____

Mail the completed form to NBA Players Association or call:

1-800-TOO-MUCH now to enroll by phone.
(Children under 18 must have parent's approval.)

Note: Sponsors are not permitted to contact the players they have sponsored, either in person or by other means including, but not limited to, telephone calls, letters, e-mails, or third-parties. Keep in mind that the basketball player you have sponsored will be much too busy enjoying his free time, thanks to your generous donations. Oh yes, contributions are not tax-deductible.

NOT ALWAYS ROLE MODELS

During the late 1990s the Suns held an open practice with more than 16,000 kids in attendance. Cliff Robinson was one of the mainstays on that particular Suns team and Toby Bailey of UCLA was a young player who was hustling and trying to earn some playing time.

During the team scrimmage on the main floor of the AWA, Bailey was quickly becoming more than a minor irritant to the veteran Robinson. I don't know exactly what prompted it, but Robinson suddenly grabbed Bailey around the waist, picked him up off the floor and violently threw him down to the hardwood. Robinson then stood over Bailey and taunted him. It was quite a fine example of unsportsmanlike conduct for the 16,000 youngsters who soaked in every moment. The open practice ended moments later.

MANAGING EXPECTATIONS

Employees of the Suns faced the summer of 1998 with much trepidation and uncertainty. If there was a labor action, would that lead to budget cuts, furloughs, and mass layoffs? Even though it was a situation that was completely out the control of the individual teams, everyone, including the peanut vendors, knew that a strike or lockout was going to impact them. Things were uneasy.

Once it was certain that there would be a lockout, Jerry Colangelo got word to all Suns employees.

"No one is going to lose their job," Colangelo said. "We are going to get through this together. We'll have to cut way back on spending and there probably aren't going to be any raises this season, but we are going to get through this."

Within the Suns organization, there was still some worry among employees. That was only natural. But when the lockout ended and the season fired-up again in January, not one Suns employee had been fired, laid-off, furloughed or down-sized because of the NBA lockout, not one.

Organizational loyalty is not something you can demand in the company's Human Resources handbook. It is something management helps create and nurture. Loyalty and respect are qualities that management earns one decision at a time.

THE COLOR OF SPORTS

One of the great memories from the early years of my career with the Suns was the first night my wife and I took our four-year-old daughter, Casey, to a Suns game. The Suns were playing the Rockets that night and I was running around, tending to my PR duties.

My wife and daughter sat in the stands at the Coliseum, a few rows up from the Suns bench. As you might imagine, the game was a magical and exciting new world for our little one and she would constantly point out and share with her mom all of the amazing things she saw.

Midway through the first quarter, as the players sprinted up and down the court, Casey suddenly shouted out, "Look mommy, there're five whites out there!"

Needless to say, my wife was in shock. Her mind was racing. "Where did my innocent little girl learn about racial differences? I've got to talk to her pre-school teachers…. we've never made race an issue…she's only four-years-old!"

But before my wife could think another thought, little Casey finished her comment… "Look mommy, there're five whites out there… and five reds!"

I am happy to report that in spite of my wife's anxiety, Casey has grown up to be a wonderful young lady who has respect and appreciation for people of all races and cultures. And the Rockets sometimes wear blue on the road.

The lesson we learned that night was that it was not important for my young daughter to distinguish the color of the players, only the color of their uniforms.

On a different level, sports have always played an important role in the advancement of minority rights. With the world rapidly shrinking, thanks to technology, the role of sports as a teacher of multiculturalism has taken on even greater significance.

If we are to expand cultural diversity by promoting global partnerships, then basketball, especially NBA basketball, is an opportunity of tremendous proportion.

NBA basketball is now seen on television in over 600 million households in nearly 190 countries worldwide, from Afghanistan to Zimbabwe. As the game continues to develop on a global basis, players are drawn to the NBA from all over the world.

Although the numbers will fluctuate annually, an average of 75 players born outside the United States will make NBA rosters each season. They will represent approximately 30 countries as diverse as Holland, Croatia, Nigeria, Lithuania, Jamaica, Australia and Serbia. This influx of new foreign players into the NBA offers a culturally varied cross-section of the world that has already helped bridge obstacles of culture, communication and race.

Echoes From the Purple Palace

The NBA and most of its athletes are not only role models for kids; they have become global role models for a modern world.

The critical element in all this is that NBA players are accepted on the basis of their ability and how well they use that ability to make their teams successful. They are not judged or recognized by the color of their skin, their heritage, or their religious background, just on their ability... and, on some nights, through the eyes of a little girl, just on the color of their uniforms.

MY BAD

I have a confession to make. I have been harboring this guilt since the early 1980s. I am hoping that the truth will, at long last, set me free.

It was in back 1982 that a gentleman called me at the Suns office. He identified himself as being "black." Today, the politically correct would say "African American."

He rambled on a bit, but he got my full attention when he suddenly called the Suns "racist." He went on to say that "the Suns think black kids are the same as monkeys."

"Where did you hear that?" I said, shocked and confused by the accusation. My immediate thought was that this guy was a "wacko."

He responded, "It was in one of your TV commercials."

"What?" I exclaimed. "No way!"

Now I was really in shock. My mind was racing, and I could not, for the life of me, figure out exactly what this guy was talking about. So I became defensive.

"Sir," I began, "I'm in charge of our ads and our advertising schedule, and I can tell you that we are not running any TV commercials at all. We haven't run any TV commercials for months. I simply don't know what you're talking about!"

The gentleman continued to rant about kids, racism and monkeys.

2 WACKO!

"I'm very sorry, sir," I said calmly. "We're not running any TV commercials and if I don't know what you're talking about, I really can't help you."

And I quietly hung up on him.

But at the very moment I put down the phone, it dawned on me what the gentleman might have been talking about.

It was a public service announcement promoting the Easter Seals Shootout, a free-throw shooting fundraiser for kids. The spot featured the Suns Gorilla, Suns guard Kyle Macy and some kids from the local Boys and Girls Club. Since Easter Seals did the media placement for the spot, it was not on my advertising schedule, nor was it top of mind. In addition, the Shootout had already taken place months before.

But I did remember setting up the taping. We secured Kyle Macy, the Suns' best free-throw shooter at the time, as the spokesperson for the commercial. Macy also happened to be white. For comic relief, the Suns Gorilla would join Macy on camera but, since "Go" doesn't speak, Macy would interpret his pantomime and body language. It was all carefully scripted.

When we recruited the kids, I asked specifically that the group have appropriate racial diversity. We wound up with one white, one Hispanic and two black youngsters as volunteers. To have some fun, we even rented a couple of mini-gorilla costumes for two of the kids to wear.

With the camera rolling, Macy delivered his lines flawlessly. The Gorilla nodded his head in agreement with everything Macy said to promote the upcoming Easter Seals shootout. The four kids recruited for the spot could be seen shooting at a hoop in the background. Then, their message delivered, Macy and The Gorilla turned around to watch the kids.

Macy turned toward The Gorilla and innocently asked, "Which ones are your kids?"

THAT was what the gentleman had been talking about.

A couple of follow-up phone calls confirmed my worst fears. More concerned with Macy's lines, I really was not paying any attention to what was going on in the background. But, apparently, when our production crew brought out the mini-gorilla suits, the two African American youngsters declined to wear them. The white and Hispanic kids however, didn't have a problem and they donned the furry suits and masks. The video crew simply took the path of least resistance.

So, a careful viewing of the spot would show two black kids and two little gorillas shooting baskets, and then, a mildly confused Macy asking the Gorilla, "Which ones are YOUR kids?"

In the end, it was my responsibility, I whiffed on it and I'm sorry. I really wasn't looking at the kids as being black, white or Hispanic. I simply saw them all as kids.

But isn't that the way we're all supposed to be, colorblind?

Didn't Dr. Martin Luther King, Jr. teach us "to judge people, not on the color of their skin, but on the content of their character?"

BEST ASSIST

During his time with the Suns, Anfernee "Penny" Hardaway was probably better known for his shooting and scoring, than for his playmaking abilities. His best assist, however, may have come, not on an NBA court, but on an airplane.

Following a mid-season game, the Suns' charter flight was stuck on the tarmac in Toronto, delayed five hours by a mid-winter storm. The team's ultimate destination would be Chicago. Finally, in the wee hours of the morning, the flight was given clearance to fly, not to Chicago, but to nearby Milwaukee. Consequently, the team would land in Milwaukee and then bus the final 90 miles into Chicago.

It was already a miserable bunch of players and coaches on that flight and the weather around the Great Lakes continued to deteriorate. Once airborne, the flight alternated between "bumpy" and "turbulent." Then it went from "violent" to "downright scary."

The window shades were all pulled down. There was nothing to see out there anyway. It was night and the plane was flying on instruments through a major snowstorm. As the airliner thrashed about through the blackened sky, hints of panic began to creep into the cabin.

As the plane began its descent into Milwaukee, worried cries came from more than one player, "Please... get this plane on the ground!"

Stephon Marbury called out to Hardaway, who was sitting near a window. "Penny, please look out there and tell me you see the ground, some buildings, some lights!"

Hardaway calmly raised his window shade a few inches and took a peek, but there was nothing to see. They were still going through thick storm clouds and the plane was still flying blind. Penny pulled down the shade and said, "It's all clear down there, man. We're gonna' be fine!"

> **It's all clear down there, man. We're gonna' be fine!**
> – Penny Hardaway

Marbury and everyone else relaxed. A few minutes later they landed safely in Milwaukee. It was well after 3 a.m.

Many on the flight that night believe that those few words of assurance from Hardaway, spoken calmly and with confidence, may have been Penny's best assist during his time with the Suns.

CONTRAST

Contrast that noble and selfless Hardaway story with team travel in the Barkley era, just a few years prior.

Suns guard Frank Johnson was an avowed, "white knuckle" flyer. He hated flying, especially when things got a little bumpy. So during particularly turbulent flights, Charles Barkley would always be sure to scream in Johnson's direction, "We're all gonna' die, Frank!"

RING OF HONOR

It was always a great honor for me to organize the Suns Ring of Honor ceremonies for former players, coaches or team personnel who made significant contributions to the franchise. Now that virtually every NBA game is televised, the league is very strict with its rules on extending halftime intermissions to accommodate special ceremonies or halftime activities. You literally have to beg the NBA and get written permission for an extra five minutes for your special ceremony.

In the weeks leading up to the Ring of Honor ceremony for Tom Chambers in April of 1999, I worried that Cotton Fitzsimmons was going to talk too much. Chambers and Kevin Johnson had been the two mainstays of Cotton's best Suns teams, so I expected Cotton to be effusive in his praise of "Tommy Gun." I implored Cotton to keep his remarks to two minutes, and as the big day approached, I was constantly reminding him to keep it short. When the ceremony finally got underway, Cotton was awesome. I had totally misjudged him. He kept his remarks to a minute and thirty seconds.

When we eventually handed the microphone to Chambers, including the time we had allotted for him, we had a seven minute cushion! No problem, or so I thought. Tom proceeded to blow through every bit of that extra time and as the TV crews were getting ready to start the second half, Chambers was still talking! The NBA was not happy and I thought there would definitely be a fine in my future.

When I told Tom afterwards, "You killed me on the time, man!"

His responded, "Oh, I forgot to tell you. When I have a microphone in my hand and I'm nervous, I tend to talk a lot."

"Jeez, Tom," I said. "Thanks for telling me... NOW!"

2 WACKO!

TOM CHAMBERS

RAM TOUGH

Over his career, I discovered that Colangelo likes to do the unexpected, the unanticipated, and many times he does it by making a very generous gift.

So, a few days ahead of Chambers' induction ceremony, Jerry asked me to detail all the things we were doing to honor Tom. I gave him the list and the script. Jerry nodded his okay and didn't say another word.

In the past, on the nights we honored other players, we had given vehicles to Connie Hawkins, Dick Van Arsdale and Walter Davis. Since Chambers is well-known as a cowboy-rancher, we planned to give him a custom saddle, along with a horse and trailer.

When it came time for Colangelo to make the presentation however, he couldn't resist doing the unexpected. He grabbed the microphone and said, "Tom we are pleased to present you with this custom saddle and a horse to put it on!"

Since we couldn't bring a real horse out onto the court (I'm pretty sure there is an NBA rule prohibiting that), we got a couple of our sales guys to dress up in a goofy-looking horse costume and clomp out onto the court for the presentation.

"Not this horse," Jerry continued, "But a real one! And a trailer to move everything around, and, by the way, I'd like you to go down to Joe Gambino Chevrolet and pick out a truck to tow your new horse and trailer!"

Now, that was all fine and dandy. The fans (and no doubt, Tom Chambers) loved J.C.'s generous spontaneity. But please understand that, in spite of the fact that Joe Gambino is one of the nicest people you could ever want to meet, in spite of the fact that his family is still involved with Phoenix area car dealerships, in spite of the fact he is Italian, a loyal Suns season ticket holder and a long-time friend and staunch supporter of Jerry Colangelo, his family's dealerships were NOT Suns sponsors.

I knew this was a huge mistake because the local Dodge dealer, who WAS the big Suns sponsor at the time, was sitting in the front row that night. Our marketing guy, Harvey Shank was the man who carefully nurtured these relationships and was very protective of them. I knew he would be upset about J.C.'s inadvertent gaffe. So, as the ceremony was winding down and Harvey and I stood in the arena's north tunnel, I said to him, "Harv, I'm so sorry about the truck thing with Jerry. That wasn't in the script."

"What truck thing?" Harvey asked.

Apparently, he'd missed it. So I told him that during the presentation Jerry invited Chambers to go down to Joe Gambino Chevrolet and pick out a truck.

Harvey turned to me, his eyes wide with astonishment and, while seeming to grow to about 6-8 before my very eyes, he stammered, "He said WHAT?"

So I repeated what had happened. Harvey turned on his heel and stormed off, but not before shouting back to me over his shoulder, "We'll see about THAT!"

A short while later, I was sitting in my regular seat behind the press table, happy that the ceremony was now over and the second half was underway, although about five minutes late, thanks to "chatty" Tom Chambers. But here comes Harvey, walking with a determined stride. He'd just spent the last 10 minutes mending the relationship with the Dodge dealer. As he walked past me with a determined stride, he barked, "It's gonna' be a DODGE!"

CHANGING THE GAME

Basketball history demonstrates that no one changes the game like a dominant big man. Sometimes change will manifest itself as an adjustment of the rules, while at other times it might be a catalyst for development of new and innovative equipment. Regardless, the intention is to improve the game while keeping both players and fans safe.

In the early 1950s George Mikan's size and skill forced the fledgling NBA to change its rules. The primary reason why Mikan dominated the early NBA game can be narrowed down to the lane in front of the basket. It was only six feet wide!

That meant, when Mikan lined up in the low post, even standing outside of the free-throw lane, he was only three feet from the basket! It was literally child's play for the 6-10 Mikan to turn and drop the ball through the hoop, or spin and bank it off the backboard glass. So, in order to push Mikan and other big men away from the basket, the NBA widened its foul lane to 12 feet in 1954.

About the same time (1955) the stellar play of University of San Francisco center, Bill Russell, caused the NCAA to widen their free throw lane to 12 feet. That change was often referred to as "Russell's Rule."

Then came the dominance of Wilt Chamberlain in the 1960s. In response, NBA rule-makers widened the lane once again in 1964, this time to its current width of 16 feet.

When Lewis Alcindor (later known as Kareem Abdul-Jabbar) began to emerge as basketball's next dominant big man, rules began to change again. Beginning in 1967, just as Alcindor was starting his collegiate career at UCLA, the NCAA banned the dunk shot. That rule remained in force until 1976.

Although most basketball fans believe that the anti-dunking legislation was precipitated by Alcindor, his UCLA coach, the legendary John Wooden, claimed that the NCAA Rules Committee outlawed the dunk at that time because of players hanging on the rim, glass backboards breaking and rims bending. As mere mortals, who are we to question the wisdom of the "Wizard of Westwood?"

Meanwhile, in the NBA, powerful players like Gus Johnson in the late 1960s and Darryl "Chocolate Thunder" Dawkins in the 1970s, had been shattering backboards with their aggressive dunks. It was becoming increasingly obvious that both collegiate and pro basketball needed rims that could absorb the power of a violent dunk and instantly snap back into position without shattering backboards.

The so-called "breakaway" rim was first used in NCAA competition in 1978. The NBA quickly adopted the new snap-back rims in 1979 after Dawkins shattered two more glass backboards.

Incidentally, on one of Dawkins' trips to Phoenix with the 76ers, the entire front row of Suns fans sitting under one of the Coliseum's baskets, donned construction hard hats and unfurled a banner that said, "NO DUNKING ZONE."

They could have used those hard hats again, a decade and a half later, when Shaquille O'Neal came to Phoenix on his first trip to AWA in February of 1993 and proceeded to bring down one of the baskets with a powerful dunk.

A FAMILY AFFAIR

One of the exciting amenities at the America West Arena was a permanent, full-sized practice court on the lower level. As the building was being designed, Jerry Colangelo insisted that this feature be included. As a young high school player, Jerry once broke into his high school gym to practice his shooting late at night. At the arena, J.C. wanted to make sure that his Suns players had every opportunity and every amenity available to them, at anytime they wanted.

I remember working late one night in 2005 and walking through the arena's lower level. I heard some balls bouncing on the Suns practice court, so I took a peek. One of our newest players, Raja Bell, was shooting perimeter jump shots. Under the basket, his wife was tracking down the rebounds and firing the ball back out to him.

It made me think of the old days, when I saw Jeff Hornacek working on his shooting at the old Suns practice facility, the Phoenix Jewish Community Center. Jeff's wife Stacy was the rebounder.

Families grow, circumstances change and wives can't always rebound for their player-husbands. But I always think fondly of those young couples, working together and putting some genuine sweat-equity into their NBA careers.

Echoes From the Purple Palace

FROM THE WACKO! FILE

201 EAST JEFFERSON ST.
PHOENIX, ARIZONA
85004

EVERYBODY SAYS STEVE IS THE KEY I AGREE, HE'S THE M.V.P., BUT LEANDRO BARBOSA HAS TO "STEP-UP" THIS SERIES NEEDS TO SCORE ABOUT 15 TO 20 PTS A GAME PLUS 10 ASSISTS OR MORE A GAME. NEEDS STAY IN ATTACK MODE ALL 48 MINS. USUALLY WHEN ONE PLAYER GET M.V.P., THEY GIVE OR ALLOW THE OTHER TO WIN THE CHAMPIONSHIP. EXPERTS SO THE SUNS CAN'T RUN

DALLAS SAYS THEY KNOW NASH CAN THEY SAY DALLAS HAS GOTTEN BETTER WITHOUT STEVE I SAY B.S. I WANT THESE SUNS TO COME OUT PROVING

GO MAKE HISTORY BY SCORING 75 PTS IN BOTH. DON'T STOP ATTACKING & RUNNING, I'M TIRED OF HEARING THAT THE TEAM IS WEAK & CAN'T WIN PLAYING UPTEMPO STYLE. IS EXCITING TO WAY. DALLAS KNOWS HOW TO STOP, STEVE IS THE TALKING, BAD, SAYING THE SUNS ARE OVERATED PLEASE "SWEEP" SEND A MESSAGE TO THE WORLD, BECAUSE ALL THE EXPERTS SAY THAT THE SUNS WILL LOOSE & FIZZLE OUT

NOT A WHISTLE BLOWER

NBA athletes are among the best in the world. Their overall speed, quickness, conditioning and athleticism is amazing, and on some nights, absolutely incredible. Yet the men who truly control the game, the referees, don't even come close to the conditioning levels or athletic ability of the players. In addition, young, inexperienced refs, like young, inexperienced NBA players, make lots of mistakes.

Generally speaking, (though not true in every case) the more experience a referee accumulates over the years, the better his judgment becomes. But as a referee's judgment and observation skills improve with age and experience, his overall physical condition naturally deteriorates. Many crucial calls in an NBA game are made by officials who are out of position simply because they can't keep up.

I have never refereed a basketball game on any level. But, after watching the NBA games for more than five decades, and seeing how NBA officials can control and influence how the game is played, I approached the chief of NBA officials, Darell Garretson with an idea to help keep older, more experienced, officials in the game longer.

During his long career, Darell was considered one of the league's best officials. After his retirement as an active ref, he became the NBA's supervisor of officials. Since Garretson lived in Mesa, AZ, he was a frequent visitor to Suns games so he could make first-hand observations of his officiating crews. One night, as Darell sat in the upper press box, I approached him with my idea.

Although two officials successfully worked NBA courts for more than 30 years, my concept called for today's standard of three officials, but positioned differently on the court.

Essentially, my idea had one official under each basket with the third official working center court. The officials on the baselines would be able to see oncoming fast-breaking action without trying to make judgment calls while racing to keep up with 25-year-old athletes. In any half-court set, two officials would be focused on the play.

The idea would keep experienced officials, the ones with the best judgment, out of retirement and in the game. With each stop in play, the officials would rotate one position. They wouldn't have to run, just walk to their new spot on the floor.

Darell listened patiently, but judged it an absolutely terrible idea and immediately dismissed it (and me).

I still think it makes sense. Two officials cover the half court, while the third official is in position for any fast-developing, breakaway play coming to the other end. Since the refs don't have to endure the constant, heart-pounding, end-to-end transition with younger athletes, the older, more experienced referees, hopefully with more fully developed judgment skills, can prolong their careers and even improve the game. It was just a thought.

RUBBER CHICKEN CIRCUIT

One thing that team executives frequently do is represent their franchises at numerous fund-raising luncheons and dinners. So it was not unusual for me to be at a dinner, sponsored by the Arizona Black Chamber of Commerce, honoring a respected member of Phoenix's African American community, Cloves Campbell Jr., and the community newspaper his family had published for many years, *The Arizona Informant*, formerly known as *The Arizona Black Informant*.

The master of ceremonies that night was Ernesto Salazar, a handsome gentleman who was a pillar of the local Hispanic community and, who bore an uncanny resemblance to the actor Victor Mature. On the surface, it seemed an incongruous match, until Ernesto explained it.

"A lot of people have been asking me, what connection I have to the Black Chamber of Commerce, to Cloves Campbell, Jr. or to the *Arizona Informant*. Actually, Junior and I grew up together in South Phoenix and we have been friends our entire lives. In fact, we are planning to start a new business together and I am happy to announce that here tonight."

The audience, well acquainted with both men, buzzed in anticipation of the announcement.

"It's going to be a combination Hispanic and African American restaurant," Ernesto revealed, "We're going to call it, 'NACHO MAMA!'"

2 WACKO!

FROM THE WACKO! FILE: THINGS TO DO

AUTHOR'S NOTE: Nothing escapes our ever-helpful, ever observant fans, as this note to the Suns broadcast team exemplifies.

THINGS TO DO TODAY

Date 11/22/99

☒ 1. LEARN TO ANNOUNCE THE NAME
☐ 2. OF PLAYERS — ESPECIALY NOTE:
☐ 3. SUNS DO NOT HAVE A PLAYER
☐ 4. BY THE NAME OF "GUGLIANA"!!
☐ 5. IN THE PAST YOU MURDERED "AIMS" FOR
☐ 6. AINGE

"MAKE A NOTE TO REMEMBER"

Echoes From the Purple Palace

A HAWK IN THE CUCKOO'S NEST

It was the Suns vs. the Lakers in a 2000 playoff game at Staples Center. The Suns played brilliantly, but in the end, Kobe Bryant delivered the winning basket for the Lakers and broke the hearts of Phoenix fans. Connie Hawkins and I were at the game, sitting just a few rows behind the Suns bench.

When the game ended, we decided to just wait near our seats until the crowd cleared out and the players got ready to get on the bus and head for the airport for our return flight to Phoenix.

As we waited, here comes the Lakers' number one fan, Jack Nicholson, wearing his signature sunglasses and walking down the sideline past our seats on his way out. Nicholson looked up, saw Hawkins, and began to slowly flap his arms up and down in an exaggerated motion. As he did that, he grinned and mouthed the word, "Hawk."

Connie cracked up and I added, "Hawk, do you know how big you are? You are HUGE, man, HUGE!" It turns out that Hawk got to know Nicholson when he played parts of two seasons in a Lakers' uniform back in the mid-70s. Still, it was a most impressive Hollywood salute to my man, Hawk.

REFUELING

The 161st Air Refueling Wing of the Arizona Air National Guard, nicknamed "The Copperheads," has served the country with distinction during NATO missions in Kuwait, Iraq and Afghanistan. It has been a tradition for the unit's air crews to dedicate and identify their planes with local sports teams. The Suns were honored, not only to be invited to place their new logo on one of the unit's KC-135 tankers, but to have team representatives be part of the dedication ceremonies.

Connie Hawkins and I had become an excellent PR team at these events. For me, the most exciting part of the ceremony was that all the Suns representatives would get to go on a "dedication flight."

As a pilot and aviation enthusiast, I loved the idea and couldn't wait to take off. Hawk was a bit more apprehensive. Even after we were airborne, I could tell that Hawk was still uneasy. I tried to reassure him as we headed toward northern Arizona where our flight-mission was to practice refueling near the Grand Canyon.

OUR KC-135 CREW

"Hawk," I said, "What's the problem?"

"I'm just afraid that something will go wrong," he responded.

"Hawk," I reassured him, "this plane is an airborne tanker. It holds over 30,000 gallons of high octane jet fuel. If something goes wrong, it'll be over quick! We won't even know it. We'll be toast, literally!"

Hawk looked at me and said facetiously, "Thanks, Tom. That makes me feel so much better!"

Once things settled down and Hawk understood that we were in the hands of some very competent and professional airmen, we all enjoyed the flight.

Hawk and I both had the opportunity to observe a refueling operation from an observation port in the tail of the aircraft, adjacent to the boom operator's position. I don't want to say that these were precision operations, but the aircraft being refueled was so close to us that not only could I read the nametag on the pilot's flight suit, but also I could clearly see that he had blue eyes!

Eventually, we returned Hawk safely to Earth.

EAGLE BASE

A few years ago, the NBA pulled together a tour of former players to visit U.S. troops stationed in Bosnia. Two other retired NBA players, Pearl Washington and Charlie Scott, joined Connie Hawkins on the trip.

2 WACKO!

Together they toured some military installations including one base on the front-line of the conflict. When Hawk returned to Phoenix, I asked him the name of the base he visited.

"Eagle Base," he told me.

"Where's that?" I asked.

"No idea. They wouldn't tell us."

"What was it like?"

"Well, all the players had to wear military uniforms and helmets anytime we went outside," Hawk said. "They even gave us guns!"

"They gave YOU a gun?!" I asked incredulously.

"Yeah. They wanted us to look like everyone else on the base."

"OK. They gave you a gun. Did they give you a clip?" I asked.

"No, man!" Hawkins laughed, "They didn't give me any clip!"

I breathed a retroactive sigh of relief.

RARE BIRD

It was Jim O'Brien, a long-time Pittsburgh sportswriter, who played a huge role in Connie Hawkins' election to the Naismith Memorial Basketball Hall of Fame (HOF). O'Brien would probably tell you that he was just one of many people who supported Connie's candidacy. But the reality was that O'Brien was the guy who shepherded Connie's nomination and all the letters of support through a process that took several years.

O'Brien's relationship with Connie went back to his American Basketball Association days with the Pittsburgh Pipers (1967-68) when Connie led the league in scoring (26.8 points per game) not to mention an amazing 13.5 rebounds per contest. Hawk was named league MVP as Pittsburgh defeated New Orleans for the ABA Championship.

O'Brien was a virtual bulldog when it came to recruiting support for the Hawkins' nomination. Without advocates like Jim O'Brien, Wayne Embry and Jerry Colangelo, I doubt Connie would have had the broad-based support he needed to become a Hall of Famer.

HALL OF FAME

The Naismith Memorial Basketball Hall of Fame (HOF) informed us that Connie would be named to the HOF Class of 1992. The official announcement would be made in New York City, several months ahead of the May 11 induction at the Hall of Fame in Springfield, Massachusetts.

I was honored to accompany Hawk to New York City for the press announcement. It was my job to make sure that Hawk was at all official functions and coordinate media requests for interviews. Imagine my consternation when I arrived at the first official Hall of Fame function, a breakfast in our hotel, and Hawk was nowhere to be found! I called his room. There was no answer.

I then learned that an elevator full of hotel guests was stuck between floors. Upon hearing that news from the hotel staff, I remember just standing there shaking my head, thinking that we'd have another story for Hawkins' long and checkered history of missed curfews, buses, airplanes, wake-up calls and even missed tip-offs! Just then, who comes walking across the hotel ballroom toward me, but the Hawk, with a big smile on his face!

"Connie! I was worried you were caught in that elevator!" I said.

"N-a-a-a," Connie replied, "I knew you'd want me here early. So I came down about an hour ago. I was having coffee with some of the guys!"

After that, I never let him out of my sight.

NO WAY

Connie Hawkins is often described as "a New York City playground legend." But even young, developing legends had a tough time finding large-sized basketball shoes in the 1950s. A businessman in Connie's Brooklyn neighborhood helped the budding star secure some size-14 Chuck Taylor Converse All-Stars, the best and, at that time, pretty much the ONLY basketball shoe available. Hawk always had those sneakers with him, but he only wore them to play ball.

During our trip to New York, Hawk told me about a night when he traveled from his home in Brooklyn up to Harlem for a YMCA game. After the game was over, Connie changed his footwear, slung his prized basketball shoes over his shoulder and was about to leave the gym and head for the subway. Suddenly, a guy walked right up to him, stuck a gun in Hawkins' face and said, "Gimme them shoes!"

Hawk looked at the guy, then looked at the gun and said, "No!"

The gunman was stunned, "What chu mean, no?! I got a gun, man! Gimme them shoes!"

"No," Hawkins repeated firmly, knowing how hard it was to get these shoes in the first place, "I'm NOT givin' you my shoes!"

Connie turned and walked away.

The gunman shouted after him, "Are you crazy, man? I got a gun."

Hawkins just kept walking, bracing for a shot that never came.

When Hawk first told me the story I said, "Man, that took a lot of guts! Weren't you scared?"

"Not really," Hawk confessed. "I was just a kid and I didn't know what I was doing. The only thing I was thinking was there was no way I was going to give that guy my shoes! When I got home and thought about it later, that's when I got scared!"

A REVEALING STORY

Following the Hall of Fame announcement, on the return flight to Phoenix, Connie and I were sitting across the aisle from one another. He was playing around with my computer and I was reading a proposed movie screenplay, based on the book *FOUL!*

by David Wolf. The book could have just as easily been titled, *The Tragic Story of Connie Hawkins*.

I have always known Connie to be a great guy, but one of the passages I read on that flight confirmed everything I ever thought I knew about him, and more.

A New York City high school and playground legend, Hawkins got a full scholarship to the University of Iowa. When he first arrived at Iowa, the athletic department assigned a tutor to help him with his studies. Hawkins, inexperienced in bookish matters, was excited about it, but for all the wrong reasons. "Great!" Hawk enthused, "You can go to class for me, take my tests, and I can focus on playing ball!"

"Sorry, Connie," the tutor said, "But that's not the way it works."

It didn't take long for the tutor to discover Hawkins' most closely guarded secret. He was functionally illiterate. Connie had always assumed that basketball would provide everything he needed. Indeed, basketball helped get him through high school without much book time or worry about grades. Connie would always carry a book or a newspaper with him and no one ever suspected he couldn't read.

It would have been easy for the tutor to give up on Connie and ask for a different athlete to mentor, but instead, he diligently went to work, teaching Connie some new fundamentals in the game of life. Connie was a quick learner and the basic reading and writing skills he had ignored in grade school and high school, were quickly assimilated.

This was a time before the NCAA allowed freshmen to play varsity ball. Hawkins enjoyed a sensational year on the freshman team at Iowa and everyone was looking forward to Connie joining the varsity the following season. Additionally, a world of literature and reading was opening up for Hawk. He was as excited about getting back to Iowa to continue his progress with the tutor, as he was to step up to the varsity basketball team. Well, almost. But Connie was clearly growing as a person.

When Hawkins was on break from school and back in New York City, he was suddenly swept up in an investigation regarding a college basketball betting scandal. Hawkins was one of the biggest names to ever come off the playground courts of New

York City and, consequently, that made him an attractive target for prosecutors. The only problem was that Hawkins was only guilty of being young and naïve. He was completely innocent of any point-shaving, gambling or wrongdoing.

But when he finally was allowed to return to the Iowa campus, the betting scandal followed him. The administration took away his scholarship and told him that he was no longer welcome at Iowa.

As you might imagine, Connie was devastated. His entire world was crumbling around him and he really did not know what he was going to do next.

But, knowing that he would not be returning to Iowa, he took the time to sit down and write a note to his tutor, expressing his appreciation for all the time, patience and extra-effort that he had invested in him.

When I finished reading that story, I looked over at Hawk and I was literally moved to tears. Connie Hawkins, the player, is in the Basketball Hall of Fame and his on-the-court exploits are legend. But that one story, that one thank you note, told me everything I ever needed to know about Connie Hawkins, the man.

PARDON THE INTERRUPTION

The new AWA had a beautiful office lobby which not only served guests visiting the Suns executive offices, but it also served as a nice backdrop when TV outlets were interviewing Suns players, coaches or executives. Such was the case one day as a visitor waited for his appointment with someone in the Suns front office and the *Greatest Sports Legends* show was getting ready to interview the Hawk.

The chief interviewer and host, baseball great, Reggie Jackson, "Mr. October," was not actually on-site. One of the show's assistants would interview Hawk and later, through the miracle of technology and editing, it would not only look like Jackson asked the questions, but that he was actually on the set with Hawkins.

Echoes From the Purple Palace

The camera light went on, the tape began to roll and the interview began. The first question asked was, "Connie, why do you think it is that Julius Erving, 'Doctor J,' doesn't seem to be as appreciated here in Phoenix as he is elsewhere around the league?"

But before Hawkins could respond, the visitor waiting in the lobby, long-time Suns fan and local printer, Thom Meaker just couldn't help himself. He jumped up and blurted out, "Because everything 'Dr. J' does, Connie Hawkins did 10 years ago!"

Hawkins laughed and said, "Yeah! Listen to that man!"

Hawk genuinely appreciated the support, but the director, unamused, said, "OK, let's rewind the tape and take it from the top!"

Because that's what killjoy directors always say.

READ TO ACHIEVE

The Suns had successfully promoted the NBA's Read to Achieve program in elementary schools throughout the Valley of the Sun. A special reading contest had produced a winning school in Buckeye, Arizona. Those over-achieving students earned a pizza party, an appearance by the Phoenix Suns Gorilla and a Q & A session with a Suns player.

The day's activities were being coordinated by the Suns VP of Public Relations, Debra Stevens. The Gorilla had done his usual high energy routine by acting out a special story that was read to the assembled students. They loved it.

The kids were now digging into their pizza and anxiously awaiting the arrival of the Suns player, Shawn Marion.

In a scenario that NBA PR people know all too well, Debra met Shawn on the loading dock outside the school cafeteria to give him a 30-second overview of what had already happened and outline what he was supposed to do. She reminded him about Read to Achieve and that the kids would be asking him questions.

2 WACKO!

SHAWN MARION

"I got it. I got it. No problem," Marion said as they walked inside.

As the teachers, school administrators and a few members of the news media watched, the kids settled down and Shawn offered to answer any questions they might have.

Because of the day's reading theme, the first question from a young student to the Suns forward was, "Mr. Marion, what books do YOU like to read?"

Shawn seemed a little embarrassed. He looked down at his sneakers and shook his head.

"Aw-w-w, man," he responded, "I don't read books!"

When Shawn looked up, he saw the shock and puzzled looks on the faces of everyone in the room, and the abject disappointment on the face of Debra Stevens. He quickly tried to cover his gaffe.

"But, I read *Sports Illustrated* and *ESPN Magazine*," he added hastily, in a lame attempt to recover.

Shawn was a good guy and was trying to be a good role model for the kids, but on that day, he may have been just a little too honest.

FROM THE WACKO! FILE: AN ATHLETIC JOB APPLICATION

Dear US Airways Center,

I'm applying for a position as an equipment manager with your Phoenix Suns Basketball Team. In the past I have been athletic and I understand the players' needs. Please inform me of any openings that become available. Thank you.

Sincerely,

J. Strap

CLEARED FOR TAKEOFF

It was January 21, 2004, and President George W. Bush (#43) was making a visit to Phoenix.

As every pilot and most folks across America now know, since 2001 and the, 9/11 attacks, when a President visits your city, air traffic comes to a virtual standstill.

The Federal Aviation Authority imposes what they term a TFR, or Temporary Flight Restriction, over the region during the times of the President's arrival and departure. Take-offs and landings for regularly scheduled flights are delayed and inbound flights are often held on the ground in their departure city.

Jerry Colangelo had just come out of a long meeting with Arizona State University President, Michael Crow. When he checked his cell phone he saw that he had two messages, one from his son Bryan and the other from Washington, D.C.... the White House.

J.C. called the White House first and found out that President Bush was in town and "43" wanted to invite Jerry to dinner that night.

"Well," Colangelo responded to the White House staffer, "I've got a little bit of a problem. Tonight is my wedding anniversary and my wife and I had plans. Let me get back to you."

So Jerry called his wife, Joan, and she said, "Absolutely! Go to dinner with the President."

At that point, Jerry thought it might be a good idea to see why Bryan, the Suns' general manager, was calling.

When Jerry connected with Bryan he found out that the Suns were still in Denver, but not allowed to take off because of the Presidential TFR.

"We're just sitting here on the tarmac, waiting," Bryan said. "Can't you call Bush and do something?"

So, Jerry made his callback to the White House to tell them that he would be delighted to join the President for dinner that night. But then he added, "Oh... and I've got another situation you might be able to help me with."

Within minutes, the Suns' flight was cleared for takeoff in Denver. The Suns' charter was the only flight allowed to head toward Phoenix's Sky Harbor International Airport before the TFR was officially lifted.

Apparently, it's not only good to be the king; it's good to have connections in high places.

TEE PEE SUMMIT

As the one-time president of Major League Baseball's Texas Rangers, President Bush was an avid fan who wanted to meet with some of Arizona's top baseball people. In addition to Colangelo, the invitation list for the President's dinner included: Diamondbacks manager, Bob Brenley; D-Back's general manager, Joe Garagiola, Jr. and the new owner of the California Angels, Phoenix resident, Arte Moreno.

An east Phoenix, Mexican eatery, the Tee Pee, was quietly selected as the venue. How secret was the Secret Service's selection process? Well, when Tee Pee owner Art "Zip" Killeen walked in the back door of his restaurant that day, he was surprised by a Secret Service agent who asked him, "Who are you?"

Zip fired back, "Who the hell are YOU?"

Once informed of the pending arrival of his special guests, Zip thought they would isolate the President's table from the other restaurant patrons, but "43" insisted that they keep it "business as usual." So, customers waiting for tables that evening were somewhat stunned when asked by the hostess, "Would you like a table next to the President?"

Sports were the main topic at the table, causing Colangelo to later observe, "For as powerful and important a man that he is, I was struck by how well versed he is in the world of sports, how much he follows baseball and the amount of up-to-date information he had."

For the record, the President ate enchiladas, rice and beans.

TOP TOUR GUIDE

Al McCoy was walking through the arena one morning when he saw Jerry Colangelo leading a tour for a group of men, all well-dressed in suits and ties.

McCoy couldn't resist and shouted out to Colangelo, "Hey, Jerry! Are you a tour guide now?"

No sooner did the words leave his mouth, than McCoy realized that one of the gentlemen in the group, happened to be the current President of the United States, George W. Bush.

That is what you call a VIP tour.

PRESIDENTS' ROW

It was China vs. U.S.A in basketball at the 2008 Olympic Games in Beijing. This particular contest would prove to be the most-watched televised basketball game in world history. As the managing director of the USA men's basketball team, Jerry Colangelo was invited to sit with the President of the United States, George W. Bush; former President, George H.W. Bush and the Prime Minister of China, Wen Jiabao. Nearby, Colangelo spotted the former U.S. Secretary of State, Henry Kissinger, who was so comfortable with his surroundings that he was fast asleep in his seat and actually snoring before the game began. Nevertheless, Colangelo recognized that he was in some pretty impressive company.

From the beginning, the Chinese security staff in the arena was struggling with crowd control and there was lots of pushing and shoving. The elder Bush was knocked off-balance several times and almost went down, but on each occasion, Colangelo grabbed him by the arm and prevented him from falling.

J.C. was scheduled to do a courtside interview at halftime with ESPN. He knew that it would be relatively easy to get down to the court for the interview, but he had a hunch that returning to his seat among the Presidents and VIPs might be a little more challenging. His hunch proved correct.

Echoes From the Purple Palace

Although he was wearing every media, team official and VIP pass imaginable Colangelo's return trip was stopped cold by a virtual wall of the suddenly efficient Chinese security force. He tried to talk his way past them and kept pointing to his seat and showing his credentials, but they didn't speak English and Jerry's Mandarin needed work.

Just then, the Prime Minister of China walked down the aisle, perhaps on his way to the men's room. J.C. waved and shouted at him, "Hey, tell these guys that I'm sitting with YOU!" The PM barked a few quick words in Chinese to the security guards and the gates to the great wall opened to allow Jerry to return to his seat and enjoy the second half of a big U.S.A. win.

HAIR RAISING TALES

One night, my wife and I joined Joe Garagiola, Sr. at a charitable fund-raising dinner. I had just come from the barber shop where, on whim, I had decided to go for a total buzz cut. When I walked in, Joe exclaimed, "Tom, my gosh! What did you do to your hair?"

"I just thought I'd try a new look, Joe."

The balding Garagiola responded enviously, "Man! If I had hair like yours, I'd spend 20 minutes a day just runnin' my fingers through it!"

***

A short time after the success of the 1987 movie, *Wall Street* I decided to go for the slicked back, "Gordon Gekko" look. In the NBA, some might refer to it as the "Pat Riley" look. With a healthy dose of "goop" in the morning I could keep my hair slicked back all day! But once the goop dried, it hardened into a sort of hair helmet!

Naturally, I became the target for plenty of intra-office derision. One morning, I walked into the office to find that every guy there, not only had his hair slicked back in a full-Gekko, but was also wearing a white shirt, tie and suspenders, all in my honor! I walked into the

2 WACKO!

men's room and there was a two-gallon dispenser of green, industrial grade, hair goop with instructions for all the guys to use it liberally. To paraphrase Gordon Gekko in *Wall Street*, "Grease is good!"

***

That was also around the time when, on Halloween, Suns CFO, Rich Dozer came into the office, fully made-up with a false nose, salt-and-pepper colored hair and dressed in costume as … Tom Ambrose!

And a fine lookin' lad he was.

Rich never did tell me the results from his trick-or-treating that Halloween night, but it was still a nice compliment. At least, I think that's what it was.

DOZER AS TA

42 OF 50

When the NBA celebrated its 50th Anniversary in 1996, they released a list of its top 50 NBA players since the league's inception. Casting votes in the process were select media members, players and coaches.

It was the league's Golden Anniversary, but the list made me realize that I grew up in a "golden age" of pro basketball. I'm sure there are many NBA fans who have had the honor and privilege of watching, in-person, all 50 of the NBA's all-time best. I am envious.

Of the 50 players on that list, I missed seeing only eight play in-person: George Mikan, Bob Cousy, Bill Sharman, Sam Jones, Bob Pettit, Paul Arizin, Bill Russell, and Elgin Baylor. However, with the exception of Mikan, I saw them all on TV and, I could have seen them play in-person, but at 12-years-old, even with my own profitable newspaper route, I just didn't have the money for those big-time NBA games at the Garden!

Later, while working for the Suns, I had the opportunity to close my all-time-great gap a little bit by meeting Mikan, Cousy, Russell and Baylor at games, meetings and various NBA events.

Now, there's whole new generation of NBA stars… and perhaps the beginning of a new "golden age." of basketball. Compare and contrast the old with the new, but most importantly, enjoy. NBA players are, unquestionably, among the world's greatest athletes.

NOT TIRED

Invariably, when I was out in the community, the conversation always turned to basketball – Suns basketball. A question or comment addressed to me was always pre-qualified with the statement, "I know you must really get tired of talking about basketball, but…"

My honest answer was always, "No, I love talking about it. I've been involved with it for more than half my life. If I didn't love it, I never would have hung around for this long!"

The Suns teams that will always hold a special place in my heart and mind are, of course, John MacLeod's 1975-76 "Sunderella Suns" who took the franchise's first trip to the NBA Finals against the Boston Celtics.

Then, it's the 1988-89 Suns who, in their first year under Cotton Fitzsimmons, made the third biggest turn-around in NBA history. Led by Kevin Johnson and Tom Chambers, they went from an anemic 28-54 record the year before, to a glittering 55-27 mark and a playoff run that took them all the way to the Western Conference Finals.

After that, consider the 1992-93 edition of the Suns, coached by Paul Westphal. It was Barkley's first year and resulted in a dynamic run to a league-best 62 wins and an NBA Finals trip against the Chicago Bulls.

In 2004-05, a high-scoring, run-and-gun version of the Suns made another dramatic turnaround, literally shooting their way to a 62-20 record under Coach Mike D'Antoni. The previous year they had stumbled through a dismal 29-53 season.

For all four of those teams, it was their ability to rebound from horrible seasons to achieve great success that won my admiration. Colangelo often called it "going from the outhouse to the penthouse." They were also fun teams to work with and to be around. Winning will do that.

Given a choice, I guess I'll always root for the underdog. Over their long and successful history, the Suns have rarely played the role of the "overdog." So, we were a perfect match.

DUNK YOU VERY MUCH

Looking back, there were many key plays, clutch shots and spectacular dunks that I will never forget.

Among the more memorable dunks for me were: Tom Chambers' tomahawk slam while literally flying over Mark Jackson of the Knicks; Dan Majerle soaring high over Golden State's 7-7 Manute Bol; Kevin Johnson's not-to-be-denied playoff "whammo" over Hakeem Olajuwan of the Rockets; any of Larry

Nance's dunks in the 1977 NBA Slam Dunk Contest in Denver and the "Hocus Pocus" blindfold dunk by Ced Ceballos in the 1985 NBA Slam Dunk Contest in Orlando.

Regarding Ced's controversial winning, "Hocus Pocus" dunk in '85, I can personally attest to the fact that the original blindfold worn by Ceballos still exists and is locked up in a secure location somewhere in Phoenix. Please don't mention that to Geraldo Rivera.

I regret that I only heard about, but did not get to see, some of Connie Hawkins' gravity-defying dunks during his years with the Suns. Otherwise, I have little doubt that he'd be right at the top of my "best-dunk" list.

DISCLAIMER

Arthur Woodstone was a friend, a dyed-in-the-wool New Yorker, an accomplished author and, a guy who simply loves the game of basketball. Even into his 60s and 70s he would participate in lunchtime pick-up games at his local gym in the city.

Somewhere along the line, knowing his love for the game, I sent him a pair of socks with an "official" NBA logo embroidered on them. The socks became so special to him that he referred to them as his "magical" socks. It seemed that whenever he wore them in those pick-up games, he felt that he played better. So like a kid with a "woo-ee" blanket, he wore (and washed) those socks until they literally disintegrated.

Arthur was well into his 70s when his wife Pam politely asked me if I could get him another pair of NBA socks. I did, of course, but I decided that for safety's sake, I should include a disclaimer and attach it to the socks.

NBA MAGICAL SOCKS

This product guarantees the wearer that he will be able to soar to the basket for two-handed, tomahawk slams, swipe nickels off the top of the backboard just for fun, and, in general, jump higher and shoot straighter than the NBA's best players.

DISCLAIMER: This product should only be applied before going to bed and should be used only in connection with R.E.M. sleep. The NBA, its teams, the manufacturer and the little Chinese lady who made these socks, deny any responsibility for any actions performed in these socks while you are awake, or even in a semi-conscious state (like Connecticut).

PER DIEM

Whenever NBA players go on the road they receive a daily cash per diem to cover the cost of their meals. Today, players receive $121 for every night the team is on the road. That dollar figure is negotiated as part of the league's collective bargaining agreement with the NBA Players' Association. The idea is that players should have sufficient funds to purchase healthy and nutritious meals at good restaurants, while they are traveling.

That was the concept. The reality was that as the team bus made its way from the airport to the team's road hotel, many players, especially the rookies and young veterans, would be scouting out the fast food joints near the hotel. They planned to fill up on an inexpensive fast-food meal and then pocket the rest of their per diem.

Good trainers and coaches are always alert to this type of behavior and quickly swoop in to offer some good counsel for the young players. There is simply no way that a professional athlete in the NBA can sustain performance at a high level while consistently using fast-food as his primary fuel. Sorry, Ronald, Wendy and Jack.

Clearly, since the first player per diem was negotiated through the players' union in 1957, much has changed. How much? Well, the NBA's first per diem was $7 per day.

Now, even though NBA teams travel via charter flights, where food and snacks are constantly available, the per diem is an unshakable perquisite for players. In addition, generous, catered spreads are also available in NBA locker rooms following games. Be assured, no active NBA player will ever starve to death.

> **"... the NBA's first per diem was $7 per day."**

A player who sticks with his team through the pre-season and regular season and makes every road trip, would be paid about $8,200 in per diem for the year, with taxes due on about 40% of that amount.

It all seems kind of silly, when the average annual salary for NBA players is somewhere between five and six million dollars. But remember, there are players at the bottom end of the salary scale, who have to "scrape by" on a little less than a half-million dollars per year!

Often, players consider the per diem as just "walkin' around money" and they spend it on music CDs, video games, movie DVDs, headphones, batteries and other "essentials."

Veteran Suns players like Charles Barkley, Danny Manning, Joe Kleine, Jason Kidd and Rex Chapman would frequently give their per diem money to the team trainers and locker room personnel as a "thank you" for their hard work.

Jazz center, Greg Ostertag paid out his per diem in gratuities for valets, clubhouse boys and, especially, waiters. "I might be the best tipper in the league," Ostertag once joked. "It keeps them from spitting in your food."

Per diem money is paid in cash and distributed to the players as they begin each road trip. Not surprisingly, a lot of the money quickly finds its way into (and out of) the card games that are a regular feature of every NBA charter flight. There has been more than one flight, when a player's entire per diem for a road trip has been lost before the team plane taxied out to the active runway for takeoff.

But, at the five-star hotels frequented by NBA teams, a room service steak can go for $80 to $100. So for a player who is conscientious about eating right and getting his rest, the NBA per diem, like Goldilocks' porridge, seems "just right."

THE JOKER

There is a side to Jerry Colangelo that most people don't see, J.C. the "joker." April Fools' Day always seemed to bring out the best in Jerry. Typically, he would work with the local sports media to expand his gag into a community-wide "gotcha!" He once convinced everyone in town that the Suns would be moving to San Diego. That one backfired a little bit when some fans responded, "Great! We'll help you pack!"

But I think his best may have been when the Suns organization had just gone through a spring from hell as they tried to introduce Suns fans to Pay-Per-View television. Suffice to say, the concept did not go over well. So imagine the outrage when on the morning of April 1st, during an "exclusive" interview on the Suns' flagship station, KTAR 620 AM, Colangelo announced plans for a "Pay-Per-Listen" concept for radio.

Colangelo explained that fans would be issued a coin box that would be attached to their home radios. Just drop a couple of quarters into the slot and you'd be able to listen to Suns games featuring Al McCoy's radio play-by-play. Jerry reported that they were still developing technology for car radios.

Fans were outraged! "How could he do this?! Why that money-grubbing #%!*@!"

Even when fans were quickly reminded of the date of the announcement, April Fools' Day, it took a long time to calm them down. There are just some things you don't joke about, and don't you dare take away my Al McCoy!

THE JUMPER

Colangelo was in a local Phoenix hospital for some "minor" surgery. That's what the doctors called it. Personally, about the last thing I would consider to be "minor," would be a doctor approaching me with a scalpel.

Anyway, following the procedure, J.C. was in his hospital bed on one of hospital's lower floors. He was still a little groggy from the anesthesia, when his good friend, Bill Shover, came by to see how he was doing.

Even before pleasantries could be exchanged, a wide-eyed Colangelo excitedly told Shover, "Bill, I think I just saw somebody fall past my window!"

> **"I think I just saw somebody fall past my window!"**
> **– Jerry Colangelo**

Shover assured him that everything was okay and that the drugs from his surgery were probably making him hallucinate.

But Colangelo insisted that he saw what he saw.

So, Shover, wanting to put his friend at ease, but at the same time thinking that Jerry was delusional, went downstairs to see the hospital's chief administrator, an old friend.

"I know this sounds crazy," Shover said, "but Colangelo is insisting that he saw somebody fall past his window."

The administrator looked at Bill, totally surprised, and exclaimed, "He SAW that?"

It turns out that there was an alcohol rehabilitation center with an outside patio on one of the hospital's upper floors. Unfortunately, one of the patients undergoing treatment there, decided to take his own life. His chosen path to the next world went right past Colangelo's window.

Shover returned to Colangelo's room to tell him what he'd learned.

"I told you so!" Colangelo said with a knowing grin on his face.

Shover never doubted Jerry again.

THE DINKA DUNKER

Manute Bol, who passed away a few years ago, began his NBA career playing for the Washington Bullets in 1985. Years before, as a rite of passage in his native Sudan, the 7-7 Dinka tribesman actually killed a lion with a spear!

Adjusting to his new life in the NBA, learning a new culture and a new language, things did not always go perfectly for Manute. He would sometimes scramble his English phrases. Friends and teammates credit him with originating the enduring NBA phrase, "my bad!"

At 7-7 and a stunningly skinny 225 pounds, Bol was a basketball curiosity to be sure. When the Bullets were on the road, they tried to tamp down the media side show surrounding Bol by staging off-day news conferences at their team hotel.

Such was the case when the Bullets arrived in Phoenix at Metrocenter's Westcourt Hotel. The local media gathering was in a small meeting room just off the hotel lobby. The ceilings in the room were a standard eight feet high, which made it appear that Bol was almost brushing the ceiling with the top of his head.

Manute was still struggling with his English, so the media session was really more of a photo-op and the newspaper and TV photographers were enjoying the assignment.

At one point I found myself standing close to Bol and I noticed that there were several fine lines across his forehead. Initially, I guessed that they might have been caused by a constantly furrowed brow. Upon closer inspection however, I discovered that the lines were actually a series of closely spaced dots, a sort of tattoo, deliberately stamped into his skin.

Following the media gathering, I did some research and discovered that even ancient skulls of Dinka tribesmen were found to be scored with that same type of needle mark design. It was simply another Dinka rite of passage.

I'm sure that's something to which every young Dinka looks forward... having a tribal design tapped onto your forehead with a rudimentary ice pick and a hammer, right after you kill a 400-pound lion with a spear!

And you were worried about your kids texting too much or playing violent video games.

SING IT

One of the eight different positions I held during my 37 years on Planet Orange, focused on handling the Suns annual advertising campaign. I worked in concert with our advertising agency, Owens & Associates and their vice president, Marty Laurel.

There were years when we focused our print campaigns for season tickets on star players like Walter Davis or Paul Westphal.

Then there were other years when the Suns didn't really have any notable stars or we didn't know exactly who was going to be on the team for the coming season. In those cases, we'd take a more creative approach.

Often, during some of those "no star power" seasons, we went with a music theme, focusing our ad dollars on radio and television.

One of my all-time favorite Suns songs was the country-themed "Ain't goin' down 'til the Suns come up!" written and performed by the talented team of Tim Hattrick and Willy D. Loon.

There was another year when the organization went with "I'm a Suns Fan," based on the Sam and Dave hit, "I'm a Soul Man." That song was written and performed by one of the hit's original artists, Sam Moore.

Another notable chapter in Suns musical advertising history came when we hired a Patti LaBelle sound-alike to re-make the hit, "New Attitude" for the Suns campaign theme in 1984-85. It was an awesome rendition!

However, after the Suns went 36-46 that season, I can remember explaining to all the Kiwanis and Rotary Clubs on my regular speaking tour, "Yes! Last year the Suns did indeed have a 'new attitude' but, unfortunately, we found out quickly... it was a BAD attitude!"

2 WACKO!

During the mid-90s, Suns forward Wayman Tisdale, also a talented jazz musician, wrote and recorded the theme music for the Suns pre-game show. He called the song "Playin' with Fire!"

There were other years we had so many stars on the team that we couldn't really pick one or two over the others because precious egos might be bruised, so we'd include the whole team.

The Suns opening theme music, used on both radio and television, has really stood the test of time. With only the occasional "tweak," or change of pace, it's the same music that Bryan Colangelo helped develop around 1990, more than two decades ago.

NO DRAFT EXPERT

Dwight Clay of Notre Dame gained some notoriety when he hit the jump shot that ended UCLA's record, 88-game winning streak in 1974.

At that time, the PR departments of each NBA team were responsible for developing their own draft day information and materials for distribution to their local media.

I highlighted most of the sure-fire, first-round talent in that year's draft but I was deliberating over which players to list under "Other Prospects."

I wanted to show my fellow "Domer," Dwight Clay, a little love, so I put him on my "Other Prospects" list. In my mind, there had to be an NBA team somewhere that would take a look at him.

But after 10 rounds had gone by and well over 200 players were drafted, my man, Dwight Clay, had not been selected. He would never play in the NBA. I'm not sure if he ever got a tryout. But Clay did enjoy a long and successful career with the Pennsylvania Gaming Control Board. There is nothing wrong with that.

But after that blow to my basketball ego, I decided to focus strictly on PR and leave NBA talent scouting to the NBA talent scouts.

Fortunately, a few years later, the league's PR directors were rescued from this kind of embarrassment, when NBA headquarters in New York became the central clearing house for all information on NBA draft prospects.

THE MIDWEST SCOUT

Author's Note: The NBA's annual meetings were always a great place to catch up with old friends, meet the faces behind those phone voices from around the league and, of course, pick up some new stories. It was at a league gathering in San Diego when I first heard this gem of a tale. Names have been discreetly omitted.

In order to evaluate prospective college players, NBA general managers work hard to develop a nationwide network of basketball talent scouts. These scouts are basketball guys, many of them former coaches and players, whose judgment the GM respects and whose experience he values.

Typically the scouting system divides into geographic areas of the country and, in today's game, geographic regions of the world. In the United States it is quite normal for a team to have scouts who focus their coverage on the East Coast, the Midwest and the West Coast. On many occasions, the team GM would also get out on the road to scout some of the top prospects. Sometimes the GM would join one of his scouts to watch games or cover tournaments, compare notes and chat about prospects.

Such was the case one winter's day as a team GM got ready to step off the curb at Chicago's O'Hare International Airport and into the automobile of his somewhat neurotic but talented Midwest scout. Together they would be making the two and a half hour drive to Milwaukee to check out a Marquette game.

As the GM mentally prepared himself for the long, boring drive, anticipating nothing but a steady stream of basketball small talk, he had an idea. He mischievously concocted a tale of pure fiction designed to "yank the chain," of his long-time Midwest scout. But not even the GM's fertile imagination could have predicted "the rest of the story."

2 WACKO!

It was a typical winter day in Chicago, cold, slushy and overcast. The scout's car pulled over near the curb where the GM was anxiously waiting to get out of the biting cold. The GM opened the rear door to toss his bag onto the back seat. But he hesitated to let go of his luggage because the back seat was littered with newspapers, scouting reports and the crumpled remains of more than a few fast-food meals. He couldn't help but notice some dried-out bones from an old order of Buffalo chicken wings, scattered on the floor behind the front seats.

He pushed some of the papers around, clearing a spot for his bag. He tossed it in and slammed the door in disgust. The GM then opened the passenger's side door, checked the front seat for any errant food items, and then, with some trepidation, sat down.

The Midwest scout greeted his boss warmly.

"How ya' doin'?!" the scout said as he steered his car out into traffic.

"OK," the GM said stoically, buckling his seatbelt, but staring straight ahead and effectively casting the bait.

As he drove toward the Interstate, the scout sensed something was wrong.

"Is there some kind of problem?"

"No. No problem," the GM said, not even looking over.

"C'mon, man!" the scout implored, "I can tell when something is wrong!"

"I don't want to talk about it." The GM said curtly.

They drove on in silence for several miles, until they were free of the airport traffic and now settled in for the drive to Milwaukee.

The silence was deafening, so, once more, the scout tried to discern just what was bothering his boss.

"Did I do something to tick you off?" he asked.

The GM hesitated for a long while before responding, "Well, I heard something that really bothered me. But I don't want to talk about it."

The hook was set.

"What was it? What did I do?" the scout said, his voice rising with emotion, one of his chubby fists pounding on the steering wheel in frustration. "You gotta' tell me!"

Knowing that he was fully in control of the situation, the GM let a little time pass, until the only sound in the car was the hum of traffic whizzing past them on the highway.

Finally, the GM began, "Well, I heard something from one of the other NBA scouts, but I almost hesitate to bring it up."

At this point, the scout was holding onto the steering wheel with both hands, but was literally bouncing up and down on his seat. "What? What did I do?"

"Well, you know the Holiday Inn in Little Rock where all the NBA scouts stay?" the GM asked calmly, skillfully beginning to reel in his catch.

"Yeah! Yeah! I know the place. What about it?" the scout asked impatiently.

"Remember that all the rooms face an inner courtyard and you can see across into the other rooms?"

"Yeah, I know. I stay there a lot."

"Well," the GM began, "one of the other team scouts told me that a few weeks ago, he had just checked into his room. He looked out his window and he said he could see into one of the rooms across the way. He said that the curtains were open, the lights were on, and he could see YOU in there... playing with yourself!"

A few seconds passed before the nearly-crazed scout shouted, "That's a lie! That's absolutely not true! I ALWAYS close the curtains!"

FROM THE WACKO! FILE: THE SHANGHAI CONNECTION

Dear Mr. Ambrose,

How do you do! I'm Nu, an ordinary girl from China. I hope that the distance will not become the obsolete that we associate.

Sometimes, I can envy the basketball fans in Phoenix. They have an opportunity to watch the matches each week and meet the stars with their own eyes. I often feel that you are so far from me. And because of the limitation of distance and the different time zone, I can only watch your match from the TV. But I still catch all the chances to collect items of your team, never miss them. Pay a lot of attention to the stars, I select everything of them and survey your page.

As your loyal fan, I hope one day the Suns will have an official shop in our city. We want more convenient. And it will greatly shorten the distance between us.

May you the best of luck of everything all time! Go Suns!

NO TEAM SHOP...NO PROBLEM

Arizonans travel all over the world and sometimes they find evidence of Suns support in the oddest of places.

Consider the traveling fan who visited a remote village high in the Andes Mountains of Chile. On a dirt road just outside the village, he encountered a local who was wearing a t-shirt with a big Suns logo on the front.

Why was that so unusual? Well, in addition to the far-flung location, the villager, using colored markers, had actually drawn the Suns logo, freehand, on a blank, white t-shirt!

I guess if you are a genuine Suns fan and there are no officially licensed NBA team shops around, you just make your own!

The name of the village and the name of the villager remain confidential because I fear that the NBA might dispatch to the mountains of Chile, a team of attorneys armed with cease and desist orders for creating unlicensed NBA products.

Echoes From the Purple Palace

SUNS FAN, MOUNTAIN MAN

2 WACKO!

LEFTY'S DUNK

Professional golfer Phil Mickelson has always been a big fan of the Suns and the Suns organization has always tried to return that respect. In fact, Phil was a Suns season-ticket holder and before they were married, his wife, Amy, was a member of the Suns Dance Team.

PHIL MICKELSON

Phil was a senior at Arizona State University, and still an amateur golfer, when he captured his first PGA win at Tucson and was getting ready to participate in the upcoming Phoenix Open. The Suns wanted to recognize his success, so our VP of marketing, Harvey Shank, dreamed up a clever way to salute Mickelson at a Suns home game.

Shank's plan called for the Gorilla and his crew to go through their high-flying dunk routine. At the end of their performance, the Gorilla would invite Mickelson onto the court and offer him the ball to try a dunk off the trampoline. Naturally, Harvey thought, Mickelson would politely refuse and then, we would announce, "Ladies and gentlemen... please welcome the winner of the Northern Telecom Tucson Open... from Arizona State University... Phil Mickelson!"

"from Arizona State University... Phil Mickelson!"

It was a nice plan. And when Harvey approached Mickelson at the next home game and told him that we would honor him at the break between the third and fourth quarters, Mickelson was very, very appreciative, thinking that the gesture was "very cool."

"That is so nice," he said to Harvey. "I really appreciate that!"

Well, everything went according to plan, but when the Gorilla offered Mickelson the ball, "Lefty" grabbed it and took off, headed for the trampoline at the other end of the floor!

Phil, having absolutely no idea of how it all worked, sprinted toward the basket and jumped onto the trampoline. But he didn't hit the trampoline with enough downward thrust. There was no way he created enough spring to reach the basket and dunk the ball.

So, fully committed and hanging in the air about halfway to the basket, Phil just kind of heaved the ball at the rim. Then, as gravity exacted its inevitable pull, Mickelson landed awkwardly on the Gorilla's big, foam landing pad. Shank, along with every other Suns executive, had his heart in his throat, fearing the next morning's headline would read, "BUDDING PGA STAR INJURED IN STUPID SUNS' STUNT!"

Miraculously, Mickelson bounced to his feet, uninjured, and the entire crowd exhaled. Only then did we announce him as the winner of the Tucson Open.

DETERMINED

We quickly found out that Phil Mickelson is nothing, if not determined. It wasn't too long afterwards that Phil was playing in the Pro-Am at the Phoenix Open. One of the other players in his group was Suns boss Jerry Colangelo. Suns marketing chief, Harvey Shank was walking with the foursome. During the round, Mickelson was like a little kid, absolutely begging Harvey for another chance to work with the Gorilla and dunk the ball off the trampoline at a Suns game.

Harvey refused to consider it but Phil was not to be denied. After Colangelo teed off, Phil walked up the fairway with him and implored Jerry to let him come back for another slam dunk try. As he frequently did, Jerry finally said, "Sure!" leaving the details to Harvey, or me, or whomever.

Mickelson quickly found Harvey and told him excitedly, "Jerry said I can do it! Jerry said I can do the dunk!"

Harvey looked at Mickelson as if he just stepped off a space ship that had landed in the middle of the fairway.

"What?" Harvey exclaimed. "Are you insane?"

> **" Jerry said I can do it! Jerry said I can do the dunk! "**
> – Phil Mickelson

Then Harvey added, "Phil, there's not enough paper and not enough ink in this world for you to sign an indemnification form that would cover that. The answer is, 'no'!"

The thought of the PGA's rising young star jamming a finger, spraining an ankle, tearing a cartilage, or worse, was enough to make any risk management team blanch. Over the years, we did many golf-related Gorilla skits with Mickelson, but we never again let him get anywhere near that trampoline.

SPAWN

It is fair to say that Major League Baseball's (MLB) Phoenix franchise was spawned by the National Basketball Association's Phoenix Suns.

It is well-documented that Joe Garagiola, Jr. and Maricopa County Supervisor, Jim Bruner approached Jerry Colangelo in 1993 and asked him to lead the charge to bring a major league baseball franchise to Arizona. It is equally well-documented that J.C. initially said, "No."

But after thinking it over for a few days, Colangelo decided that the timing and circumstances were right. Phoenix was establishing its position on the national sports map and this might be the best chance for Phoenix to land a major league baseball franchise.

With legislation already in place to fund the construction of a new stadium, Colangelo accepted the challenge.

Echoes From the Purple Palace

To help him build the case to present to the baseball owners, Jerry turned to the resources that helped him turned the Suns image around following a drug scandal in the late 1980's. The Suns in-house advertising and public relations firm, SRO Communications, capably headed by Ray Artigue, went to work.

The Phoenix "pitch" was convincing. Their materials, surveys and commitments from the greater Phoenix community made a big impression on the major league owners.

Then Artigue, dressed as a bat boy, entered the MLB owners' meeting and distributed personalized, custom-engraved bats to each of the team owners.

It was clear that a new franchise in Phoenix, headed by Jerry Colangelo, was going to be well-run and successful. In fact, the MLB owners liked what they saw so much, that in the final minutes of the eleventh hour, just prior to granting the franchise, they tried to jack-up the price. J.C. would have none of it and walked out.

A few hours later, the owners called Colangelo back into the meeting and the Phoenix franchise was approved, at the original price. I guess they were only joking. What a fun bunch of guys to have as your business partners!

So, Major League Baseball's Arizona franchise officially came to be in March of 1995. The first game for the fledgling team would be in the spring of 1998.

In the meantime, there was much work to do. Build a stadium, organize a minor league system, hire a staff, get some players and, of course, start selling suites and season tickets.

The Suns organization was stocked with lots of enthusiastic and talented, young executives. Colangelo would give many of them an opportunity to lead and manage the new baseball franchise.

I was proud to have been a mentor to many of the young people who would be invited to cross the street and join the staff of Colangelo's baseball club.

That helped create a collegial and remarkably cooperative relationship between the Suns and the new baseball team.

DIAMONDBACKS OR SCORPIONS

As the baseball team was taking shape, J.C. would frequently consult with Suns execs to brainstorm, evaluate ideas, or ask opinions. Selecting the name for the new baseball franchise was one of those times.

As you might imagine, baseball fans were excited and full of suggestions for names for the new franchise. One of my personal favorites was the "Arizona Dry Sox." But in the end, it came down to two names, "Diamondbacks" or "Scorpions."

> **"... it came down to two names, 'Diamondbacks' or 'Scorpions."**

Even though the "Scorpions" had a very cool logo concept, Colangelo just couldn't get over the creepy, crawly insect thing. Why he felt more comfortable with the hissing, rattling, slithering snake thing, I do not know.

As we sat in the Suns weekly executive meeting, J.C. asked us about the two names. Which one did we like and why? We batted the two names around for a while, but there was no consensus.

Colangelo called for a vote. Someone suggested that it be a secret ballot, so that we could get a true reading, not influenced by the votes of others. Small bits of paper were passed around, quickly filled out and then returned to Colangelo.

One by one J.C. read the ballots out loud and then placed the scraps of paper in two piles on the desk in front of him. The final tally was "Scorpions" six votes and "Diamondbacks" three. I was one of the six.

Jerry looked up and said, "Thank you gentlemen. I am happy to make it official. The name of our new baseball franchise will be … (he paused for effect)… THE ARIZONA DIAMONDBACKS!"

There was only one thing you could say after that.

"It's good to be the king!"

SUNS UNDERCOVER

Suns Productions created an entertaining in-game segment called *Suns Undercover* where players took on roles and jobs that nobody expected.

Rex Chapman once entertained Diamondback fans on their way to a game at the ballpark, dressed as "Chappy" the itinerant street musician. "Chappy" was simply an awful musician and his tips, or lack of them, proved it. As fans picked up their pace to avoid him, nobody recognized him as Rex Chapman, Suns shooting star.

Rodney Rogers once posed as a 6-7, 260-pound, pizza delivery guy with a hidden camera in his hat. When the customer answered the door, Rodney opened the box to show the customer that he was getting exactly what he ordered. The only problem was that Rodney had already taken a huge bite out of the pizza! He explained, "I'm sorry man, I didn't mean to do that, but I was really hungry. Let me give you two dollars off."

Faced with a giant pizza delivery guy, who filled up his entire doorway and, who had already taken a big bite out of his pizza, all the customer could say was, "No, no, that's OK. It's fine. Don't worry about it!"

In another episode, 6-10 Suns forward Corie Blount, played the role of a Subway counterman who asked a customer if he wanted chips with his Subway sandwich. When the customer said, "Yes." Blount opened the bag, poured the chips all over the sandwich and then smashed the chips into the sandwich… with his elbow!

Shawn Marion once played the role of a pedicab driver waiting outside a Diamondbacks game. He picked up a couple, but before he could pedal ten yards, he feigned a leg cramp, got off the bike and stretched out a little as his passengers waited patiently. Marion then climbed back on the bike and resumed pedaling. But before he could go another ten feet, he was once more "seized" by leg cramps.

This time he not only got off the bike, but actually fell to the ground, writhing in pain. His two customers slowly looked around and then quietly climbed out of the little pedicab. They not only didn't offer to help, they never even looked back as they walked away.

Suns forward, Tom Gugliotta was cast in the role of a car wash attendant who would offer customers a choice of scents for their car's interior… "new car" or "locker room." He actually had an old smelly sneaker for customers to sniff if they were undecided.

Guard Casey Jacobsen once pretended to be related to tennis great Jimmy Connors, calling himself "Casey Connors." As he was giving tennis lessons to a group of elderly women, he instructed them that the object of the game was to "hit every ball over the fence." They followed his instructions with unbridled gusto.

One of the *Suns Undercover* crew's favorite episodes was Oliver Miller playing the role of an aerobics instructor at LA Fitness. Wearing a floppy, fisherman's hat, Miller led his aerobics class through a workout set to music like *Do the Hokey Pokey*. When he didn't know exactly what to do next, the 340-pound Miller just hopped around, waved his arms and commanded his students to "freelance!" They did and the totally absurd skit became an instant classic.

A MINUTE WITH JOE

Though his time with the Suns was just four-and-a-half seasons, Joe Kleine established himself as a favorite of teammates and Suns fans alike. His popularity was such that he even secured a special feature on Suns broadcasts called, "A Minute with Joe."

Film crews would follow him into unusual locations and ask him if they could talk to him. "Hey Joe, you got a minute?"

Perhaps the weirdest episode was when the film crew actually followed Kleine into the showers. Wearing a shower cap, Kleine conducted the interview amidst the water, steam and soap bubbles.

KLEINE WATCH

One night, as the Suns were lined up parallel to the half-court line, standing at attention for the National Anthem, Kleine became light-headed and passed out. When a seven-footer weighing 270 pounds collapses in a heap, it is neither safe, nor pretty. Joe, apparently falling prey to the flu and a brutal NBA travel schedule, was unhurt. However, for the next ten games, at home or on the road, whenever the Suns would line up for the anthem, two of Joe's teammates would stand on either side, and about a foot behind him, ready to catch him, just in case.

KLEINE AND AINGE ON GOLF

In the 1990s, Joe Kleine and his golfing buddy, Danny Ainge teamed up for some outrageous Suns TV golf features. Basically, in each episode, they offered new and creative ways to pick up a couple of strokes each time you play golf. This is also called "cheating."

During one show, Ainge, ensconced in a deep, green-side bunker and out of Kleine's direct line of sight, demonstrated how to secretly pick up the ball along with a handful of sand, and then toss both, gently and accurately, toward the hole. If done properly, and if your opponent is Joe Kleine, no one will suspect a thing.

The "pager ploy" episode outlined how to wear down your opponent mentally. Have a paging device planted somewhere in your golf cart with the volume turned to the max. The basket behind the seat is a good spot, Ainge explained.

Enter the pager's number on your cell phone's speed dial. Wait until your opponent is deep in concentration – in his backswing, hunkered over a critical shot or maybe a crucial putt. Be sure that you are standing well away from the cart where the pager is stashed. Then, hit speed dial and call the pager. If timed properly, it can be worth several strokes per round.

If your opponent hits his ball into some of Arizona's thick, desert brush, and then he goes in looking for his errant shot, have a little baby rattle handy. If the rattle is timed correctly, your opponent will quickly walk out the rough and declare that he will take the penalty stroke.

In another feature, Kleine explained why a can of white spray paint should be an essential tool in every golfer's bag. You discover that your drive has rolled up behind a tree and you have no shot. Whip out your can of spray paint and make a large white circle around your ball. Call your opponent over and tell him that the ground around your ball is obviously "under repair" and you're taking a free drop. Then pick up your ball and give yourself a clear shot at the green.

DISCLAIMER: These golf tips are presented for purposes of amusement only. The author is not responsible for consequences, or personal injury, should these techniques be implemented during your next round of golf.

THE TV CONSULTANT

The Suns television broadcast team was constantly striving to improve. So it was no surprise when two former Suns players-turned-broadcasters, Tom Chambers and Eddie Johnson, learned that the team was bringing in a consultant to improve the overall "look" of the TV broadcasts. The session would focus on ways to improve their on-air appearance and their broadcasting styles.

Chambers and Johnson knew that they would be brought in separately for the consultation. What they didn't know was that the "consultant" was actually an actress hired by *Suns Undercover.*

Of course, everything would be recorded for review and critique.

Even Suns president, Rick Welts, stopped by to lend credibility to the scam. The crew set up their cameras and built a stage-set in one of the arena's large dressing rooms. There were make-up and wardrobe people on hand and practice scripts to be read, but there were no mirrors. They had all been removed.

With Chambers sitting in a chair, the make-up artist asked him to close his eyes and then applied what Tom thought was a basic, make-up foundation, but in actuality was a dark-colored goop that gave him a "blackface" look that would have made Al Jolson envious. It was a minor miracle that the cameraman could keep a straight face. Chambers was oblivious.

Then it was Eddie Johnson's turn. He got the same kind of treatment, but with a "square Afro" hair style remake and some bright red lipstick.

Separated by both time and space, each of the broadcasters was asked to read, on camera, assorted tongue twisters, nursery rhymes and a selection of Dr. Seuss' silliest passages.

In both cases, when they got to the second page, the copy was amended to read "You're on *Suns Undercover*!" But both Tom and Eddie read right through it. The consultant had to ask each of them to repeat that last line…"You're on *Suns Undercover*."

That's when it hit them. They'd been had, and they were going to be "punked" on the next broadcast of *Suns Undercover*.

UNASSUMING

While the Suns basketball staff was busy inviting players to their pre-draft auditions in 1996, Suns Productions was pulling together a feature story idea to follow one of the potential Suns draft picks through the whole process.

Dave Griffin of the basketball staff suggested that young Steve Nash of Santa Clara might be a good subject for the feature, even though the Suns were not 100% sold, as yet, on drafting the 6-1 point guard.

Tom Leander and photographer Dave Grapentine, of Suns Productions, showed up at Sky Harbor International Airport to greet Nash and begin filming him as he arrived in town. They waited at the gate as Nash's flight disembarked and a steady stream of passengers flowed into the terminal. Nash was so "un-NBA" in size and appearance that he walked right past the cameraman and Leander without a glimmer of recognition.

The steady stream of passengers exiting the plane slowed, then stopped.

Leander, quickly realizing their mistake, whipped around and said, "Wait! I think that was him!"

They chased after and caught up with the very normal looking Nash, who ultimately became the Suns first-round pick that year (#15 overall).

Undoubtedly, Nash's days of walking through airports unrecognized and unbothered, have been over for quite some time.

ALMOST INVISIBLE

Early in the 1996-97 season, the Suns Gorilla and his assistant Brian Larive were making a promotional appearance at a local radio station. The Gorilla, of course, does not speak in costume, so when the program manager met them in the lobby, he was a little upset. A silent Gorilla doing pantomime simply doesn't play well on radio.

"I thought we were going to have a player!" the manager protested.

"I know! I'm sorry," Larive said, "I thought so too!"

Just then, from the corner of the lobby, someone wearing a hooded sweatshirt that all but covered his face, said, "Uh, I'm a player!"

Everyone stopped and looked toward the small, non-descript figure who had been sitting, unnoticed, in the corner of the lobby.

It was Suns rookie, Steve Nash, who was making his very first community appearance as a member of the Suns. Nobody knew who he was.

NOT WHITE

During a 2011 interview with actor James Caan, sportscaster Dan Patrick asked Caan if he had ever played sports. The actor, who grew up in New York City, confessed that he did play some basketball in his youth.

Patrick pressed him to describe his playing style. Caan offered that he played "like a white Steve Nash."

A somewhat puzzled Patrick observed, "Wait! Steve Nash IS white!"

Caan quickly responded, "No. He can't be. He doesn't play that way!"

> "...like a white Steve Nash."
> – James Caan

STEVE NASH

NOTHING BUT RESPECT

Nobody, not even a referee, has a bad word to say about Steve Nash. In his 2010 book, *Personal Foul*, published by Clerisy Press, former NBA referee, Tim Doneghy, talked about the Suns point guard.

"Steve Nash was always a mild-mannered guy, at least until he got his two MVPs. That's when he started playing the Kobe game, wanting a foul called on everything. Still, he was one of the players you'd want your kids to meet. When we were walking out of the arena at the same time, the players to their private jets and us heading out to the airport to fly coach, he'd always have a good word for us. 'All right, guys, take care, have a good night.' A classy guy.

I believe that it hurt him being white. If he'd been black, he might have gotten more calls. From a referee's standpoint, white players aren't expected to be good, especially a relatively short point guard. Nash is listed at six-foot-three on the NBA website. But I'm five-ten and he's barely taller than I am. Let's face the facts – professional basketball is predominantly a black sport. A lot of people were saying that Nash got the NBA awards because he was white, but the reality is the opposite. He doesn't get the respect he deserves, from the referees and from the league office, because he isn't black.

From my standpoint as a ref, I never saw him get the respect, the star treatment that the superstar black players got. When in doubt, the superstar always gets the call. Nash never got that. Maybe it was because he was just too nice a guy. He tried to start the bitching and complaining thing after he got those MVPs, but it just wasn't in his personality."

CONSPIRACY THEORY

Disgraced, defrocked and de-whistled, Donaghy was convicted on assorted gambling charges and for influencing the outcomes of NBA games. Prior to his conviction, he had a 13-year career as an NBA official. That was long enough to understand the culture and certainly long enough to develop opinions on players, coaches and owners around the league.

I had the opportunity to read one of Donaghy's early manuscripts of *Personal Foul*. Frankly, I was neither shocked nor surprised by anything I read. I had previously heard about or suspected, virtually everything he detailed in his book.

PRE-DRAFT WORKOUTS

Once comfortably ensconced at AWA, Jerry Colangelo was proud to show off the facilities that rivaled any in the NBA. He wanted young, NBA prospects to see and experience the Suns first-class operation. Even if the Suns didn't sign or draft a young prospect, their first impressions of the professionalism at AWA might count for something in player relationships or free agent signings down the road.

About a month before the NBA Draft, Colangelo and the basketball staff would frequently bring in prospects to for workouts that would showcase their skills.

In 1996, a young Kobe Bryant, fresh out of high school, was applying to be part of the NBA draft class and was invited to Phoenix for a pre-draft workout. I remember passing J.C. in the hallway, just after he had watched Bryant work out for an hour on the Suns practice court.

"Hey, Jerry," I said, "How'd that Bryant kid look?"

J.C. put his hand to his mouth and gently bit down on the knuckle of his index finger.

"U-h-n-n!" was all he could say.

Loosely translated, that meant, "He's so good, I don't know where to begin."

Regrettably, Kobe, the boy-wonder, was drafted #13 by the Charlotte Hornets and then traded to the Lakers. But the Suns didn't do so badly two picks later, when they selected Steve Nash.

A few years went by before another young high-school athlete was under consideration by the Suns, Amar'e

Stoudemire. There were more questions than answers about Stoudemire and drafting a high school player to come straight into the NBA was always a huge risk. So the pre-draft tryout was an important element in the Suns decision-making regarding Amar'e.

The basketball staff always brought in a few other players to measure against and challenge the key draft prospects.

Things were no different in 2002. In addition to Amar'e, the Suns brought in a 6-10, junior college player who unfortunately, had already spent a considerable amount of his young life in prison. He was one tough dude, with nothing to lose.

> **That's it! We're drafting him!**
> – J.C. on Amar'e

The informal tryout, basketball's version of "show and tell," began to heat up. Amar'e tried to clear some space and viciously elbowed his nemesis right in the mouth, knocking out two teeth. The ex-felon didn't react. He simply picked up the two teeth from the basketball floor, handed them to Suns assistant coach Phil Webber and said, "Hold these."

He then returned to step up his defense on Amar'e. A few minutes later, the two players sprinted for the rim, the 19-year old Amar'e intent on scoring, the grizzled ex-con determined to stop him and exact his revenge. The two met at the rim in an explosive collision that almost brought down the basket. But Amar'e powered the ball through both the hoop and his defender, with a violent slam dunk.

Instantly, Colangelo turned to Suns' lawyer Tom O'Malley and said emphatically, "That's it! We're drafting him!"

A few weeks later O'Malley represented the Suns at the NBA's Draft Lottery ping-pong ball drawing. The bouncing balls determined that the Suns would select ninth and, a few weeks later, the Suns made good on Colangelo's pledge by selecting Amar'e Stoudemire.

REMODEL

After ten years had passed at AWA, Suns' management took a look back at their original design concepts for the arena. They felt that the only mistake they made was not putting the Suns locker room and training facilities contiguous to the practice court instead of a few yards down the corridor.

But as comfortable as the America West Arena had become for the Suns and for Phoenix fans, after a decade in a new home, you notice how a few adjustments might make things a little better or more attractive. In addition, the Suns staff was growing and in need of additional office space. There was a pent-up need to expand the number of ladies' rest rooms and it was also time to update the overall look of the arena.

When it opened in 1992, AWA was widely considered the standard for arena design, with stacked suites on private concourses and integrated structure parking. AWA was the model to which other cities looked to revitalize their urban centers and bring fans back to downtown.

By the end of the decade, there were newer and better facilities out there, many borrowing ideas directly from AWA. It was already time, perhaps even past time, for an upgrade. So Mike Hallmark and his team of architectural wizards went to work.

Because of a tight budget, the original design of the arena was simple and somewhat utilitarian. There was lots of concrete block and small windows. That's not a bad thing when considering the extreme heat of Phoenix summers.

But the original design also lacked a major entry, a "wow" lobby that would give fans the feeling that they were entering a special place – big, bold and spectacular. There was also space on the east side of the arena that was being under-utilized. Hallmark would address all those issues and give the building a new transparency.

First was the lobby. Builders reclaimed a big chunk of the outdoor plaza bordered by Jefferson Street on the North and by 1st Street on the West, and turned it into a glass enclosed, fully air-conditioned, four-story atrium that would soon bear the name, Casino Arizona Pavilion. Ticket windows were now comfortably indoors, with new escalators leading to every seating level. A new Suns office lobby was created on the fourth floor and, within the Pavilion, new opportunities were carved out for advertising signage that promoted sponsors and arena events.

Next was the new office space. Running along Jefferson Street, new construction, jutting out 18' from the original structure, would provide additional room for retail shops and restaurants on the ground floor, while creating three floors of office space above. The entire arena façade would be converted from cinderblock to clear glass. The architectural vision was to open up the arena, and make the activities within totally transparent to the downtown community.

Finally, on the eastside of AWA, architects created the Bud Lite Paseo, which runs from Jackson Street to Jefferson Street. It helped create a second major entrance for fans parking and entering from the eastside. One of the most popular features for fans is an indoor-outdoor television studio for Suns pre-game, halftime and post game shows. The entire Paseo side of the building also was opened up by clear glass panels.

Although I wondered how adding so much glass to a building in a hot, desert environment could possibly be both comfortable and economical, Hallmark convinced me that new, modern technology and materials now made glass an excellent insulating material.

Echoes From the Purple Palace

A BLEND OF OLD AND NEW AT THE REMODELED AWA / USAC

I think Hallmark's vision for the remodel of the arena hit the mark and its realization was exactly what the building needed to carry it forward, well into the 21st Century.

On January 6, 2006, America West Arena was renamed US Airways Center following the merger of the two airlines. As time goes by and sponsors morph through mergers and acquisitions, there is always the likelihood of future name changes for the arena. But for many Suns fans, simply calling it, "The Purple Palace," works just fine.

FLASH IN THE PAINT

Rookies and young prospects attempting to make an NBA team must go through a non-stop series of tests and challenges.

2 WACKO!

The steps include rookie camp, summer league, informal workouts, training camp, pre-season games and finally, the regular season. If they can adjust and improve their game at each level, they stand a pretty good chance of making an NBA roster. But more often than not, at some point, they'll hit a wall and then, they're gone.

Several players come to mind. In the mid-1970s, Suns coach John MacLeod absolutely fell in love with a young point guard named Duane Reade. Duane handled the ball well and was an excellent middle-man on the fast break. He excelled during rookie camp, summer league, informal workouts and training camp. But during a pre-season game against Los Angeles in Oklahoma City, in front of a huge, sellout crowd, veteran Lakers' guard, Lucius Allen, picked Reade's pocket in the backcourt on three straight possessions. Each steal led directly to a Lakers' basket. Regrettably, Duane never recovered. He was done.

In 1980, the Suns were desperately looking for a "bad" rebounder (NBA translation: *a really GOOD rebounder*). We signed a young, 6-7, journeyman forward named Wiley Peck. In an intra-squad scrimmage during training camp in Flagstaff, Peck hauled down 15 rebounds. We all looked at each other optimistically, thinking that maybe the team's rebounding woes had, at last, been solved. But when Coach MacLeod tried to add a few other basketball concepts to Peck's repertoire, it was too much. Peck proved not to be the "bad boy" we all desperately wanted. He was waived a few days later.

One of the most exciting training camp flashes of brilliance came in 2004, when the Suns signed a 5-9 (almost), 165-pound (maybe), Japanese-born, firebrand, named Yuta Tabuse (pronounced: *Utah*).

He had played two seasons at BYU-Hawaii, a Division II school, before trying out with the Denver Nuggets in 2003. As the NBA's first Japanese player, Yuta commanded amazing media attention. In addition to the Suns' usual press entourage, as many as 33 Japanese media members were attending Suns pre-season games. That number doubled when the Suns headed to the East

Coast for some pre-season games and additional credential requests came in from the rest of the international media.

Tabuse was off the charts when it came to internet "hits," and his Suns uniform (#1), quickly became one of the top three selling Suns jerseys worldwide.

He played with a high-energy, "street-ball" flair, complete with no-look passes and accentuated by a wild, hip hairstyle. The Suns were looking for Yuta to fill some minutes at point guard behind the newly reacquired Steve Nash. But Tabuse suffered a few injuries that slowed his progress and opponents consistently exploited his size. He appeared in just four regular season games before the Suns waived him in mid-December.

The team's brief fling with Tabuse was another example of a training camp flash that couldn't hold up under the day-to-day grind of an NBA season. Too bad, he was an exciting tribute to the little guy in sports.

STATS ALL FOLKS

A basketball box score is a lot like a balance sheet. The total number of missed field goals and missed free throws in a game must equal the total number of rebounds. If a rebound cannot be clearly credited to an individual player, it is recorded as a "team rebound."

Here's an example. A player is fouled and goes to the free throw line to shoot two. He misses the first free throw; the rebound from that miss is not credited to an individual player, but instead, goes down as a team rebound. Our shooter then misses his second attempt and Dana Hooper grabs the ball. Hooper gets credit for a rebound.

NBA players fully understand that they get paid for results. That fact is even more important to those players who have performance bonuses built into their contracts. At the very least, NBA players take pride in the numbers they post, so believe me, they pay close attention.

The Suns' Leonard "Truck" Robinson was one guy who would occasionally chide our statistical crew for missing some of his rebounds (they really didn't). But Truck would suggest that, to make up for their errors, the crew should just "give" him some of those team rebounds. The crew would simply chuckle and ignore his request, knowing that Truck didn't need to be greedy. He was one of the best rebounders in the league.

Truck can now look back with pride at his accomplishments and his impressive rebounding numbers, and know that he legitimately earned every single one of them.

Another player who had his issues with stats was Mike Bibby, a 6-2 guard who played collegiately at the University of Arizona. The Suns had a pre-season game in Tucson, against Bibby and his Sacramento Kings. The teams had met several times the season before and Bibby thought that the Suns' stat crew was not doing a very good job when it came to accurately counting his assists.

During team warm-ups prior to the game, Bibby was standing near the press table, expressing how he thought he was being short-changed by the stat crew. Everyone knew what he was doing. Call it "politicking." Call it "the power of suggestion." Call it "planting a seed." But while he attempted to gain an edge, Bibby was also calling into question the integrity and professionalism of what was an excellent and experienced statistical crew.

Finally, one of the stat crew guys, Bryan Neddoff, had heard enough.

"Hey, Mike," Neddoff began. "I have an idea how you can get credit for a lot more assists."

"Really?" Bibby said, "How's that?"

"Do you see those guys over there in the Kings uniforms?" Bryan added.

"Yeah... my teammates. What about them?" Bibby asked.

"Well, during the game tonight," Neddoff continued, "when you pass them the ball, tell them to MAKE THEIR SHOTS!"

The Suns Danny Manning was also a bit of a whiner when it came to his assists. Our stat crew became so fed-up with his season-long haranguing that, in his final Suns game, the play-by-play stat sheet showed this late entry: "Basket by D. Manning, assist from D. Manning."

It was not only a statistical impossibility, but a final, tongue-in-cheek "good bye," courtesy of the Suns stat crew.

CHAPTER 6

DON'T BLINK

THE ESSENCE OF THE GAME

In all my years with the Suns, one of our most exciting teams was the 2004-05 club, coached by Mike D'Antoni. They turned a 50-loss season the previous year into a 62-win campaign, only the second team in NBA history to accomplish that feat.

I was energized because I hadn't seen our fans that excited in years. People would stop me on the street just to tell me how much fun it was to watch the Suns again. After several down seasons, and a whole bunch of coaching changes, the "Purple Gang" was back!

D'Antoni's strategy was to push the ball up the floor and take a shot within seven seconds or less. In the NBA, that is a relentless, nearly impossible, pace. But Steve Nash was an absolute wizard with the ball, almost never failing to find the right man in the right spot for the right shot, and that shot was usually a "three."

Led by Amar'e Stoudemire, Nash, Shawn Marion, Joe Johnson and Quentin Richardson, they turned that philosophy into a 31-4 start and finished the season with a 62-20 mark.

Clearly, for this team, the three-point shot was their weapon of choice and they used it with deadly efficiency. They led the league in long-range bombing accuracy (.393) and broke the NBA record for most three-pointers in a season (796). As might be expected, they led the league in scoring with 110.4 points per game, the highest scoring average in the NBA in a decade.

But the basketball cognoscenti turned up their noses at the Suns success because playing defense was only a passing thought for that team. But isn't the first concept of basketball to outscore your opponent? Isn't that the essence of the game? D'Antoni and the Suns thought so, and they proceeded to do so 62 times that season, not only leading the league, but also tying the franchise record for wins.

> **The three-point shot was their weapon of choice.**

Still unimpressed, the critics would only say, "The playoffs are different. You have to play at least SOME defense."

Nevertheless, during that season, the most frequently asked question in the basketball world was, "Can the Suns win a championship without playing ANY defense?"

The pundits said, "No!"

D'Antoni and the Suns set out to prove that they could. Suns fans just smiled and fastened their seatbelts.

The 2005 playoffs began with the Suns sweeping the Memphis Grizzlies four straight, in the first round. Despite losing Joe Johnson to an injury in the second round, Phoenix defeated the talented Dallas Mavericks in a thrilling six-game series, winning the final game on the road.

In the Western Conference Finals, the San Antonio Spurs simply could not handle the Suns' Amar'e Stoudemire, who averaged 37 points per game. But the Spurs did an effective job of limiting the rest of the Suns' high-octane offense. The Spurs took the series 4-1 and a few weeks later, went on to win the NBA Championship.

The Suns' season-long excellence earned Steve Nash the league's MVP Award and Mike D'Antoni NBA Coach of the Year honors. Bryan Colangelo was named NBA Executive of the Year.

SUNS COACH MIKE D'ANTONI

BARISTA

Coaches and athletes are a superstitious lot. They have their routines and, especially when things are going well, they will never deviate from them.

2 WACKO!

As the Suns were rolling to a 31-4 start during the 2004-05 season, coach Mike D'Antoni would stop at the same Starbucks store every morning his team was in town. He would be served by the same young lady and he would always order exactly the same thing. Over several months, it was a friendly, "Hi! How are you this morning?" type of relationship. The young barista was not really a sports fan and she had no idea who she was serving.

As luck would have it, a friend invited her to a Suns game. It would be her first.

As they settled into their lower level seats at the arena, the young barista was suddenly shocked to see one of her regular customers standing on the basketball court, right in front of the Suns bench.

"Hey, look," she said to her friend, "That's double latte over there!"

FROM THE WACKO! FILE: WHAT'S A FEW EXTRA ZEROS?

Author's Note: Included with this letter to Amar'e Stoudemire was a copy of what was once thought to be a winning Powerball ticket. On it, the writer had scribbled a note, "I hit all these!" His "almost" lucky numbers were 01 12 23 36 49 – with a Powerball number of 09. Stamped on the bottom of the ticket was a very official looking declaration by the Lottery Commission, "NOT A WINNER." Scribbled next to that was the writer's reaction, "this made me sick!"

Amar'e was doing OK financially, but not nearly as well as this desperate proposal suggests. Maybe they thought he wouldn't notice.

Hello Amar'e,

I would like to ask you to pay for the house that we had built in Mesa, Arizona. The house is almost ready to move in.

What happened is I hit the Powerball for 55 million dollars, so we put down money to have a house built.

Now the D.C. Lottery sent the ticket back and said it was not a winner. I just don't know what else to do.

Could you buy the house for us?

It is only $236,000. I can send you or fax you all the information that is needed to send the check. If not, could you please send us a check for $220,000,000 overnight by FedEx?

Please, Amar'e.

Thank you,

A FAN

KEEPING THE ROLL GOING

NBA stats and records are available everywhere. You can look 'em up. But for pure enjoyment, energy and excitement, the Suns' run under Coach D'Antoni, from 2004-2009, was one of the best thrill rides in Suns history.

But I thought the whole thing was over after just one sensational season. As the team opened its 2005 training camp, word came down from the medical staff that Amar'e Stoudemire would be lost for the season, due to a nagging knee injury. The mood at the training camp gym that morning could best be described in a single word, "depressed."

"Put a fork in it, we're done!" was the prevailing sentiment and, by the time the news aired that evening, the media had written off the Suns as possible contenders.

But even with a completely overhauled roster, the Suns didn't miss a beat. They continued their run-and-gun style and went on to win their second straight Pacific Division title with a 54-28 record.

2 WACKO!

Maybe there was something to this "shoot in seven seconds or less" thing.

Phoenix became the first team in NBA history to lead the league in scoring (108.4), field goal percentage (.479), three-point field goal percentage (.399) and free-throw percentage (.806). Nash won a second straight MVP trophy, while Suns newcomer Boris Diaw was named the NBA's Most Improved Player.

> **"D'Antoni's magic was still working."**

D'Antoni's magic was still working.

When the playoffs started, the Suns won back-to-back, seven-game series against the Lakers and Clippers, earning another trip to the Western Conference Finals. But it was there that the battling Suns fell to the Dallas Mavericks in six, hard-fought games.

SEEING STARS

During the playoff series with the L.A. Clippers, the Phoenix Suns Gorilla got to meet one of L.A.'s glitterati, but I don't think he enjoyed the experience.

Penny Marshall, who played "Laverne," in the 1970s TV series *Laverne and Shirley*, was a big Clippers fan who traveled to Phoenix for the first two games of the series. She was sitting in a front-row seat right under the basket. This was territory frequented by the Suns Gorilla. He'd bang his drum incessantly, put on extra-long gorilla arms to distract Clipper free throw shooters and do the many things that the Gorilla does to fire up the crowd.

Marshall was incensed. She sought out Suns management and, in very colorful language, demanded that the Gorilla be told to cease and desist. Her protests were ignored.

The Gorilla continued with his antics and Marshall continued to brood as the game ended in a Suns win.

Afterwards, one of the members of the NBA's security staff saw that the Gorilla was cleaned up, out of costume and wearing his "civilian clothes." With Penny Marshall waiting nearby, the security official thought it might be a good idea to have the two meet and mend fences. He thought that once Marshall understood what a nice guy the Gorilla's alter-ego was, she wouldn't be so upset.

So the introduction was made. But the instant that it registered with Marshall that the guy she was meeting was actually the Suns Gorilla, she reared back and slapped him, hard, right in the face!

The Gorilla was staggered. The slap was so loud that it caught the attention of arena staffers, who raced over to help.

"Are you OK? What happened?" they asked the Gorilla, who was still stunned by the blow. A dazed and bewildered Gorilla responded, "I just got smacked by Laverne!"

> **I just got smacked by Laverne!**
> –The Suns Gorilla

The next day, the Gorilla was discussing the incident with the Suns in-house counsel, Tom O'Malley.

"On a scale of one to ten," O'Malley asked, "How hard did she hit you?"

The Gorilla moved the ice bag off his jaw long enough to respond, "An eight!"

In the future, the Gorilla plans to use a stunt double for all celebrity introductions.

FROM THE WACKO! FILE: FAN BACKLASH

Dump the commish and all the refs!

July 25, 2007

Attention: Phoenix Suns, Administrative Offices, and Register Sports Editor,

I have given up my naïve belief that the NBA is honest. I believe that the Suns would have won the series championship if it hadn't been for that sleazy Donaghy cheating.

I also don't believe that this was an isolated incident. I don't see how Commissioner Stern was ignorant about the entire matter. I believe that a large group, including all the referees, was involved.

I believe that Commissioner Stern should step down along with all the referees who reviewed the games and who went along with the "crazy calls." This would be especially true in the game where Stevie Nash was kicked in his private area. And, to be just thrown in a rough manner on the floor, Horry should have been kicked out of basketball. And, then in same game, Nash was hit on the nose. The Spurs played like they were brutal heathens. How could they accept a championship after their behavior. I believe that this incident will forever taint the Spurs and the trust in basketball. This hitting, kicking and cheating are unforgiveable.

I blame the Commissioner, David Stern, for what happened. Until he steps down, the cheating and scandalous behavior will continue. He obviously turned his head, and said, "It is part of the game in the finals, and ganging up on Stevie Nash was OK."

Steve Nash was abused and roughed up because he is white and a great player. I can't see how he coped with the reverse discrimination that he has had to endure during his playing years and. I believe that the Black Spurs players planned to bring him down.

What was D'Antoni, the coach, doing by playing Nash so much right before the finals? By the time the finals arrived, Nash was dead tired.

As I said before, I believe that this was not just one rogue, or isolated criminal acting. I believe that a whole network of people was involved.

Clean up the NBA, get rid of the commissioner, Stern, and do a complete, honest investigation. I don't know a whole lot about the game of basketball, but any idiot who was watching could have picked up that it was a cruel, fixed game. The Spurs set out to hurt Nash.

I believe that the championship should be played over again. I believe that Spurs should relinquish their title of being champions. They are just a bunch of brutal players.

Signed,

D.D. Cardone

SHIRLEY YOU JEST

The 2004-05 Suns produced the best record in the NBA (62-20). The team included stars like Steve Nash, Shawn Marion and Amar'e Stoudemire. Yet, the team's media darling that season turned out to be a little-used reserve named Paul Shirley.

Shirley was a 6-10 forward who graduated from Iowa State with a degree in mechanical engineering. He then bounced around the basketball world with stops in Greece, Spain, Russia, the CBA, and three NBA teams, before joining the Suns at training camp in the fall of 2004. When his basketball odyssey was done, Shirley wrote a book, *CAN I KEEP MY JERSEY? 11 Teams, 5 countries, and 4 years in My Life as a Basketball Vagabond* (2007, Villard Books).

During his somewhat fragmented season with the Suns, Shirley was signed in October, waived in November then, re-signed in January. He created a national media stir when, during a Suns road trip, he began writing a blog for the team's website, www.suns.com.

Here are some samples from Shirley's journal:

> **March 19** – Our little plane ride poker game has become a road trip fixture … The poker games started way back in the preseason. I think I had the idea while Casey Jacobsen had the chips. I probably got to play in about six games (poker, not basketball) before I was sent packing, released just days into the regular season. The fact that I am here and available for poker games on the Phoenix Suns' charter plane (along with being theoretically available to play in basketball games) is a little remarkable.
>
> **March 20** – Since I do not play much, I have some time on the bench to think about the things that are going on around me… I am afraid Memphis may get kicked out of the league. I could be mistaken, but I think they started three white guys – three American white guys at that. I am pretty sure there is a rule against that somewhere – some kind of quota, I think.

> **March 22** – I play for (I use the term loosely; play for/cheer for – same thing) arguably the best basketball team in the world. My responsibilities include: 1. Showing up for buses, practices, games, etc. on time. 2. Refraining from causing undue stress to anyone by misbehaving on road trips or wading into the stands to attack fans. 3. Practicing hard when given the opportunity. 4. Entering games when my team is up by an insurmountable margin and attempting to break the shots-per-minute record.
>
> **March 26** – Based on the crowd at the game, the use of silicone per capita in Miami has got to be the highest in the U.S. All in all, a good night for testing one's ability to focus through distraction.

Shirley's on-the-court contributions that season added up to nine appearances, averaging 3.3 minutes each. He took 11 shots and made five. He connected on exactly half of his four free-throw attempts. The Suns designated blogger grabbed two rebounds, dished out a total of three assists and averaged 1.3 points per game. But it will be through his words, not his stats, that Paul Shirley will be remembered on Planet Orange.

CHAPTER 7

SHAQ ATTACK

NO PEACH BASKET

Shaquille O'Neal's Arizona debut as a rookie for the Orlando Magic was at the brand spankin' new America West Arena in 1993. Fans couldn't wait to see the NBA's next dominant big man and O'Neal did not disappoint them.

In the first half, Shaq attacked the basket with a powerful dunk. The rim gave, then snapped back, as it should, but something else broke, causing the basket hydraulics to fail. The whole basket assembly seemed to pitch forward and then slowly collapse, folding down upon itself until the rim was only four feet off the floor. The culprit was identified as a 300-pound counter-weight, which was not properly connected to the basket assembly by its solid steel, ring and hook assembly.

Conspiracy theorists claim that someone sabotaged the ring-hook because, when they inspected the damage, the hook was bent to a nearly straight position and could not possibly have held when slipped through the steel loop.

Could the steel hook have been bent by the strength and leverage of a single NBA player? Could the metal have been fatigued after just one-half of an NBA season of use? It was an implausible scenario, but that's how legends are shaped. Come to think of it, Shaq does have a Superman "S" tattooed on his bicep.

As the national TV audience waited and watched a spate of commercials, Phoenix fans in the arena were buzzing about what they had just witnessed. It took 35 minutes for the AWA crew to replace the basket with a completely new structure rolled out from storage.

A failed basket standard was such an unlikely circumstance that the staff had never gone through a full rehearsal of the replacement scenario. Of course, when they tried to push the new basket through the tunnel and onto the main court, the crew found out that they could do that only when some of the end-zone seats were retracted. After several frustrating stops and starts, the new hoop was finally erected and the game resumed.

For the record, the Suns won 121-105, but the legend of Shaq was already beginning to grow.

A WORD FROM SHAQ

On his abysmal career free-throw percentage, Shaq once observed, "Me shooting 40 percent at the foul line is just God's way to say 'nobody's perfect.'"

Echoes From the Purple Palace

AWA CREW RESPONDS TO SHAQ ATTACK

FROM THE WACKO! FILE: THE EYES HAVE IT

To: Mr. Kerr and whoever else had something to do with the trade for Mr. O'Neal

Mr. Shaquille has strabismus of the eyes.

If you look up close to him as he is trying to shoot a free-throw, you will see that one of his eyes turns inward. When he played the first game against the Hornets, he was one for eight on his free-throws.

I watched him carefully and I saw that each time he threw the ball at the free-throw line, one eye turned inward. This occurs when he has to perform close up, such as throwing a free-throw. Look at the tape of his performance.

When he looks you straight on at a distance, his eyes look perfectly normal. But then, he isn't trying to throw a free-throw.

Did you give him an eye test before you hired him?

He breaks out in a full-blown sweat every time he has to run up and down the court. His blood pressure must be highly abnormal.

He is truly a liability on the court. He might just have a heart attack on you right there on the floor.

You hired a cumbersome clod. Once he was great, but now his is a disaster. All he has shown me is that he is capable of injuring one of his own teammates. Poor Raja Bell.

You really bought into the bravado of Shaquille O'Neal.

Shaquille O'Neal is bull in a China shop. He has ruined the rhythm that the Suns had before he joined the team.

He causes such congestion near the basket. He can't move fast enough to get out of the way.

You can just forget about even getting to the playoffs with this "Mess" on the floor. You need to check his vision, his balance, his coordination and how much he had to drink the night before a game. Did he even get a physical before you hired him? That's a legal way out of the deal. You bought damaged goods.

He is an overweight "oaf," a boob on the floor. After fouling on a play, he twirls around, like he's thinking, "Where am I? Where am I?"

You might also consider checking his mental status also, because I don't think he comprehends what is going on around him.

It is just pitiful when the public sees a living legend of his stature make such a blatant fool of himself. He should get down off of his soap box, and admit to everyone that he can't perform as he used to, or feign some fatal disease.

But, really, if he wants to be a real hero, he should step down gracefully, but I can't see that ever occurring.

Face it, you bought into his past bravado, and it is only going to get worse. I feel sorry for the rest of the team.

A Concerned Fan,

Cher M.

2 WACKO!

THE BIG SHAQTUS

SHAQ MAGIC

The Suns traded for Shaquille O'Neal in February of 2008. A month later, he joined the rest of the Suns players and coaches at the historic Arizona Biltmore Resort for the annual Suns & Stars Gala, to raise money for Phoenix Suns Charities (PSC).

As part of the evening's entertainment, PSC board member, Melissa Leonesio secured the services of Dan Dunn's PAINTJAM. Both an artist and an entertainer, Dunn spins a giant six-foot square canvas on a special easel, while spreading paint with brushes, or his fingers, in a paint-ballet set to music. The act is five minutes of controlled chaos, with paint flying everywhere and the subject of the painting remains unknown until the final moment. Dunn's act is a YouTube favorite.

We had secretly arranged with Dunn to paint a portrait of one of the Suns. I was one of only a few people in the room that night that knew the painting we'd auction off would feature Shaq. As I watched Dunn go through his gyrations, I simply could not figure out how his seemingly random splashes of paint could turn out to be an image of Shaq that anyone would recognize.

All of a sudden, bing, bang, boom, a splash here, a brush slash of paint there. Dunn spun the canvas right-side-up and there was a fantastic painting of a grinning Shaq! Along with everyone in the audience that night, I was stunned.

Tom Chambers was serving as our auctioneer and he immediately fired-up the live auction for the painting. After only a few minutes, Chambers had worked the bidding up to $14,000. I was happy because that meant we had already covered our expenses and made a little money for Suns Charities – anything more would be "gravy."

Just then, a very deep, amplified voice boomed from backstage, "That's TOO LOW, Tom! That's TOO LOW!"

It was Shaq!

2 WACKO!

DAN DUNN PAINTS AT SUNS & STARS

The big guy emerged from backstage to join Chambers on stage and immediately began working the crowd. The bids climbed to $25,000, then $32,000, then up to $37,000!

Shaq and Chambers were working two hot bidders, but the momentum stalled at $41,000. We'd already made arrangements with Dunn to do a second painting if needed. So our capable auctioneers got both bidders to accept a Dan Dunn painting of Shaq for $41,000 each.

The winning bidders were invited to come up on stage for photos with Dunn, Shaq, Chambers and the portrait. However, before they could get up there to snap the shutter, a third bidder came out of the audience, requesting that a third painting be done and he'd be happy to fork over another $41,000!

It was pure Shaq magic. He had taken the bidding from $14,000 to a $123,000 payoff for Suns Charities.

That, ladies and gentlemen, is quantifiable "star power."

LOU'S WHEELS

Lou Amundson was a little different from your average NBA player. He was a hustling, 6-9 Suns forward who, in spite of limited playing time, quickly played his way into the hearts of Suns fans. Lou had graduated cum laude from UNLV with a degree in University Studies and a focus on English and Philosophy. He enjoyed drawing and painting in his spare time and, he wore his hair in a distinctive pony-tail. For some reason, Shaq took a liking to the free-thinking Amundson.

But the differences didn't end there. Walk through the players' parking lot at any NBA arena and you'll see the very latest in high-end transportation: Mercedes, Cadillac, Ferrari, Aston Martin, Maserati, Bentley, and Rolls-Royce to name a few. But Amundson rode a beach cruiser bicycle to practice every day. That impressed everyone in the Suns front office until we found out that Amundson's downtown condo was located about a block from the arena.

Nobody knows how it began but, as a practical joke, Shaq started taking Lou's bicycle and hiding it. This went on for several days before Steve Koek, Josh Greene, Stefan Swiat and the crew at suns.com got word that Lou was going to retaliate. They grabbed their cameras and headed for the parking garage adjacent to the arena's practice court. There, they discovered that Lou had filled the inside of Shaq's truck with thousands of those little, foam packing peanuts.

Actually, a whole bunch of people had been tipped off, so there were cameras everywhere, including a crew from the A&E cable channel that was following Shaq around, shooting footage for a potential reality show. Shaq hammed it up to the full extent of his acting ability.

When O'Neal came out to get in his customized GMC van, he saw all those packing peanuts and laughed. Building maintenance was quickly summoned and they cleared the vehicle of the packing material, at times using big snow shovels. I have no idea why the arena crew would need snow shovels in Phoenix, but they proved to be effective tools for removing the packing peanuts. They filled an entire dumpster with the stuff.

That was when Shaq decided to pick up Greene and Swiat and toss them into the dumpster with the peanuts. If you're

Shaquille O'Neal, 7-1 and 325-pounds, you can do stuff like that. A few minutes later, playing to the cameras, Shaq jumped into the dumpster himself. Then, making sure that the cameras were still rolling, Shaq conspired with teammates Jared Dudley and Alando Tucker to plot his revenge on Amundson.

O'Neal was threatening to cut off Lou's pony-tail. Koek and his camera went into to the Suns Clubhouse to find Shaq sitting there, electric razor in hand. Shaq looked directly into the camera and said, "We're gonna' get him."

Amundson quickly became aware of Shaq's threat and, was more than a little concerned about his personal safety and well-being. The team went into a closed-door meeting as Koek waited outside the room.

Within a couple of minutes Koek heard a ruckus on the other side of the door and burst in to see what was happening. He discovered several Suns players, including Goran Dragic, holding Amundson down while Shaq was kneeling over him with the electric trimmer. The big guy buzzed a couple of hairs from one of Lou's eyebrows but he also took a pretty good chunk of hair from one side of Amundson's head. The pony-tail survived. Coach Alvin Gentry quickly declared The Case of the Purloined Bicycle "over."

Koek was happy that his video footage of the event was picked up by ESPN that night, but his prized piece of memorabilia from the incident was a little, foam packing peanut, autographed by Shaq.

A few days later, Shaq was seen sporting a T-shirt with a photo of Lou's face superimposed on a woman's body, the shirt had the tag line "Louisa Amundson."

One cannot help but wonder what Shaq would have done if he DIDN'T like Amundson.

END OF THE RUN

Shaquille O'Neal was the largest player to ever lace-up a pair of sneakers for the Suns. Those sneakers, by the way, were a mind-boggling size 23.

Echoes From the Purple Palace

With the benefit of 20/20 hindsight, Suns fans can look back to the signing of Shaquille O'Neal, in the spring of 2008, as the beginning of the end for the team's spectacular run under D'Antoni.

It was a gamble to bring in the aging giant. The rationale for the move seemed to be that O'Neal could help a finesse team bludgeon its way through the playoffs. But it was a dramatic change in direction and proved to be a horrible clash of styles. The end result was the basketball equivalent of a train wreck.

The Suns went from a fan-pleasing, free-wheeling, full-court, up-tempo, run-and-gun style, to a more deliberate half-court game that wasn't nearly as much fun.

Consequently, Phoenix was eliminated from the playoffs in the first round. Frustratingly, for the third time in four years, it was the San Antonio Spurs who sent the Suns packing. It was apparent that Shaq would not be the answer to the Suns championship aspirations.

For four years, D'Antoni turned Suns basketball into an art form of offensive basketball. He had the right players, with the proper skills to make his high octane system work.

It certainly didn't hurt to have NBA MVP playmaker, Steve Nash, running the show. Did Nash "make" D'Antoni, or did D'Antoni's system make Steve Nash? Does it matter? Not really.

It all came together for a sensational run that Suns fans can stack up against any other team, or time period, in Suns history. During those four, full-seasons under D'Antoni, the Suns made the playoffs every year, including two appearances in the Western Conference Finals. That is bangin' hard on the NBA's championship door.

But when D'Antoni's contract was up at the end of 2007-08, the magic and energy that once captivated the basketball world, seemed spent. So the Suns and D'Antoni parted ways.

Shaq stayed around for another season and posted some impressive numbers in 2008-09. He played in 75 games averaging 17 points per game, averaged 8.4 rebounds and 1.4 blocked shots. But the Suns, even with Nash at the helm, were becoming a hodge-podge of players who did not necessarily complement one another.

Terry Porter replaced D'Antoni as coach and lasted half a season before he was replaced by Alvin Gentry. Taking over for the final portion of the 2008-09 season, Gentry did the best he could, given the roster talent he had, for three full seasons and a portion of another. But right in the middle of the 2012-13 season, he was supplanted by Lindsey Hunter who was anointed the franchise's fifteenth head coach. Expect many more to follow.

There was no doubt that the lightning which once defined Suns basketball, had escaped its bottle. It would prove to be impossible to recapture.

GATE CRASHERS

Ever wonder who gets invited to those "closed" VIP events, where all the players and celebrities go during the NBA All-Star Weekend?

Two Phoenix-area friends, both Hispanic businessmen and big fans of the NBA, desperately wanted to find out. TNT was planning their big All-Star Weekend party at Corona Ranch, a former working horse ranch in South Phoenix, converted to a special events venue.

Remember Tareq and Michaele Salahi, the two White House gatecrashers who conned their way into an invitation-only event early in the Obama administration? Well, our All-Star gate crashers called themselves Nacho and Escolito.

Nacho telephoned Escolito, "Meet me at the kitchen door at Corona, and wear your white coat!" That was code for sneaking into the event dressed as a couple of waiters.

The TNT event was hosted by Ted Turner himself. Security was high, and the bouncers were muscle-bound and seemed very serious. Nobody noticed as Nacho and Escolito boldly walked through the kitchen at Corona Ranch, waved at a few people they knew and then walked out into the celebrity-heavy crowd. It was so easy that they never even bothered to put on their waiters' coats.

It was Valentine's Day and Nacho and Escolito were definitely feeling the love as they hobnobbed with NBA stars, team officials, hot babes, agents and sports dignitaries of every stripe. There was plenty of food and all the drinks you wanted, all for free. Later in the evening, they would sit down to enjoy an exclusive, private concert featuring Maroon 5.

Nacho and Escolito topped off their evening at TNT's Corona Ranch party by enjoying expensive cigars and shots of premium tequila, with NBA stars and celebrities they didn't even know. For two curious guys who grew up in Phoenix, it was an All-Star night to remember.

FROM THE WACKO! FILE: INEPT

To Steve Nash, Guard,

Oh, I finally understand why the trade was made with O'Neal. How could the "Owner and the big executives" not know about O'Neal's inept ability?

This was all a big con on the public. Who ever made the worthless trade knew just what they were doing. They did so to bring down your team, and they have accomplished just what they set out to do. They don't want another "playoff" season like last year.

Unless, you, Steve Nash, try "a little bit harder." That comes from Janis Joplin. Another lyric of hers I like is, "take another piece of my heart, baby, if it makes you feel good." Or, "freedom is just another word for nothing left to lose." Why don't you listen to her before you play your next game? Her spirit and common sense will justify your pain.

There must be absolutely no satisfaction in what you have been put through, and now this ludicrous trade with O'Neal.

Don't think for a second, that the owner didn't know this, along with his other limitations.

What I'd like to know is what the payoff was? Your team won't make the playoffs with this "oaf."

Did it have something to do with the official who was sent off to jail with all his "secrets?" Was it a compromise to make sure that the Suns would not make the playoffs?

Now, I'm just speculating here. I have no proof that the above occurred. But, why would they make such a trade? The men who made this trade know basketball and what makes a good player...

It must be like playing with a retarded elephant.

Keep out of his way. He will injure you like he did Bell. I think he is disoriented... I think he is in the early stages of dementia.

So, whoever dreamed up this trade did it not for the benefit of the Suns winning the championship.

Someone will finally realize this, and see how duped the public was, along with any other fans feasting on his old glory days. Reality is just starting to take its ugly stance.

Oh, well, there is always St. Jude to pray to, but I wouldn't count on any miracle to happen.

Basketball honesty is about as honest as professional wrestling.

You are a great performer, the best, and people like you come around once in a lifetime.

God bless you, Steve, and look for the truth.

"Truth-Beauty, Beauty-Truth. And that is all you need to know." (Keats)

Sincerely,

M.U. Stang

RAMBLER

If they had really thought about it, Suns fans would have realized that it was probably too good to be true. As Steve Nash got ready to start the 2011-12 NBA campaign, everyone in Phoenix knew his Suns contract was in its final season. Would the Suns re-sign him, trade him, or let him go to free agency?

Once the lockout-shortened season was scheduled to begin, the media began to turn up the pressure on Suns management. Would Nash stay or would he go?

On the day after Christmas 2011, the Suns responded by saying that they would love to have Steve, now approaching 38 years old, remain with the Suns. Nash said he would like to re-sign and remain in Phoenix. Suns management called Nash "the sun, the moon and the stars."

In the new Suns-speak, all of that blather added up to mean... Nash was gone. The only remaining questions were when and where.

Echoes From the Purple Palace

During Nash's time in Phoenix, Suns broadcaster Al McCoy creatively dubbed him, "the Nash Rambler." But, with apologies to both the Voice of the Suns and American Motors, Nash was more like a high-performance sports car, rather than that quirky, little 1950s sub-compact that was the star of the 1958 Playmates' song, "Beep, Beep."

Nash was the consummate playmaker and team player. His now-you-see-it-now-you-don't passes thrilled Suns fans and made his teammates better. In a game known for its over-inflated egos, Nash really didn't seem to have one.

He would never fail to credit his coaches and teammates for the Suns many successes. And, as the team's leader, he would never fail to shoulder the blame for Suns losses. In addition, win or lose, Nash rarely avoided the media, not standard behavior in professional sports today.

When the NBA moves into its playoff season, every fan knows that the game changes and becomes more physical.

Opponents knew that if they wanted to stop the high-octane Suns, they had to stop Steve Nash, by whatever means possible.

As opponents lined up to take their shots, Nash steeled his resolve to never back down. In spite of being consistently held, punched, shoved, throttled, smacked and otherwise grossly abused, Nash kept going.

During Game 1 of the 2007 playoffs against the Spurs, Nash inadvertently banged heads with the Spurs' Tony Parker, resulting in a bad nosebleed for Nash. Suns trainers, working feverishly for several crucial fourth quarter minutes, couldn't stop the bleeding. Without Nash's court leadership and clutch shooting during that critical time, the Suns fell to the Spurs in the game's final minute.

Perhaps the most egregious incident came in Game 4 of that same playoff series, with just seconds left and the Suns on their way to a win.

The Suns old nemesis, Robert Horry, picked that moment to violently hip-check Nash into the scorer's table. Nash's teammates reacted instinctively and left their bench to protect their team leader. The result, unfortunately, was that both Amar'e

2 WACKO!

Stoudemire and Boris Diaw were suspended for the next game, which the short-handed Suns would lose.

Graphic photos of the battered and bloodied Suns point guard became a rallying point for Nash's teammates and outraged Phoenix fans, but victory was not to be, as the Spurs defeated the Suns and then went on to claim the NBA Championship.

In the 2010 playoffs against the Spurs, Nash took a Tim Duncan elbow to the face that forced his right eye swollen-shut. Seconds later, Nash drained a clutch, one-eyed, three-point field goal that sealed a win for the Suns and eliminated the Spurs from the playoffs. It didn't result in an NBA Championship, but darn it, it felt good to finally beat the Spurs.

A BATTERED AND BLOODY STEVE NASH

NASH'S LAST NIGHT

At the end of 2011-12, with Phoenix eliminated from the playoffs for a second straight season, Suns fans turned out in force for the campaign's final game. In an ironic twist, the game was against the Spurs. Fans were there to salute Steve Nash in what they rightly suspected would be his last game in a Suns uniform.

Late in the contest, chants of "We want Steve!" broke out at US Airways Center and continued to grow until the entire arena was on its feet. It was, many thought, a request for one more curtain call for their hero and perhaps a final, desperate plea for Suns management to keep him in Phoenix.

After the game, Nash responded, "It was obviously amazing to get that type of reception and support. It's very special because it's not something that I asked for or imagined to get that type of spontaneous reaction. It's authentic – the relationship that I thought we had, so it's great. It really feels special and the fans have been phenomenal. It meant a lot to me to play in a city like this for as long as I have and to feel important to the fans and the community. And I just feel like a really lucky guy."

Suns fans knew Nash would be moving on, but a few weeks later, their already heavy hearts were dealt one final, devastating blow by Suns management, when their beloved point guard was traded to the Suns' perennial arch-rival, the Los Angeles Lakers. Really?

I know, I know, the Suns have done it before... Gail Goodrich to L.A. for Mel Counts... Corky Calhoun to the Lakers for draft picks... Connie Hawkins to the Lakers for Keith Erickson. In another sport, the Boston Red Sox even traded Babe Ruth to the arch-rival New York Yankees. But Steve Nash to the Lakers... for draft picks? As Al McCoy might say, "O-o-o-o-o-h brother!"

2 WACKO!

BOARD WORK

The Colangelos knew they needed someone to work the boards.

One day in 1999, I met with Suns Chairman Jerry Colangelo and team President Bryan Colangelo. They told me that given the tremendous popularity and success of the Suns since the 1992 opening of the arena, the 1996 importation of the Coyotes and then the 1998 start-up of the Diamondbacks, they were both overwhelmed by requests from the community to join boards, head task forces and be catalysts for new community projects. They freely admitted that in spite of their strong desire to remain deeply involved with the community, they simply did not have the time to do it all.

"Tom," Bryan said, "that's why we want you to be the Suns' face in the community. We don't think there is anybody who could do a better job of representing us in that way."

I was managing Phoenix Suns Charities as well as the Suns Community Relations department, so I was already well-acquainted with the Phoenix non-profit community. But the Colangelos wanted me to put even greater focus on community boards and committees, giving the Suns even more involvement with the city that had supported the Suns franchise so well, over so many years.

Nevertheless, in spite of my "community face" being what it was, the new assignment grew quickly. Since I was already committed to some of my own favorite organizations, the number of boards with which I was involved expanded to as many as 28. Many people I know have scoffed at that number, because they felt that I could never serve any of the organizations effectively. But with the Suns "having my back," and no other daily obligations within the Suns organization, I could … and did.

My thoughts raced back to my days, and my old boss, at *The Arizona Republic*, Bill Shover, who once showed me a list of his community boards. It counted nearly a hundred organizations and, in virtually every case, he had, or was, serving in a leadership role. That was how a company or a franchise got out and truly served their city. It was a subtle sermon on community involvement that both Shover and Colangelo preached often. I listened and learned.

So, for the next five years of my career, I was the Suns' Vice President for Community Affairs. It was a fabulous run that taught me much and introduced me to hundreds of fellow Phoenicians who I now call friends.

In my years with the Suns, among the organizations I served were: the Children's Museum of Phoenix; Phoenix Zoo; Partnership for a Drug Free America; Drugs Don't Work in Arizona; Governor's Council on Health, Physical Fitness, and Sports; American Heart Association; United Blood Services; University Club of Phoenix; Phoenix Children's Hospital Foundation; America West Airlines Educational Foundation; Community Care Connections; Valley of the Sun United Way; Combined Metropolitan Arts and Sciences (COMPAS).

I was also involved with the Fiesta Bowl Committee; Boys and Girls Clubs of Metropolitan Phoenix; the Arizona Coalition for Tomorrow; the Arthritis Foundation; the Greater Phoenix Chamber of Commerce; the St. John Vianney School Development Council; Cystic Fibrosis Foundation; the Challenger Space Center; the Hon Kachina Board of Governors and the City of Phoenix Human Relations Commission.

Like Shover, I found myself serving in leadership roles for nearly all of those organizations.

When ownership of the Suns changed in 2004, there were management changes within Phoenix Suns Charities and I returned to my former position of executive director. Although my community board obligations decreased, the Suns continued to stay deeply involved in the community by expanding the reach and impact of Suns Charities.

CHAPTER 8

FLASHBACKS OF LIFE IN THE NBA

THE FLIP

One of the most significant events in the early history of the Suns franchise was the coin flip to determine which of the two newest teams in the NBA, Milwaukee or Phoenix, would pick first in the 1969 NBA Draft. The prize for the winner of "The Flip" would be UCLA's dominant big man, Lewis Alcindor.

The Suns invited players, local media, season-ticket holders and sponsors to watch the Phoenix end of the flip. The coin toss itself would take place at NBA headquarters in New York. Milwaukee and Phoenix were dialed-in via conference call.

As the Phoenix contingent gathered at the Suns offices, one of the team's early season-ticket holders, Vince Watson, found himself standing next to Suns guard, Gail Goodrich. Everyone, especially the players, knew the kind of positive impact Alcindor could have on this fledgling Suns team.

The Suns, by virtue of their league-worst 16-66 record, were given the honors of calling the toss. A few weeks earlier, through

2 WACKO!

a contest sponsored by *The Arizona Republic,* Phoenix fans voted for the Suns to call "heads."

So, over the phone, the Suns made the call and then waited for NBA Commissioner, J. Walter Kennedy to toss the coin.

In Phoenix, the atmosphere in the room was heavy with anticipation.

Then, a single word changed the course of Phoenix Suns history.

> **"There goes the easy money!"**
> – Gail Goodrich

"Tails!" came the word from New York. Simultaneously, over the conference call connection, you could hear loud cheering from the Milwaukee contingent.

At the Suns offices, there were only a few quiet groans.

"There goes the easy money!" Goodrich declared to Watson, before walking out of the office and into the bright, Phoenix sunshine.

And that was that.

CUSTOMER SELF-SERVICE

Alvin Scott, a former Suns player (1977-1985), nicknamed "Bone" during his playing days, worked for a time selling season tickets for the organization.

It was standard procedure for Suns sales reps to take their prospects to the Coliseum to show them their seat locations and then actually walk them up into the arena so they could sit in the very seat they were considering buying.

One day Alvin brought a prospective family to the Coliseum. As the family stood courtside, Scott gestured toward some available seats in two different spots on opposite sides of the arena, each location about 40 rows up.

"There are some seats up there and some seats up over there," Alvin pointed out.

"You can go walk up and take a look at them."

Then he pointed to a courtside seat just a few feet away. "And while you do, I'm gonna' be sittin' down right here."

Alvin's knees paid the price for his eight seasons in the NBA, but I'm not sure that "Bone" made that sale.

BIRD MAN

Suns Coach John MacLeod was always loyal to the guys who played for him at the University of Oklahoma. Players like Alvan Adams, Garfield Heard and Clifford Ray always held a special place in John's heart.

In the early 1980s, the Suns were looking for some help at center and Clifford Ray, near the end of his NBA playing days, was available. MacLeod invited him to training camp in Prescott, Arizona. The coaches looked at him as a possible candidate for the back-up center spot, but Clifford was way out of shape and he struggled to keep up.

When camp ended, the team bus was loaded with players and equipment. It began to pull away from the hotel for the one-hour drive back to Phoenix. Suddenly, the air brakes hissed, the bus lurched to a stop and the main door flipped open. They'd left somebody behind.

A lone figure came jogging out of the shadows, headed for the bus. It was Clifford. He came trotting across the parking lot in a wobbling, jogging, shuffling sort of gait. He was half-dressed and half-undressed in sloppy sweats and flip-flops, but he was toting a huge bucket of Kentucky Fried Chicken.

Clifford caught up with the bus, and climbed up the steps to the mock cheering and jeering of his teammates. Standing next to the driver, he held up the bucket of chicken and proclaimed to all, "I had to get some bird, man!" He really didn't need it; though I'm sure his teammates appreciated it.

Clifford was waived the following day. He never played a regular season game for the Suns, but he is still working in the NBA as an assistant coach.

EAST VS. WEST

Although I did not know him personally, I certainly was familiar with the famous quote of newspaper editor Horace Greeley (1811-1872) who once said, "Go West young man, and grow up with the country." Ninety-eight years after Greeley's death, that's exactly what I did, moving to Arizona in 1970.

> **"Go West young man, and grow up with the country."**
> – Horace Greeley

Unlike Greeley, most of the New Yorkers with whom I grew up have a rather existential view of the West. That attitude seems to be, "anything west of the Hudson River, doesn't really exist, or it certainly isn't worth worrying about."

Eastern perceptions of the West are, at times, amusing. When my wife attended St. Mary's College in South Bend, she was unique. Most students at St. Mary's and Notre Dame came from the East or the Midwest. Those numbers have been gradually changing in recent years, but back then, someone attending those schools and hailing from Arizona or California was an anomaly.

My wife was once asked if she rode horses "out there in Arizona." Her response was, "Sure, we ride horses once in a while." But the questioner rephrased, "No, I mean do you ride horses more than you drive cars?"

No! And believe it or not, the mail in Arizona is delivered by the U.S. Postal Service and not by the Pony Express!

That leads me to the time that I was on the phone with a HOOP magazine editor from New York City. We were going over edits for stories that would appear in HOOP, at the time, the official game program of the NBA. I had to give her my home address so the "blue-line" proofs could be express-mailed to me for final approval over the weekend.

Many of the street names in our Phoenix neighborhood were drawn from Arizona's rich Hispanic heritage: Calle Tuberia, Calle Redondo, Calle Feliz. By the way, "calle" means "street" and is pronounced "kye-yaye."

When I started to give this New Yorker my street address, she interrupted me and said, "Calle...is that like, 'Yipee-eye-yo-kye-yaye?'" I just shook my head and spelled it out for her.

Evidently, she had grown up watching too many old TV re-runs featuring "The Singing Cowboy," Gene Autry. It was one of his trademark songs.

A LEGACY

When Jerry Colangelo and his group of investors purchased the Suns from the team's original owners in 1987, one of the first things J.C. wanted to do was create a team foundation.

I huddled briefly with Suns CFO Rich Dozer on the matter and he thought we should use our law firm, Miller-Pitt of Tucson to develop the required IRS paperwork.

While that was underway, we began recruiting board members from the community to join us in the effort. Our first recruit was Jim Taszarek, the general manager of the Suns flagship radio station, KTAR 620 AM. "Taz" and I hit the road to visit several NBA teams that already had established non-profit foundations. We returned with lots of great ideas and a commitment from Taz to be our first chairman of the board.

With a provisional blessing from the IRS, we moved forward aggressively to form the board. Stepping up enthusiastically to join Jerry Colangelo, Taz, Dozer and me as directors were many familiar names in the Phoenix community including: Joe Garagiola Jr., Armon Mills, Ira Lavin, Bill Shover, Bill Lavidge, Rolf Norman, Ron Bergamo, Jerry Braet, Charles Bogar, Bob Caltabiano, Mark Coleman, Sally Cooper, JoAnn Fitzsimmons, Jim Frazier, Fr. Dale Fushek, Pete Garcia, Charles Green, Jeff Hornacek, Mark Hughes,

Kevin Johnson, Marlene Klotz, Kathy Kolbe, Eddie Lynch, Wayne Manning, Lonnie Ostrom, Lillian Suffolk, Charlie Thompson, John Vandevier and Linda Dillard, as well as Paul and Cindy Westphal. Nobody turned down our invitation.

During training camp in Flagstaff in 1988, Dozer presented me with a pile of papers to sign. They all related to the establishment of our 501(c) 3, which Colangelo had christened, "Phoenix Suns Charities." I noticed that our law firm had documented a number of the required organizational and board meetings, with my name liberally sprinkled throughout the application. I asked Rich, "Did I do all this?"

Rich looked at me and responded, "Yes, you did!"

I shook my head and began signing the papers.

"There are times," I muttered to no one in particular, "when I even amaze myself!"

In the years since it was founded in 1988, Phoenix Suns Charities has raised and distributed over 10 million dollars in grants and scholarships to worthy non-profit organizations and students throughout Arizona. That is a legacy that we can all point to with pride.

THAT'S NOT ALL

Over the last 25 years, Phoenix Suns Charities has developed into a valuable resource for the Phoenix non-profit community, but it's not the only Suns community program with staying power.

Another is the Wheelchair Suns, which started in 1988, when an experienced wheelchair basketball player named Gary Venjohn, moved to Phoenix only to discover that there was no organized wheelchair team in the area.

Venjohn knew how important wheelchair basketball had been to his personal rehabilitation and morale. He wanted to be able to offer to others, the same opportunities he had used to help his recovery.

Working with Bill Byron at Good Samaritan Medical Center's Samaritan Rehabilitation Institute, Venjohn approached the Suns about developing a wheelchair basketball team. The Suns jumped at the offer, supplying uniforms and warm-ups as well as financial support.

The team name evolved from "Samaritan Wheelchair Suns" to the "Banner Wheelchair Suns," reflective of ownership changes at the hospital.

There were the expected growing pains, but the team not only survived, it flourished. For 25 years, the Suns team has competed in the National Wheelchair Basketball Association. Today, additional registered teams include the Banner Wheelchair Mercury, the adult, coed Banner Wheelchair Suns and the Banner Wheelchair Suns, both JV and Prep. The teams total 40 to 60 participants.

The Banner Wheelchair Suns/Mercury teams also perform community outreach and education. Presentations on anti-bullying, safe driving and wheelchair skills are offered by individual team members in Valley classrooms throughout the school year.

A second organization that has grown deep roots in the community is the Junior Suns/Junior Mercury Youth Basketball Program. We pulled it together in the mid-90s and it now boasts over 18,000 boys and girls playing in leagues around the state. The YMCA is a major partner in this Suns program, but the outreach also extends to the Boys and Girls Clubs and the Jewish Community Center. The affiliated summer camp program for young hoopsters, teaches the fundamentals of the game to over 600 kids every June and July.

Lastly, Suns Nite Hoops is a program designed for young men between the ages of 18 and 25, a group that falls between the cracks of youth programs and adult counseling. Competitive basketball is the hook, but hoops are integrated with essential life skills training.

Since it began in the mid-1990s, Suns Nite Hoops has benefited thousands of young men, who are offered an alternative to violence, drugs and gangs, by furthering their education and employment opportunities, as well as giving them the chance to play competitive basketball.

2 WACKO!

Nite Hoops began as a Suns' collaboration with Maricopa County Adult Probation and the Phoenix Police Department. At its core, the program was designed to offer guidance and a helping hand to young men who may have made mistakes early in life, but who wanted to turn their lives in a positive direction. The program now has a long and proven record of success.

DESERT STORM

On the night Suns Charities was scheduled to hold their Courtside Classic, the United States government and its military decided it was time to take back Kuwait from Iraq's Saddam Hussein. They launched Operation Desert Storm.

> **"Jerry just wiped us out!"**
> – Armon Mills

The date was January 17, 1991. U.S. forces had been building up in Saudi Arabia for many weeks and the threat of war was palpable. There was no doubt there was going to be fighting in the Middle East. It was not a question of "if," only "when."

But throwing a party, even a charitable fund-raising gala, on the day that war breaks out is generally considered to be bad form, so we were monitoring the situation very closely. The decision was made that if the U.S. launched military action before noon, Phoenix time, on January 17, we would call each of the 600 guests slated to attend the Suns Charities event and tell them that the fund-raiser was postponed. If war broke out after 12 noon, we were going ahead with the party as scheduled.

High noon came and went. The Suns Courtside Classic was "on." War did indeed break out that day, but the first strike came late in the afternoon, Phoenix time. During the cocktail hour at The Pointe-Squaw Peak, we watched on big screen televisions as President George H.W. Bush (#41) addressed the nation regarding the conflict.

The Middle East was a virtual powder keg and nobody really knew how this action was going to turn out. It could be a minor skirmish of short duration or possibly Armageddon for planet Earth. The fear was that many U.S. servicemen would be killed, severely impacting American communities and military families.

Suns Charities was in its formative years and was just a year or two into the process of building its financial base. When President Bush concluded his televised remarks, Suns President Jerry Colangelo took the podium to address the assembled Suns Charities supporters. Colangelo committed Suns Charities to a donation of $50,000 from that night's event to help U.S. military families in Arizona.

Hearing Colangelo's off-the-cuff pledge, and knowing exactly, to the penny, what the Suns Charities' bank balance was at that moment, the chairman of the Suns Charities board, Armon Mills, leaned over and whispered to his fellow board member, Jim Taszarek, "Jerry just wiped us out!"

Of the 600 people who purchased tickets to the 1991 Suns Courtside Classic, there were only two "no-shows." After the event, Suns Charities made good on Colangelo's promise by donating $50,000 to the American Red Cross.

A FINE WAY TO DO BUSINESS

Long-term relationships in business don't seem to count for much anymore. It's all about the bottom line. And that's a shame.

"Here are the specs. Submit your bid and we'll get back to you. Maybe"

That's cold.

Whatever happened to the handshake that closed a deal without any lawyers in the room? Whatever happened to the job that you could just give to a trusted vendor without soliciting three competitive bids that might vary by a percentage point, or a dollar, give or take?

The Suns and pro sports teams in general, require a significant amount of printing. Newsletters, magazines, schedules, game programs, media guides, marketing materials, stationery and business cards comprise just some of the basic printing needs.

When I started with the Suns, the team was already working with Thom Meaker of Meaker the Printer for much of their printing business. I quickly learned that I could trust Thom to deliver a quality product at a competitive price. We were constantly approached by other printers who offered to shave a bit off this price or that. I found it a far better use of my limited time and resources to work consistently with Meaker. I trusted him completely and I was never disappointed.

When we wanted to publish a 25th Anniversary book on the Suns, Thom suggested the designers, printers and bindery that could best pull the book project together, even though most of those resources were outside of his own company. He was simply helping one of his good customers, even if he didn't benefit financially.

As one of our season ticket holders, Thom also knew the team and our front office philosophy well. He was a valuable sounding board for many of our ideas, some good, some not so good, but Thom could explain the difference to us.

Over more than three decades, his ideas, creativity and perspective was of invaluable help to me and a tremendous benefit to the franchise. Meaker saved the Suns tens of thousands of dollars, back when tens of thousands of dollars were really worth something.

There were too many tight deadlines to count and more than a little stress to endure, but that made this trusted relationship even more rewarding. It was an efficient and enjoyable way to get things done, that is, until the accountants, lawyers and bankers took over.

MY WORD IS MY BOND

In the late 1960s and the early 1970s, Jerry Colangelo was on the road scouting college games, first for the Bulls and then a few years later, for the Suns. During his travels, he frequently would cross paths with Kansas State Coach Cotton Fitzsimmons.

Echoes From the Purple Palace

COTTON

Jerry loved the idea of bringing successful college coaches into the pro game, but he'd been burned by several coaches who used his interest to go back to their schools and negotiate new and more lucrative deals for themselves.

One night, when he was seeking Fitzsimmons's opinion on some potential college coaching candidates, Colangelo asked Cotton if he would have an interest in coaching pro ball. When Cotton said "yes," Jerry asked him, "Are you serious?"

Cotton responded, "If I give you my word, then I'm coming!"

In 1970, Cotton proved that he was very serious indeed, taking Jerry up on his offer to become an NBA coach and then leading the Suns to two consecutive winning seasons with 48 and 49 wins respectively.

Even at the end of his career, Cotton's "contract" with J.C. and the Suns was a handshake deal. No papers, no lawyers, no contract, just an undeniable trust between two people. Integrity and trust work.

MY DEAL

My deal with Colangelo was a little bit different.

In this world of rapidly diminishing corporate loyalty, people were often amazed to learn that I had been with the Suns franchise for 37 consecutive years. I would patiently explain to them that I actually had the advantage of a "lifetime" contract with the organization.

However, as part of that arrangement, I used to joke that Suns owner, Jerry Colangelo, reserved the right to have me declared "legally dead" at any time of his choosing.

LITHUANIAN

As Jerry Colangelo was speaking at a 2012 fund-raising dinner, he referred to me, his old PR guy, as I sat in the audience.

"I see Tom Ambrose is here tonight. He's a guy I hired years ago, because I thought he was Italian. Then, years later, I come to find out that he's actually Russian or something."

"Lithuanian!" I shouted from the audience.

J.C. glanced in my direction and responded, "Whatever!"

FINE LINES

Perhaps it is born out of frustration, perhaps it is an intellectual challenge, but when reporters create different ways to ask the same question, NBA PR Directors are often forced to create new ways of answering. Sometimes those answers become a permanent part of the NBA's lexicon.

Take the example of John White of the Portland Trail Blazers who, after fielding dozens of daily media calls about the status of his often-injured star Bill Walton, came up with the response, "he's day-to-day." John rode that answer for years. It was simple, yet somehow elegant in its simplicity. It proved to be much better than saying, "I have no idea. Call back tomorrow." Best of all, it is now a permanent part of the NBA dictionary.

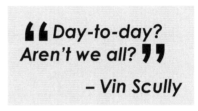

Of course, as Dodger announcer Vin Scully once observed, "Day-to-day? Aren't we all?"

***

Sports columnist Joe Gilmartin reported that one of his favorite lines from a PR director came from his inquiry into some aspect of the Suns drug scandal in 1987. That was when I, on advice of counsel, responded, "I am precluded from answering that!"

***

Another time, Gilmartin asked NBA PR chief Brian McIntyre if the league was going to investigate some rumored misbehavior by an NBA player.

"We're looking into it," McIntyre said.

"So you're investigating?"

"No, we're 'looking into it.'" McIntyre responded, "I'll let you know when we start an 'investigation.'"

***

2 WACKO!

The Suns 1976 Rookie of the Year, Alvan Adams, played 12 years with the Suns and offered many clever quips during his career. One of my favorites came during a season when the Suns suffered through a rocky start. Even 20 games into the season, the news media were still referring to the Suns poor start. That prompted Alvan to ask an inquiring reporter, "Exactly when does a 'start' stop?"

***

The Suns President and CEO received many letters addressed to "Jerry Coal And Jello" or "Jerry Co-Angelo." Once, I received a thank you note addressed to "Mr. Tom Oink-Rose." I guess that letter was intended for my male chauvinist alter-ego.

***

The NBA salary cap has introduced a lot of new language into trade deals and contract negotiations. But in 2009, the Suns announced that they had reached an agreement on a contract "divorce" with both Sasha Pavlov and Ben Wallace. That was new NBA nomenclature for me. I wondered… who gets custody? And of what?

THE HECKLERS

Around the NBA, there are some leather-lunged fans who become as well-known for their well-placed barbs as players are for their precision shooting. Two of them leap to mind immediately, Leon "the Barber" in Detroit and Robin Ficker from Washington, D.C.

Wayne Witt, the long-time PR director for the San Antonio Spurs, remembered Leon the Barber sitting directly behind the visitors' bench in Detroit.

"He was loud and obnoxious but extremely creative and funny," Witt recalled with a smile. "He rode our coach Stan Albeck, relentlessly, always calling him 'Albright.'

Echoes From the Purple Palace

"At the time, Albeck had one of those popular, 'frizzy' hairdos. Leon would loudly comment that Albeck reminded him of Shirley Temple.

"One night Stan called a time-out and Leon shouted, 'Don't call a time-out Albright, you'll just screw 'em up!'"

But Witt also remembered that Detroit wasn't the only arena where Albeck had interaction with fans.

"Another night, coaching in the Forum in Los Angeles, Albeck was on his feet moving up and down the sideline. He felt a tug on his pants leg but jerked away and ignored it. About the second or third time it happened he turned around to come face-to-face with actor Jack Nicholson who said most politely, 'Excuse me coach, but I can't see.' Albeck sat down.

"Here in San Antonio, at the old HemisFair Arena, there was a couple, season ticket holders, who sat in the first row, literally with their feet touching the court. She was a blond who constantly got up and down, parading around to somewhere. Who knows where?

"Finally one night, a fan named George Valle, otherwise known as 'Big George' of San Antonio's infamous 'Baseline Bums,' had enough. In a booming voice that could be heard throughout the arena, even over the crowd noise, George yelled, 'Hey blondie, sit down! You're not THAT good lookin'!'"

There was yet another night when Detroit's Leon the Barber went after Boston superstar, Larry Bird.

"Hey, Bird," Leon shouted, "Why don't you take some of the money from that big contract of yours and go buy yourself a CHIN!"

JUST PLAIN IRRITATING

Robin Ficker was a well-known attorney in the Washington, D.C. area, but he became even more renowned for his antics as a heckler at Washington Bullets games. He felt that if his heckling could distract the opposition, he was doing his job as a "sixth man."

Ficker never cursed or used bad language and was always knowledgeable, well prepared and loud. Targeting opposing players from his spot behind the visiting team bench, he would often read aloud... VERY ALOUD... from books or articles written about his nightly targets of ridicule. Michael Jordan and the book, *The Jordan Rules*, were two of Ficker's favorites.

The Pacers' Reggie Miller was no fan of the rubber chicken that Ficker would occasionally brandish in a taunting fashion. And Indiana coach, Larry Brown never truly appreciated the art of Ficker verbally assaulting his team through the megaphone he'd use during time-outs.

Ficker became somewhat of a media sideshow, especially on nights when the Bullets were visited by NBA superstars like Jordan. TV crews would come in and actually put a microphone on Ficker, in order to document his every word.

Finally the NBA had heard, and had, enough. They instituted what is commonly referred to as, "The Ficker Rule," which prohibits fans from engaging in verbal abuse that interferes with communication between coaches and players. A violation results in the fan's ejection.

GUEST PEST

As Charles Barkley and the Suns opened the NBA Finals in 1993, who shows up in a near-courtside seat at America West Arena? Like a moth to a flame, it was attorney-heckler, Robin Ficker, who continued to incessantly exercise his right to free speech, much to the consternation of all those sitting within earshot.

But that's not the entire story.

From his many years playing in the NBA's Eastern Conference, Charles Barkley was well-acquainted with Ficker. Even though he had been the target of many a Ficker zinger, Barkley, in some, warped way, still respected the guy.

Charles also knew that Ficker was one person who could really get under the skin of his friend, Michael Jordan. So, in a somewhat twisted act of "gamesmanship," Barkley invited Ficker to Phoenix for the start of the NBA Finals against Jordan's Chicago Bulls. Barkley not only bought Ficker a plane ticket, but he also got him a prime seat, right behind the Bulls' bench. I don't know if Ficker stayed at Barkley's home during his time in Phoenix, but he might have.

Ficker was appreciative of the opportunity Barkley presented him and he embraced his anti-Jordan role with *mucho gusto*. But once he started his routine, AWA security swooped in and removed him from the arena before the end of the first quarter of Game One.

I thought that would be the last time we'd see Robin Ficker. I was wrong.

ONE HEALTHY CHEER

As the second game of the NBA Finals got underway at America West Arena, I noticed a fan standing up and waving what appeared to be a large bunch of raw broccoli.

I thought that was just a bit unusual, even for the NBA Finals, so I moved in for a closer look.

The first thing I noticed was that the fan in question was none other than Robin Ficker, who had been summarily ejected from the first game. He was back! But he wasn't sitting behind the Bulls' bench and he wasn't being his usual, vociferous self.

Then, I noticed that there was a hand-lettered sign attached to the veggies he was waving around. It read, "Charles Broccoli."

> **"That may not be grounds for ejection but, it's just plain WACKO!"**

What? I'm sorry. That may not have been grounds for ejection, but it was just plain WACKO!

MEXICO...OLD OR NEW

NBA trainers are the most valuable members of a team's traveling party. They are the ones who make sure everything on a road trip goes smoothly. That includes hotel check-ins, on-time arrivals and departures for planes and buses, the transportation and cleaning of uniforms and practice gear. They also take care of the shipping of video and medical equipment and luggage transfers. Don't forget they also coordinate practice sessions and treat injuries.

With international travel more and more part of every NBA team itinerary, the trainers will often hold onto all player passports during the season, just to be certain that paperwork is up-to-date and nobody will forget to bring their documents on a trip when the team crosses an international border. A few years ago, one star Suns player went to the team trainer to ask for his passport because he was taking a short trip out of the country.

"Sure," the trainer said, "Where are you headed?"

The player confided, "New Mexico."

THE McCOY ROAST

In 1999, the House of Broadcasting paid special tribute to the Voice of the Suns, Al McCoy. It wasn't exactly a "roasting" of Al, because how do you roast an all-around great guy and a broadcasting icon? The event turned out to be more of a "light toasting," but great fun nevertheless.

> **"Al is the only broadcaster in the NBA who can sleep in a pillowcase."**
> – Cotton Fitzsimmons

"Toaster" Cotton Fitzsimmons, vertically challenged in his own right, focused on McCoy's height, pointing out that Al is the only broadcaster in the NBA who can sleep in a pillowcase.

Echoes From the Purple Palace

Cotton also explained that Colangelo hired McCoy because he knew the team would save money. Al could room with trainer Joe Proski and sleep in the chest of drawers. Cotton went on to point out that McCoy had a clothing deal with a local clothing store, GAP for Kids.

Jerry Colangelo later added that, after one year in Phoenix, he knew there was only one guy who he wanted to be the Suns broadcaster. That guy wasn't available, so he hired Al McCoy.

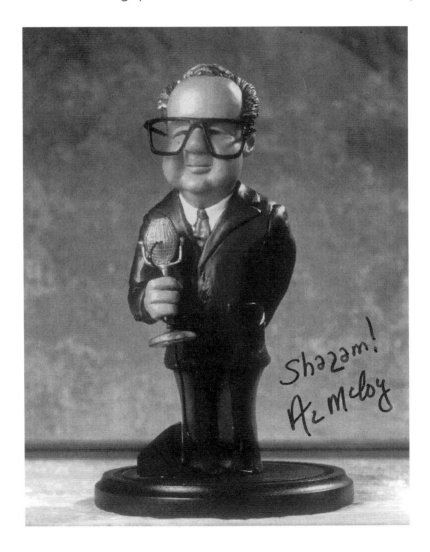

AL McCOY

THE STUNT DOUBLE

During my career with the Suns, I had the privilege of holding eight different positions and titles within the organization, from director of public relations to senior vice president and executive director of Phoenix Suns Charities. One of the "unofficial" titles I never put on my resume was "stunt double for Jerry Colangelo."

In the late 1990s, the Suns had spawned Major League Baseball's Arizona Diamondbacks and Jerry Colangelo headed both organizations. Jerry was going to be the focus of a roast at a major fundraiser called "A Night at the Barbershop," which would support the charitable foundations of both teams. As part of the fundraiser, Suns Productions went to work on a video that would answer the burning question every sports fan wants to know, "What does a sports mogul do behind the scenes after the crowds have gone home?"

The video spoof first showed Colangelo mimicking the Tom Cruise air-guitar-in-his-boxer-shorts scene from the movie, *Risky Business*. The next scene was Jerry shooting baskets at the arena in the wee hours, with Suns broadcaster, Al McCoy, rousted out of bed and on hand, to call J.C.'s personal play-by-play. The Gorilla was also there to face off with J.C. in a slam dunk contest, where Jerry did a full, mid-air somersault off a trampoline before he dunked the ball.

Then it was on to the ballpark, where, with Randy Johnson pitching and Joe Garagiola catching, Colangelo put on a hitting display, the likes of which Bank One Ballpark had never seen, before or since. His final blast was going… going… gone…into the swimming pool in right-center field. Jerry then raced across the diamond, scaled the outfield fence and cannon-balled into the pool to retrieve his home run ball.

The video was a smash hit and the highlight of the evening. Many people told me afterwards that they were amazed that Jerry could do all those things. They had no idea.

Echoes From the Purple Palace

With a masterful editing mix of Jerry's close-ups and longer shots of his stunt double, Suns Productions made Jerry look like a cross between Michael Jordan and Babe Ruth.

Jerry and I are about the same height and with both of us sporting light or grayish hair, all it took was a close match of the clothing and nobody could tell it wasn't J.C. in some of the crazier scenes.

But pity the weary stunt double who began his evening moonwalking in his boxer shorts and ended a long night of video-taping by climbing a fence and plunging, fully-clothed, into a frigid pool at Bank One Ballpark.

I was not asked to bungee-jump from the roof of the ballpark, but if they had requested it, for J.C., I would have.

FROM THE WACKO! FILE: A WALK-IN WACKO!

Author's Note: Sometimes an item for the WACKO! File comes in the mail. Sometimes it arrives via the Internet and other times it can walk through your office door, like this 1998 story from long-time Milwaukee Bucks PR man Bill King (BK):

2 WACKO!

I'm relating this tale of an interview that took place in the Bradley Center. Every year we hire six college students to serve as game-day publicity interns. We have a list of questions we pose to each interviewee. Here's how this one particular conversation went:

BK: What year are you in?

Him: 98

BK: No, you don't understand…freshman, sophomore, junior or senior?

Him: 98

BK: So you're in the Class of 98…you're a senior.

Him: No, I'm a freshman.

BK: OK, next question. I see where you are going to college in Madison (which is an hour and half drive from Milwaukee). Most of our interns come from colleges in the Milwaukee area. Where do you live?

Him: The Faircrest Apartments.

BK: And where are the Faircrest Apartments?

Him: South Street.

BK: (Biting my pen to avoid busting out laughing) And just where is South Street?

Him: In Madison.

BK: With 41 home games, how do you plan to get from Madison to Milwaukee?

Him: I-94.

BK: OK. (Now I'm starting to think that this is a setup) How many hours are you taking?

Him: Four

BK: Let me rephrase the question. Most students take a minimum of 12 credit hours per semester. Sixteen credits per semester and you'll graduate in 4 years with 128 hours. How many hours are you taking?

Him: Four. I go to class 4 hours straight through, every day.

BK: OK. Why are you going to college?

Him: I want to learn how to program video games.

BK: (It dawns on me that I might have a computer genius on my hands, which would be a good thing – even if he's not reality-based). So what kind of software do you know how to run?

Him: Well, we're just now learning DOS.

BK: Do you know how to operate Windows, Microsoft Word, Word Perfect or any other standard office software?

Him: We're just now learning DOS.

At that point I quickly pare down the remaining questions, thank him for coming in and tell him that we'll be in touch. I escort him to the lobby and (silly me) asked him where he parked. He said he walked. Somehow, I believe he might have.

STUCK ON YOU

Author's Note: This story first appeared as a feature in Suns "Fastbreak Magazine."

One of the new innovations making its appearance in NBA basketball arenas is a unique footpad, usually found lying on the sideline, right in front of the scorer's table. The device, about 18 x 36 inches, is a pad of clear plastic sheets, each lightly coated with a tacky adhesive. When a player steps on the pad, the adhesive removes any lint or dust from the treads of his basketball shoes, giving him optimum traction on the hard court. If the top sheet is no longer tacky, the player can just peel it off and go to a fresh sheet.

Like most truly great ideas, the concept is simple. But what people never see, is the extensive research, development and marketing that goes into these "simple" products.

Under the NBA's Freedom of Information Act, *Fastbreak* has obtained heretofore sealed files regarding early field tests of competing products that didn't quite make the cut. The names of players and teams involved in these tests have been redacted, and the product name has been changed to eliminate the potential of embarrassing lawsuits. What follows is a look at an early test-game, based on information culled from these heretofore secret files.

It was a dark and stormy night in Akron. Well, actually it wasn't Akron and there was only a light drizzle falling, but our story begins in the research and development department of a struggling chemical company somewhere in the Midwest.

There were problems and there was pressure surrounding an experimental product for basketball.

"We had some real difficulty in finding a consistent adhesive product," said one R & D engineer in a later deposition. "We were constantly battling with suppliers. Our formula was either too tacky or not tacky enough."

Back and forth the battle raged. Management at the small company was beginning to come, well, unglued. Perhaps it was the constant sniveling by the R & D staff that caused one irate supplier, with a sadistic sense of humor, to ship the laboratory a deliberately mislabeled barrel of cyanoacrylate ester (a.k.a. "super glue"). That's when the real problems started.

Because of the repeated delays, the marketing department was hyper–anxious to rush their new product to market. So, it wasn't too surprising when the R & D boys decided to press on with field tests before the proper lab work was completed. Quality control would come later. Their collective attitude would prove to be an embarrassing mistake.

An NBA preseason game in a non-league city was selected for the first test. Company reps were in the stands complete with clipboards and white lab coats. As team warm–ups concluded, interest in the new pad picked up as a rookie guard became stuck while stretching before the game. Since he had been doing a "hurdlers stretch," the pad, apparently coated with the "super" adhesive, had served to attach the outside of his right foot to an area just below his right shoulder blade.

He could not have picked a worse time for the entanglement since it was moments before the National Anthem. The anthem singer had to sidestep the writhing young player to reach the microphone at center court. Fortunately the rookie had the good,

Echoes From the Purple Palace

patriotic sense to place his right hand over his heart during the anthem and, in spite of intense leg cramps, managed to keep his movement to a minimum. As soon as the anthem was over, one of the trainers peeled the rookie off the pad and cut his leg loose. His chances of making the team were substantially diminished.

The game proceeded normally through much of the first half, but players on both sides gave the footpad a wide berth. That is, until a lumbering veteran power forward reported to the official scorer late in the third quarter and, without thinking, (standard procedure for many power forwards) sat down to wait for a break in the action.

When the horn sounded and the substitute was beckoned into the game, it didn't take long for the fans to notice the big black pad stuck to his enormous backside. Quickly, a 20–second time-out was called and the team trainer leaped to action, chasing down the hulking forward and then, with great delicacy, tried to peel off the pad. But, by this time, this cyanoacrylate ester had nearly 30 seconds to set. It was too late.

STUCK

2 WACKO!

(Editor's note: As seen on TV, it has been proven that cyanoacrylate ester needs only five seconds to permanently bond a construction worker (and his boots) to an I-beam, upside-down!)

One hard yank by the trainer not only removed the pad, but also a large swatch of the uniform shorts. Since the NBA does not permit players to play while wearing their warm-up pants, the coach was permitted 30 seconds to select a substitute.

The game was close. The remainder of the third quarter and most of the fourth, were played without further mishap, as long as you don't consider a referee losing a shoe to the pad as he raced down the sideline.

There are many conflicting accounts as to what happened next, but it seems that several players dove for the ball as it was rolling out of bounds around midcourt. As many hands grappled for the ball, several of the footpad sheets tore loose, creating the ultimate in "male bonding."

Players who moved in to help, became entangled themselves. One referee tried to straighten out the mess but he too was quickly attached to the pile. The official scorer reached out to help and was whisked out of his courtside seat. More players and both head coaches were sucked in as they tried to separate their teammates.

The more they tried to break free, the more entangled they became and the harder the glue seemed to grip. The crowd looked on in a sort of mirthful, amazed bewilderment. The scoreboard operator, mesmerized by the scene before him, seem to derive a sort of sadistic pleasure by repeating short, loud blasts on the scoreboard horn, adding to the confusion.

The remaining two referees, perhaps thinking that the glue would respond to authority, repeatedly blew their whistles while alternately making signals for "traveling" and "offensive foul." But clearly, the momentum had been established.

The ever-growing ball of humanity careened across the baseline, picking up a photographer and a team mascot like lint off a new wool suit. The pile rolled off the court, down the arena tunnel and out of sight.

Fortunately, because the game was played in a far–flung location, and finished later than normal, it received little notice from the news media. The next morning however, *USA Today* carried a wide-angle photo of a tangle of arms, legs and feet, with the caption: "NBA Melee Ends Game."

That's all most NBA fans knew about it, until now.

Author's Postscript: OK, we made up the whole thing... but it coulda' happened.

NEW YAWK, NEW YAWK

In 2006, my wife and I were in New York City, representing the Arizona Chapter of The Partnership for a Drug Free America. The national headquarters for The Partnership was in the classically beautiful Chrysler Building in mid-town. In post 9/11 New York City, all sorts of security measures had been implemented for high-rise buildings.

As we walked into the lobby of the Chrysler Building, I noticed that people who were headed for the elevators were swiping some kind of security card that let them pass through a turnstile. Well, I didn't have a security card and I didn't see any type of security or concierge desk. So, we walked up to a tall, uniformed security guard who was standing just behind one of the turnstiles. He was big guy, with a short haircut and a military bearing.

"Excuse me," I said. "We need to get up to the 16th floor to the Partnership offices."

He sized us up, no doubt making an on-the-spot assessment of our potential "threat level."

Then, he looked me directly in the eye and said in perfect New Yawk-ese, "Bolt a yuzz?"

Fortunately, growing up in nearby New Rochelle and, being familiar with the local dialect, I was able to instantly translate what he said.

The guard's question to me had been, "Both of you?"

But I just couldn't help myself when I responded, "Yeah! BOLT of us."

He waved us "trew."

I nodded as we passed by and said, "Tanks!"

I love New Yawk!

MY LAST NIGHT

Although no one, including me, knew it going in, the 2009 Suns & Stars Gala was, effectively, my last night with the Suns.

I have to say that the Phoenix Suns Charities (PSC) board made it an evening that I will always remember. The PSC board and staff always worked exceptionally hard on this annual event. Their efforts and creative input had paid off in a financial net to the charity of over one million dollars per year, for three consecutive years.

One person in particular, board member Melissa Leonesio, created the financial model that helped grow Phoenix Suns Charities from a foundation that offered community grants and scholarships of just over $500,000 per year, to one that generated over one million dollars annually.

I should also add that, since its inception in the late 1980s, Phoenix Suns Charities never received direct cash donations from the Suns franchise. It was the job of the PSC staff and board to go out and raise the funds to give back to the community. In 2012, I was very proud when PSC passed the $12 million mark in total community giving since 1989.

During the 20-plus years of PSC history, the Suns organization did, however, make substantial in-kind contributions of staff salaries, office space and a special commitment to a mandatory, full-team appearance for the foundation's annual gala. We turned that investment into handsome returns for the community.

A few weeks before the 2009 event, scheduled for the world-famous Arizona Biltmore Resort, the PSC board voted to establish an individual award for dedicated service to the community.

It would be called the *Spirit of the Suns Award*, and I would be honored as the inaugural recipient. The board surprised me with the honor at a board meeting just two weeks before the event.

Echoes From the Purple Palace

15 MINUTES OF FAME

When the announcement was made, the entire board of 40 people rose to give me a standing ovation. I was humbled. With the recognition coming from these folks, the majority of whom I had known and worked with for many years, it was an honor and an indescribable feeling.

In order to promote the event and my award, incoming board chair Brad Gould had secured some ad placements on many of Clear Channel's electronic billboards around the city. I was unaware of this until I was driving to work one day and I saw a huge picture of myself flash up on one of the outdoor boards. I nearly drove off the road.

"Was that ME up there?!" I asked myself.

Talk about a distracted driver! So, just to be sure, I made a U-turn, drove back and parked in a safe spot that faced the billboard. I waited until the displays recycled. It WAS me. Very cool.

2 WACKO!

On the night of the event, with over 900 people in attendance, I was introduced and congratulated on my award by Suns Assistant Coach Dan Majerle, who was originally drafted by the Suns back in 1988 when I was the team's PR guy.

In addition to my family and friends, two of the great mentors and role models in my life were in attendance and I had the opportunity to thank them during my remarks.

The first was Bill Shover from Phoenix Newspapers, who gave me my first job in Phoenix and taught me the essentials of good public relations. The second was Jerry Colangelo, who, during my early days with the Suns, taught me many things, but especially how to be a leader in service to the community. From these two men, I learned everything I needed to know about community involvement, mentoring, ethics, integrity and how to treat people with respect.

I only wish that my dad and Cotton Fitzsimmons could have been there too. That would have rounded out my personal Mount Rushmore of mentors.

Additionally, that night, I had the honor of memorializing one of our PSC board members, Dave Trout, who had died suddenly, just a few days before the event.

Two months later, following another successful Suns Charities distribution of more than one million dollars in grants and scholarships, Suns management asked me to step down as executive director of Suns Charities. Was it something I said? Perhaps it was something I didn't say. In any case, my 37-year career with the Suns, a fabulous run with one of the NBA's best franchises, was over.

Ironically, there was no formal award presented to me that night, as the inaugural recipient of the *Spirit of the Suns Award*. There was no etched glass trophy, no custom sculpture, no unique metal engraving... not even an official attendance certificate.

Board member, Kelly Norton, one of the chairs of the event, told me that they had prepared a Suns jersey with my name on it to present to me that night, but nobody could seem to find it.

Three years later, during the summer of 2012, somebody in the Suns office was cleaning out a storage cabinet and found a "09" jersey with the name, "AMBROSE" embroidered on the back. A few days later, the new folks running Phoenix Suns Charities, Robin Milne and Sarah Krahenbuhl, took me to lunch and presented me with the long-lost jersey. I won't soon forget their thoughtfulness and I wish them every success in guiding Phoenix Suns Charities to new heights of community support and service.

UNCONSCIOUS

In 2009, as I stepped away from the day-to-day management of Suns Charities, the newly-elected chairman of the board, Brad Gould, wanted to keep me involved as a member of the board of directors.

"How come?" I asked.

"Because you have unconscious intelligence!" he said.

"Wait a minute!" I shot back. "What does that mean exactly?"

He explained, "It just means that you know stuff that you don't even know that you know!"

2 WACKO!

AN ORIGINAL VAN ARSDALE

VAN GOUGH, VAN ARSDALE

With apologies to Vincent Van Gough, the art world has a new Dutchman to consider these days. He is "The Original Sun," Dick Van Arsdale. Since his playing days ended back in 1977, "Van" has coached and scouted for the Suns and dabbled in real estate with his twin brother, Tom, also an NBA and Suns veteran.

More recently, Dick has taken up painting and, the results have been remarkably good. After suffering a stroke in 2005, Van used art to fill some of his free time. With encouragement from friends, family and other artists, Van has experimented with several different artistic styles.

His paintings have served to not only bring back memories of his basketball playing days, but also the halcyon days of his youth in rural Indiana. His work has been featured at several local art shows, allowing him to visit with many long-time Suns fans who come by to say hello and check out his new venture.

The drawing reproduced here was one of his first. It prompted me to say to him, "Van, I had no idea that you had that kind of talent!"

His humble response was typical, "Neither did I!"

FROM THE WACKO! FILE: FANS ALWAYS TRY TO HELP

Now ya Got Skinny Tall

Rebounding is it. Don't Forget Port. and Spurs look Tough.

1 - Frye - when he's in mood!
2. Stoudimire - Don't burn him Out!
3 - & Lopez → ask him for a (Haircut) still
4 - Nash. Steve. JJ Reddick Next year!
5 → Richerson
6 - Barbosa.
7 - Pavalic
8 → Swift. - It's your time. Bound "Re"
9 → Admunson
10 → ? Griffin. (Blakes bro)
11 → ? Ya Don't Know.
12 → Luke Jackson maybe. A Plawkoswitz (clone) Eric 67 guy ya had

Oh my why ya didn't ask for Darnell Jackson

When this 7² Luke Nevill gets cut get him. Oh my Goodness Guys! How did ya get Griffin? That was a steal of A Lifetime! Let's Do it Again!

YOU'RE IN THE BOOK

One morning I received a telephone call from a young man who was attending college at a small school, somewhere on the East Coast. He was interested in finding out how he should plan his college curriculum to give himself the best chance of landing a job in sports. Once he graduated, he specifically wanted to work in the NBA.

Because people were so helpful and accommodating to me when I was just starting out, I always try to "pay it forward." So we chatted for quite a while. At one point I thought to ask, "How come you decided to call me? There must be a dozen NBA teams closer to where you're going to school."

He told me he knew that, but he called me, in particular, because my name was "in the book."

"The book?" I asked. "What book? The phone book? The NBA Guide? The PRSA Directory?"

"No," he responded. "You're in a book called, *The 50 Coolest Jobs in Sports*."

"I am?" was all I could say. But it didn't take me long to track down the book and order a copy.

The book was written by David Fischer and, sure enough, there I was on page 134, in the chapter on "Sports Marketing and Public Relations," listed as a "Success Story." The book does give an excellent overview of jobs in sports, both on the collegiate and professional level.

Somewhere along the line, I must have had a phone conversation with Mr. Fischer about the profession and his book, but it was probably one of many such chats I had while I was Suns PR director. I didn't remember our conversation, but I was grateful for the recognition.

BOOK IT

A few years later, author Clive Cussler was kind enough to use my name for one of his characters in *Atlantis Found*. Fans of Cussler and Dirk Pitt will no doubt recall Dr. Thomas Ambrose, the eminent anthropologist from Arizona State University. Unfortunately, as the plot unfolded, my namesake was killed off within 30 pages,

John E. Nordahl threw me a little love in his book, *Traveling, Three Months on the NBA road*.

I was also proud to help my Notre Dame buddy, Rich Wolfe, with the editing of Al McCoy's book, *The Real McCoy*. And I was especially proud to contribute one of my accounts to that collection of stories.

Many years ago, a free-lance writer named Dorothy Tegeler arrived in Arizona and I immediately put her to work doing feature stories for *Fastbreak* magazine. She was kind enough to thank me for that opportunity in the acknowledgements of her excellent guidebook, *Retiring in Arizona*.

When Michel Sarda did a series of books on local artists and supporters of the arts, I was pleased to receive mention in his *Angels of Arizona*.

COURAGE

On a night in 1995, the Suns filled a table at the Gene Autry Courage Awards in Tempe, Arizona. One of our former players, Neal Walk, was receiving one of the five awards presented that night. The Gene Autry Courage Awards were presented to deserving current and former athletes and coaches who demonstrate inspirational acts of courage and heroism while overcoming extreme adversity.

The patron of the evening was Gene Autry, who gained notoriety as "The Singing Cowboy." His 30-year career began on radio in the 1930s and later moved into movies and television. Autry also became involved in sports as the owner of baseball's California Angels.

Following a stellar college career at the University of Florida, and an NBA career that spanned eight seasons, including the first five in Phoenix, Neal Walk learned that he had a tumor on his spinal cord. Unless he underwent surgery to remove it, the tumor would paralyze and eventually kill him. But the surgery could cause him to lose the use of his legs.

That wasn't much of a choice for the 6-10 former professional athlete. Following his surgery, Neal was indeed relegated to a wheelchair, but as soon as Neal was able, Jerry Colangelo invited him to come back to work for the Suns in their community relations department.

Dick Van Arsdale, one of Walk's original Suns' teammates, introduced Neal that night and presented the award. Sitting in the audience, at a table directly in front of the stage, was Gene Autry, the "Singing Cowboy" himself.

Neal rolled to the edge of the stage and took the microphone from Van. During Neal's acceptance speech, he explained the emotion he had gone through following his surgery and thanked all those who stuck by him during that most difficult time. His remarks were frequently punctuated by enthusiastic applause from the audience. Finally, Neal looked down from the stage and addressed Gene Autry directly.

"And Mr. Autry, I just wanna' say one thing... ROY ROGERS COULDN'T CARRY YOUR SADDLEBAGS!"

The place went crazy!

Autry passed away in 1998 at age 91. Neal Walk is still going strong.

THE LAST KEYCHAIN

Over my Suns career I probably attended 30 NBA All-Star games. The entire All-Star Weekend is less about game competition than it is about giving the league's many sponsors their "props" (translation: proper recognition) on a national stage. There is absolutely nothing wrong with that.

Usually the league will take products and souvenirs from each league sponsor and assemble them into a nifty "goodie bag" for team officials and VIP guests to take home.

Typically, one of the major athletic shoe companies would provide the gym bags and the other sponsors would fill up the bag with promotional items.

When I returned home, my young daughter would invariably ask the same question that every parent hears when they return from a trip, "Did you bring me anything?"

That's when the All-Star goodie bag became a lifesaver. For several years I had given my daughter keychains adorned with NBA and sponsor logos. When she was about eight years old, following another All-Star trip, she once again asked the question. And, once more, I offered her a keychain to add to her growing collection of league-sanctioned trinkets.

She took the trifle in her hand, stared at it for a moment, then shook her head in disappointment.

"Great." she said. "I have all these keychains, AND NO KEYS!"

ONE LAST SHOT

Ask any kid who has ever hoisted a basketball toward a hoop. No matter what, you don't go home, you don't quit, until you make your last shot. Invariably, that final shot is "for the championship."

Dan Majerle played his first seven seasons with the Suns, before he was traded to Cleveland in the John "Hot Rod" Williams deal in 1995. Majerle had become a fan favorite and was a big part of the Suns success since 1988.

Majerle stayed with the Cavs for just one season before signing a free agent deal with the Miami Heat. He'd spend the next five seasons in Miami, before returning home to Phoenix in 2001-02, for the final season of his stellar 14-year NBA career.

When Majerle came into the league, he quickly developed a reputation as a hard-nosed defender. On offense, his basket-crashing plays and aggressive slam dunks, redefined "hustle" in the minds of Phoenix fans.

Then, after a couple of years, and tens of thousands of off-season practice shots, Majerle became a devastating three-point shooter. He would end his career as one of the best in NBA history.

In his final Suns season, Majerle's playing time was spotty, he struggled with his shooting and, his scoring average of 4.6 point per game was the lowest of his NBA career.

As the season wound down to its final few games, two things became eminently clear: for the first time in 13 years, the Suns were not going to make the playoffs and, this would be Dan Majerle's last hurrah.

Such was their admiration for "Thunder Dan" that his teammates, in spite of the disappointing season, were determined to have Majerle's career end on an upbeat note. Stephon Marbury, at the behest of every player on the roster, presented the case to the coaching staff. The team wanted Majerle to start the season finale, at home, against Dallas. Coach Frank Johnson agreed immediately. It would be Majerle's first start of the year.

To honor their guy, Suns players came out that night wearing armbands and headbands emblazoned with the number "9." The game was a sellout of 19,023, one of only five capacity crowds that season. Phoenix fans didn't forget the player Majerle had been, and they cheered every time he touched the ball that night.

Majerle didn't disappoint them, hitting a couple of early three-pointers that caused the hyped-up crowd to erupt into cheers that literally shook the rafters. Majerle now had 799 three-pointers as a Sun, the best in team history and everyone in the building knew it.

But in spite of the emotion, the nostalgia and the enthusiasm rampant in the arena that night, as the fourth quarter ticked away, Dan was clearly gassed. Everyone, especially his teammates, wanted him to go out on a high note and make that last shot, but they were running out of time.

2 WACKO!

"THUNDER" DAN MAJERLE

The fans began to chant, "MAR-LEE...MAR-LEE..." Dan fired up a three. Missed. Another. Missed. Bo Outlaw flew over the front row of seats to save a ball from going out of bounds and give Majerle another shot. Dan lined it up and fired. Missed again!

Coach Frank Johnson had seen enough. He started to look down his bench for a substitute, but he was stopped by someone who yelled at him from behind the Suns bench.

"Don't you DARE take him out!" shouted Georgia West, better known in Suns circles, as Kevin Johnson's mom.

Coach Johnson, respectfully nodded to her and returned to his seat without making any substitutions.

A timeout was called. During the break, Dallas coach Donnie Nelson came over and whispered something to Majerle.

> **Keep shooting! One of 'em is gonna' fall!**
>
> —Stephon Marbury

Play resumed. Marbury set up Dan for a wide-open three. Missed. By this time, the crowd contorted with body English on every Majerle shot and they groaned with every miss.

Marbury exhorted Majerle, "Keep shooting! One of 'em is gonna' fall!"

Dan was tired, frustrated and was simply running out of adrenaline. After seven straight misses, he launched another three-point prayer from about 28 feet. It hit the backboard first, banked downward and clanged around the rim several times, before bouncing straight up in the air. Mercifully, the ball dropped down and right through the hoop! The sellout crowd exploded, as much from relief as excitement.

Seconds later, as Majerle retreated on defense, he stopped at the center court jump circle, dropped down and did a couple quick push-ups. Perhaps he did it in celebration, or maybe it was just to prove to himself that he still had a little gas left in the tank.

After the game, a reporter asked Majerle what Donnie Nelson had said to him before that last shot found its mark.

Majerle related that Nelson told him, "If you can't score on Wing Wang (actually, the Dallas defender's name was Wang Zhizhi), you need to retire anyway."

Majerle's response to Nelson was, "You are so right. That's exactly why I AM retiring!"

Regarding his final, three-pointer as a Sun, an exhausted Majerle said afterwards, "I just hoped that one up there and, my hopes were answered."

Dan finished the game with 10 points, eight rebounds, two steals and two assists. Not a bad line for a guy who was headed to the "bone yard." The Suns won the game, 89-76.

After a career that spanned 14 seasons and 1,118 NBA games, "Thunder Dan" walked off the floor that night to a standing ovation that was… well, "thunderous."

On his final night, although, unfortunately, it wasn't "for the championship," Majerle did what every kid must do before they leave the gym or walk off the playground. He made his last shot.

STILL GOT IT

His playing days were long over, but in 2007, Majerle would continue to amaze fans with his shooting. Dan was working as a color commentator with the Suns television broadcast team prior to the second game in a Suns-Lakers playoff series. The TV crew had set a couple of chairs in front of the press table, near center court. Majerle stood by, wearing street shoes, a suit and tie.

The teams had yet to take the floor for warm-ups and there were only a few hundred fans and arena personnel milling about the stands. A basketball rolled over to Majerle, who scooped it up at half court and, in one motion, heaved it, underhand, toward the arena's south basket. Swish! The handful of fans who were there early went absolutely nuts!

Knowing he was hot, Marjerle grabbed another basketball, sat down in one of the TV chairs with his back to the arena's north basket. From a sitting position at center court, he launched a blind, backwards, one-handed, 45-foot shot. Another clean swish! Amazing!

Check it out on YouTube. He's still got it.

Echoes From the Purple Palace

FROM THE WACKO! FILE: WE GET LETTERS

I have a bundle of these letters, at least 20 of 'em. All of them were scribbled on the *outside* of a standard, business-sized envelope, completely covering the front and back. One day, Suns Community Relations legend Chris Mallory remarked, "Hey, Tom, I think there is something *inside* this envelope!"

So, with the 2001 anthrax scare in the back of our minds, we took a chance and carefully sliced open the envelope. Chris was correct. Inside the envelope there was a carefully folded, 8½-by-11 inch, standard piece of white stationery, but it was completely blank.

H-m-m-m-m... wacko? I'll let you be the judge.

WE WRITE LETTERS

Author's Note: As free-agency took hold in the NBA, just for fun, we once banged out a hypothetical letter from Jerry Colangelo to a hypothetical free-agent. Here it is:

Dear Overpriced Free-Agent,

Why Phoenix?

When Phoenix applied for an NBA franchise back in the late 1960s, the idea was met with skepticism. Many thought that Phoenix was too hot, too small and too far away for pro basketball.

So why would I give up a promising career with the Chicago Bulls to move to Phoenix at age 28 to become the general manager of an NBA expansion team? I guess the best answer to that is "opportunity." Not far behind is the fact that I put more trust in my own ability than in the opinions of critics.

The result? Thirty-six years later, the Phoenix Suns have become one of the most respected franchises in the NBA, in one of the fastest-growing markets in the country. We now play in the "new" America West Arena, offering the absolute best in training and practice facilities.

The Suns franchise has collected its share of NBA honors including, Rookie, Coach, Sixth Man, Comeback Player and Executive of the Year, in addition to numerous All-Star and All-NBA accolades.

On the NBA's all-time list of top franchises the Suns are seventh with a .542 winning percentage. Off the court, the Suns have a relationship with the local community that is second-to-none. Since its inception, in 1987, our team foundation, Phoenix Suns Charities, has donated more than $5 million to benefit children's charities, education and family programs.

From this impressive resume, there is only one thing missing... an NBA championship.

I suggest to you that the key factors that motivated me to come to Phoenix are the same for you today... opportunity and confidence in your own ability to make a difference.

I hope you enjoy paging through our historical information and learning more about the Phoenix Suns. I also hope you will consider Phoenix as your next NBA destination.

Sincerely,

Jerry Colangelo

Jerry Colangelo

A MAN OF LETTERS

Author's Note: Community support comes in many forms. Here's a letter I wrote for J.C. when the Anti-Defamation League was honoring NBA referee Tommy Nunez, who grew up in the Phoenix barrio and through his deeds, never left. That's followed by another letter I wrote for Colangelo as the United Negro College Fund honored Connie Hawkins. Both letters offer insight on how the Suns organization respected its former players and its relationship with NBA referees.

Honored guests of the ADL:

Imagine if you will, that your job requires you to be away from your family for the better part of six months a year.

Imagine that while you are on the job, every one of your many decisions must be made in the blink of an eye and in front of a crowd of people with their emotions on edge.

Imagine that every one of your split-second judgments is then reviewed in slow motion and picked apart by self-styled experts.

2 WACKO!

Imagine that if you ever get it "wrong," you will have each of the following publicly ridiculed: your intelligence, your judgment, your physique, your eyesight and even your heritage.

If you can imagine all that, then you've imagined a little slice of what it is like to be an NBA referee and what Tommy Nunez has endured for the past 30 years.

Even though he has officiated over 2,000 NBA games in his career, those who judge Tommy Nunez only as an NBA referee, simply do not know this man.

He is a loving husband to Mary Ann. He is a committed father to Donnie, Tommy junior and Colleen. To his fellow referees he is a loyal team player. To thousands of Hispanic children and young adults, along with countless other "less-chance" kids, he is nothing short of a hero. Tommy is the only Mexican-American official in professional sports, but that's not why he is a hero and a role model to these kids.

Tommy is living proof that a troubled kid from the hot, dusty streets of Phoenix, can grow up, be successful and make a difference in this world. Kids look up to him just for making it out of the old neighborhood, but Tommy didn't really leave. He has never forgotten his roots or how tough it was to be a kid. He has stayed connected to his heritage and he gives back constantly to his neighborhood and the surrounding community.

Everything Tommy Nunez does is for kids: youth basketball tournaments, mentoring, raising money for scholarships, summer jobs for youth, motivation for kids in dropout prevention programs, working with at-risk kids, not to mention raising awareness and assistance for the needs of migrant children. His constant reward is to see the happy looks on the faces of the children he has helped.

True leaders make a difference. The true measure of Tommy Nunez is the positive impact he has made on the lives of thousands of kids.

Imagine if we had a community full of men like Tommy Nunez.

Imagine the hope that could be generated… the good that could be accomplished.

Imagine the thousands of smiles on kids' faces.

Just imagine.

Sincerely,

Jerry Colangelo

Jerry Colangelo

A TRIBUTE TO CONNIE HAWKINS

"Hawk"... His nickname evokes images of soaring beauty and graceful flight and Connie Hawkins' game was every bit of that.

Tonight, we come together to support the efforts of UNCF and to honor a man who is truly one of basketball's legends.

It has been my privilege (and in some cases, my frustration) to be involved with Connie Hawkins' basketball career for nearly 30 years. As the Suns' general manager in 1969, I signed him to his first NBA contract. I coached him in the early '70s and then traded him away in 1973. In 1976 we retired his number 42 and in 1992, I brought him back to Phoenix to join our community relations staff where he continues to do great work.

During his seasons in a Suns uniform, Connie was nothing less than spectacular. But there are many who believe that his most sensational swoops to the hoop came long before he joined the NBA. He consistently dazzled fans during his years with the American Basketball Association, the Harlem Globetrotters, at Boys High in Brooklyn and on the playgrounds of New York City. It's just a shame that Connie's career pre-dated video tape and ESPN's "Play of the Day."

The limited amount of film archived on Connie from those early days just teases us with the amazing skill he displayed on the basketball court ...or while operating several feet above it. Those of us who saw him play in person must now explain to a younger generation that, for incredible, gravity-defying moves, Connie Hawkins was the Michael Jordan or the Julius "Dr. J" Erving of his day.

2 WACKO!

In 1992 Connie Hawkins was voted basketball's highest honor, enshrinement in the Basketball Hall of Fame in Springfield, Massachusetts. That only validated what we in Phoenix already knew about the legendary Connie Hawkins.

Sincerely yours,

Jerry Colangelo

FROM THE WACKO! FILE:
JUST ONE MORE THING

In addition to the community contributions of Phoenix Suns Charities, the Suns franchise consistently tried to help those less fortunate, around the state of Arizona.

During a typical season, the Suns donate thousands of tickets to community centers, charity auctions, families in need, youth and Scouting groups.

So, when we received a ticket request from the family of an elderly woman in Flagstaff, of course we wanted to help, within reason.

The lady was a big Suns fan who wanted to meet the players, tour the arena and see a game. But she could not afford it.

"How many tickets will you need?" I asked, knowing that the usual request was for two or four tickets.

"Do you think you could possibly see your way clear to make that 10 tickets?" her son, Earl, asked.

"Of course!" I responded.

"Oh yeah and, at the arena," Earl added, "we might have to ask for some accommodation for special needs, you know, like wheelchair seating."

"Not a problem." I said, wondering where we were going next.

"Uh, and since we'll be coming down from Flagstaff and staying overnight," Earl said, "Do you think you could get us 10 free passes to the Phoenix Zoo or maybe the Wildlife World Zoo?"

"Let me see what I can do," I responded while thinking that I'd better start writing this stuff down.

Earl continued, "Oh, I also want to ask, do you or the Suns have an arrangement with any of the hotels in Phoenix where they might be willing to put us up for free?"

"I'm not sure about that one," I said, "But let me make a couple of calls."

But when Earl said that he had "just one more thing," I couldn't help but think how much he reminded me of the old Peter Falk character on the TV series, "Columbo."

"Do you think you could help out with some sort of round-trip transportation, a van maybe, to get the 10 of us down there and back?"

I was beginning to think that somebody was putting me on, but I continued to write everything down.

Let's see… free game tickets, free lodging, free transportation, free admission to other attractions in the Valley, not to mention, meeting Suns players, getting autographs and a VIP tour of the arena.

I carefully avoided a discussion about a food allowance. I was afraid that Earl would ask for the standard NBA per diem for all 10 members of the family, at $121 each, per day!

Regardless, the price of being a nice guy was going up rapidly.

I was saved when the ONLY game that would work with their schedules was a crucial, Lakers-Suns showdown coming up in less than a week. The game was already a complete sellout. It would be impossible to find a few, single tickets scattered throughout the building, much less 10 tickets together.

I'm afraid that, ultimately, the trip didn't work out for Earl and the clan, and they had to enjoy the game on TV in Flagstaff. But they certainly were not shy about asking for "just one more thing."

I didn't dare ask him if he had a big screen TV to watch the game.

SPECIAL DELIVERY FOR J.C.

Reportage of the ever-escalating, multi-million dollar NBA player salaries and team finances, makes it appear to many that NBA teams are virtually bottomless wells of money, which they can haul up by the bucket-full, whenever needed.

Over the years, Jerry Colangelo received requests from almost everywhere, from just about everybody, for nearly everything. The letters were essentially asking for money, but money that would be used for many worthwhile things like mortgage payments, car repairs, surgery, business start-ups, doctor bills, college tuition, extra large shoes, house additions and new teeth.

Once, about a year after building an outdoor basketball court for a local charter school, the Suns got a call that the school's bus had broken down. They thought that, since we'd paid for their court, we should also pay to have their bus fixed. I suspect that the school's curriculum did not yet include courses in logic or gratitude.

One of my all-time favorite requests was the following "form letter."

> **FROM THE WACKO! FILE:**
> **CASH / INFORMATION REQUEST FORM**
>
> **Gentlemen:**
>
> **Please consider my request for cash, benefits, or information. I am interested in the following:**
>
> *Purchasing a house, purchasing a car or repairing one, payoff student loan, credit card, and finance company, own a few businesses, buy, sell, rent real estate, poetry.*
>
> **Use the back of this form, or additional sheets of paper, if you need more space.**
>
> *Author's Postscript: The handy form went on to outline the name, address and contact information for the "applicant," as well as lines to describe their family situation, any special health circumstances, and a place to sign at the bottom.*
>
> *The amount of cash the Suns would like to contribute was left completely to our discretion.*

FROM THE BOOK OF COLANGELO

So, what do you do when you have the opportunity to work with an iconic leader like Jerry Colangelo, one of the best minds in basketball and sports management?

If you're smart, you'll be quiet, listen and learn.

It is important that we all serve as mentors and role models for others, but if you are the mentee, you have an equally important obligation to pay attention and understand what's being given to you. Those of us working for Jerry heard variations of his observations on life and sports many times before they found a more permanent home in some of his books.

Frequently, I would integrate them into the speeches that I would prepare for him (and for me). They include lessons on sports, politics, management and community leadership, all of them worth repeating and remembering. Here's a selection:

"Life is an evolution. How people respond to situations and how people recognize opportunity has a lot to do with whether or not they're going to be successful. There is no game plan."

***

"Many people sit around complaining about opportunities that others get that they don't. You have to be ready to recognize opportunity when it's there, seize it and make the most of it."

***

"I've never forgotten my roots. I have very strong moral convictions about my priorities in life: my personal faith, my family, my commitment to the community and my commitment to people who are involved with me in business and socially."

***

"In our business, image is perception and perception is reality. If your team is a winner you can do nothing wrong. If you are losing, you can do little right."

***

"I find politics distasteful. I don't like political games. And I have a short fuse as it relates to people playing political games. People in politics have a political agenda."

***

"I'm not in this business to make money. I do what I do because I love what I do. If money were what motivated me, I would sell, cash-in and go retire in the sunset somewhere."

***

"I operate at one speed. And it's not neutral. And whatever endeavor I'm in is another challenge, another game. And whatever game you're in, you play to win."

***

(On his upbringing in Chicago Heights, IL) "I truly believe I owe a great deal to the foundation I got in the old neighborhood. On Hungry Hill, people really cared about one another. I got street educated there. I learned something about values, about what it is to work at something."

***

"Where I grew up, everyone was poor and worked extremely hard. They had nothing, but shared whatever they had. I wouldn't trade my upbringing for anything."

***

"Nothing is done with a cold, ruthless hand. That's not who I am. When I have to fire a coach, I hurt, I ache. It is a gut-wrenching experience."

***

"It was our job to earn the respect and support of the community. We took something from ground zero. We developed a great franchise. We established Phoenix as a major-league market. We've put something back into the community. And our job isn't done."

***

"Because I'm always called upon to serve, I just feel like someone has to do things. I look at the world in a particular way. It's easy to take. It's not so easy to give. I'm grateful for everything I have. It's much more than I ever could have imagined."

***

"This is truly the American Dream. If it can happen to someone like me, from where I came from, it can happen to anybody. You just have to believe. You have to be willing to take risks."

***

"To me, what is more important than making this a better place in which to live, a better environment in which to do business, a better place to raise families? People either have a penchant for doing things in the community or they don't. It's as simple as that."

***

"I think there is an advantage whenever someone can grow up in a business, whatever that business may be. Not only did I grow up in basketball, but I came into it on a professional basis when it was a mom and pop operation. I was part of watching this thing explode into a multi-billion dollar industry. I caught something at the right time and rode that. I learned, made mistakes and kind of grew with the sport, grew with the league, grew with the city."

***

"There are times when I sit back and am a little bit amused that I'm still the guy from Chicago Heights who worked in the sewer department, and went to the University of Illinois with a hundred bucks in his pocket. There's no way I could have dreamed that any of this would happen."

***

"One lesson I learned, and it was a hard one, is that you never know what the future holds. So when you do get an opportunity, don't take it for granted. You might not get many shots at it.

Echoes From the Purple Palace

You may have only one."

***

Rich Dozer, former Suns CFO and former president of the Arizona Diamondbacks, put together a list of J.C.'s favorite "buzz" words and phrases. Over the years, we heard these "Colangelisms" many times:

"Go to the bathroom on your own time... Period, paragraph... Vis-à-vis... I want you to know that... Maximize... Goals and objectives... You can do that in the off-season... He's goin' good!... If you are going to play, you've got to pay... They don't make 'em like they used to... (and usually at about 6:15 p.m.) Why don't you take the rest of the day off?"

***

FROM THE WACKO! FILE: MATCHMAKER, MATCHMAKER

Perhaps one of the oddest requests to find its way into the WACKO! File was one that came from the heir to a major American fortune. We are talking about an inheritance of limitless size and permanent renewability. His letter to Colangelo was an earnest request for Jerry and his wife, Joan, to serve as "matchmakers." The inquiry arrived before Internet dating websites became commonplace.

Even though the Colangelos had never met the man, the request was for them to consider introducing him to a woman who might be a good marital match. He admitted to being a little "old fashioned," but felt that being properly introduced was the best way to meet the "right" woman.

Included with the letter was a printed, 4"x 8" card with two photos and a quote from the heir, "I am seeking a caring partner for marriage, children, and quiet family life."

> Unfortunately, one of the photo images on the card was reversed, so the t-shirt he was wearing said proudly, "lainetneciB naciremA ehT"
>
> Smooth.
>
> But when you think of it, how does a nice, quiet, principled, single guy, who just happens to have more money than God, meet the right woman? Speed-dating? Barhopping? A tail-gate party? A letter to the WACKO! File? I don't think so.

THE ORIGINAL

Author's Note: The original Suns Gorilla, Henry Rojas, is definitely not a WACKO! In 2012, more than 24 years after his final on-court performance for the Suns, he opined in a letter to the editor of The Arizona Republic, about the Suns search for a new Gorilla. Henry also shared his thoughts with the author.

"My brother called to tell me that he just read the job description the Suns had posted for their new Gorilla character. He then told me that, according to the standards the Suns laid out, I would never qualify for the job. We shared a good laugh about that.

"The Suns said they wanted to adhere to the 'standards' established by the past Suns Gorillas. When we started, there was nothing in writing, but I think as the character developed and matured, the standards emerged.

"If I were looking for someone to carry on the Gorilla mystique today, I'd want to see the following attributes:

- A knowledge, love and respect for basketball
- A sense of entertainment and comedic timing
- An enthusiasm for life and a love of people
- Improvisational and showmanship skills
- Selfless anonymity
- A talent for visual artistic expression

- Knowledge of the Gorilla character's limitations
- A drive for research and development of new ideas
- An ability to recognize and seize the moment
- A desire to be the team's best ambassador
- A sense of team play and cooperation
- A focus upon leaving a legacy of good

"The Phoenix Suns Gorilla has grown into so much more than a 'mascot.' I hope that the Suns organization will continue to recognize and respect that fact."

SPORTS AND ART

Jerry Colangelo has always been a strong supporter of the arts and cultural community and he made sure that his teams' community relations and philanthropy were also involved. The Phoenix Art Museum, Phoenix Symphony, Heard Museum, Phoenix Zoo, Desert Botanical Garden and numerous theatre groups all benefited from Colangelo's corporate and personal largess. In the book, *Faces of Arizona*, he said:

"Arts are a vital element in shaping the quality of life that helps makes a community great. Sports teams are, at times, adrenaline for community spirit but, over the long term, it is the arts that will nourish a community's soul."

***

In a 1996 letter to the editor in *The Arizona Republic*, Colangelo was taken to task by a self-appointed, citizen art-snob, who felt that if the city was forced to support a new baseball stadium, then Colangelo should donate the money to hire the musicians needed to perform the music for the upcoming Arizona Ballet performance of *The Nutcracker*. His inference was clear, to a guy like Colangelo, sports were more important than the arts.

There was an immediate reaction, but interestingly, not from sports fans. Responses came from the leaders of the Phoenix Symphony and the Orpheum Theatre Foundation.

Joan Squires, then president and CEO of the Phoenix Symphony, swiftly answered the criticism in another letter to the editor, by saying, "Like many corporate business leaders in this community, Jerry has been a consistent and long-time supporter of the arts. Several years ago, before the Phoenix Symphony had stabilized its financial infrastructure, Jerry personally stepped forward to solicit donations on our behalf. Within several hours, he had raised sufficient funds to sustain the orchestra during a difficult period.

"It is no exaggeration to say we might not exist today without his support at that time," Squires wrote.

Author's Note: That was an extremely difficult time for Colangelo as well. When he sat down to make those fund-raising calls for the Phoenix Symphony, the Suns had just lost the first two games of a five-game series in the opening round of the 1993 NBA Playoffs against the Los Angeles Lakers. J.C. raised the necessary funds to keep the symphony going. Then, the Suns roared back to win the next three games in a row on their way to an NBA Finals matchup with Michael Jordan and the Chicago Bulls.

The then-president of the Orpheum Theatre Foundation, Bob Olson, also fired back at Colangelo's critic.

"The adage 'no good deed goes unpunished' certainly is applicable to Phoenix's premier sports entrepreneur, Jerry Colangelo.

He has contributed significantly to revitalize and energize our community, especially downtown Phoenix. He has spent 20 years building a new NBA franchise team into a major contender and, after that success, devoted his team management skills to bring baseball and hockey to the Valley.

… Yes, he has profited from these ventures and deservedly so. But he has given back to the community, supporting a myriad of charitable, social, youth, and cultural organizations.

… We believe a vibrant downtown means a variety of activities – including sports, music and theatre.

Thank you, Jerry, for supporting them all."

GOOFY GIFTS

During every holiday season it was traditional for Suns executives to get together, pool their money and purchase a holiday gift for the boss, Jerry Colangelo. The annual challenge was finding a unique gift for a guy who already had pretty much everything.

The gravity inversion system was all the rage in the 1970s and one of the first Colangelo gifts I remember. It was a see-saw-like affair that allowed you lie on your back, lock your feet and ankles down onto the base of the apparatus, then stretch back, swing your feet up and hang with your head upside down, sort of bat-like. It is supposed to reduce back and neck stress as well as improve circulation.

I was relatively new to the Suns executive team at that time, but I remember watching Bob Machen try to explain to Jerry how the gizmo worked. Colangelo just looked at him as though Machen's personal marble supply had suddenly gone missing.

"You want me to hang upside down on THAT?" J.C. asked incredulously.

It wasn't long before the inverted gravity machine was hanging upside down in the Colangelo garage. Fortunately, Machen was not strapped onto it.

Another gift that enjoyed a much better fate was the accordion. As a kid in Chicago Heights, Jerry took accordion lessons. It was a fact that he'd let slip in conversation and a note that Machen quickly filed away for future use. We all agreed that it would be a great present for Jerry but, realistically, more of a gag than a gift

Imagine our collective shock when, full of grins and giggles, we presented him with the gift. Smoothly, he lifted the accordion out of its case, pulled on the shoulder straps, slipped his left hand through the leather bass strap, flexed the bellows and started to play "O Sole Mio." It was just a few notes, but the accordion soon became a permanent part of Jerry's office décor, although I never heard him play it again.

2 WACKO!

One surprise gift came around 1990, the year that Harvey Shank discovered a supplier that offered all sorts of sports-themed telephones. Harv really liked the one that looked like a basketball with a cleverly built-in handset. It was just the thing for our resident basketball mogul. Harvey ordered the basketball phone and had it shipped.

When the phone arrived a week later, it was in a plain brown cardboard shipping box. Harvey knew what it was and, instead of unpacking it, decided to just gift wrap it and wait for the presentation to Jerry. A few days after that, we once again stood around J.C.'s desk for the annual ceremony. Jerry ripped away at Harvey's wrapping paper and then sliced open the top of the shipping box. There was a lot of packing material inside which Jerry removed before pulling out the phone. The gift was a total surprise, but nobody in the room was more surprised than Harvey.

"What the heck is this?" a baffled Colangelo asked.

JERRY COLANGELO

Echoes From the Purple Palace

It was a telephone all right, but instead of a basketball, it was a phone crafted out of a hockey goalie's mask.

Apparently there has been a mistake at the company's shipping center, or some wise-guy hockey fan who worked there, wanted to make a statement.

There were a couple of other presents we gave Jerry during the early years at the America West Arena. The first gift was a very practical, 40-foot, emergency rope ladder that Jerry could throw over the railing of his new office balcony and escape the arena in the event of fire, earthquake, hurricane, or fan protests.

Fortunately, he never had to use it. But there were times during some meetings, when we sensed an impatient J.C. was ready to grab the rope ladder and "go over the wall."

The second arena-related gift was a high-powered telescope which we gave Jerry so he could keep an eye on the mayor, who had just moved into his new, City Hall high-rise office, just a few blocks down the street.

In another year we brainstormed and came up with the idea that presidents, third-world dictators and corporate chiefs, all have their official portraits painted. Why not have one done as gift for the Suns prime mover?

Machen commissioned a well-credentialed, local portrait artist and gave him a selection of Colangelo photos from which to work. We wanted the oil portrait to be a surprise. As it turned out, it would be.

Depending on the artist, in portrait work the first priority is to capture the eyes. Our guy nailed Colangelo's eyes. The next thing to capture is the mouth, the smile. The artist got that too. Skin tone... check. Shape of the face... excellent. But the hair... oh, my gosh... the hair!

In the painting, Colangelo's hair style could only be described as a "coiffeur," one that might rival the 'do of Little Lord Fauntleroy. The hair was a golden blond color, curly, puffy and it seemed to glow, almost like a hair halo.

We all stood around J.C.'s office as the portrait was unveiled. Anxious anticipation intersected with stunned stupefaction. It was one of those awkward moments, when nobody knew exactly what to say. There were a few sideways glances, some smirks and a bit of foot shuffling, but nobody volunteered anything, until Jerry said, "Uh, thank you!"

I guess we were all a little stunned. It was that hair.

In spite of its initial reception, for years afterward, the oil painting enjoyed a special place in the hearts, and sometimes, directly in the faces, of Suns executives.

After hanging in the Suns offices for a while, the painting came down and was relegated to a storage room. But then, if you went on vacation for a couple of weeks, the painting might be hanging in your office when you returned. Open a closet and there it would be. Participate in a white elephant gift exchange during the holidays and… look out!

Close your office door for privacy and Jerry's portrait could be staring at you from the backside of the door. One morning, the painting was hanging in the men's washroom.

Every time someone swore that they "got rid of it," the painting would reappear a few weeks later. It was beginning to take on a life of its own, reminiscent of a horror film villain who refuses to die. But it was our self-inflicted nightmare and we loved it.

EPILOGUE

Author's Note: In June of 2007 Jerry Colangelo was moving away from day-to-day involvement with the Suns organization. To honor his long-time commitment to the team and to the community, a private dinner honoring him was held at the Arizona Biltmore. Hundreds of former Suns players, owners, sponsors, employees and members of the Suns family attended. We had a line-up of speakers to honor Jerry that night and I was asked to speak on behalf of all Suns employees, past and present. So, with Jerry sitting in front of the podium, about ten feet away, here's what I said:

I've had the privilege of working for the Suns and Jerry Colangelo since 1973, thirty-four years... where did they go?

And I am honored to have this opportunity to speak to you tonight.

What I'd like to do, is tell you about a letter that I wrote to Jerry Colangelo almost six years ago.

Jerry, I hope you don't mind my sharing this correspondence, but I think the letter sums up not only my feelings, but the feelings of a lot of people who are here tonight, or who have been part of the Suns organization since 1968.

The date of the letter was August 9, 2001. That was a year before Amar'e Stoudemire was drafted out of high school. It was three years before Jerry Colangelo would be elected to the Basketball Hall of Fame and almost three years before the Suns franchise would go up for sale.

I don't remember there being any deadlines or circumstances that prompted me to write it. I just remember that I needed to get my feelings down on paper and get it to Jerry. Here's the letter:

Dear Jerry,

I have started and stopped this letter to you countless times, simply not being able to find the right words.

I think that sometimes we get so busy with work and with life that we don't take the time to reach out and say "thank you" to those who have meant so much to us. That's why I'm writing this letter to you now.

A few years ago, I was lucky enough to receive mention in a book called "The 50 Coolest Jobs in Sports." The title simply confirmed what I already knew... working for you and the Suns was indeed one of the most exciting jobs in the country.

I have always believed that everything happens for a reason and that we are guided by a higher power when we make those decisions that ultimately determine our life's course. Assuming that is true, I was very lucky to have a guardian angel looking over my shoulder, because ultimately he led me to Jerry Colangelo.

I still have a copy of the letter I sent you from Tucson in the fall of 1971. You were kind enough to respond to my letter and invite me to visit you at the team offices in Phoenix. We met a few weeks later and, although I didn't know it then, that meeting would influence my personal and professional life for the next thirty years.

You helped me land my first job in Phoenix with Bill Shover at The Arizona Republic and, less than two years later, you brought me into the Suns family... your family.

First, you gave me the opportunity. Then you gave me the loyalty and support I needed, not to mention the space, to do my job. You were always willing to play along with my crazy ideas. But you also forgave my mistakes and misjudgments (which I really tried to keep to a minimum).

I remember introducing you to my father when he was visiting Phoenix a year before he passed away in 1982. You told him how happy you were to have his son as part of the organization and what a great job I was doing. Those words meant a great deal to me and I know they made my dad very proud.

When I received the NBA PR Directors' Award at the All-Star game in San Antonio, you went out of your way to come to the reception and say some very nice things on my behalf. No other team owner had ever done that for his PR guy and I was proud to have won that award for you and for the franchise.

I think of all the players, coaches, the staff and families who have been part of this great organization over the years, an organization which you created from scratch.

I think of all the time invested, the money generated, and generously contributed back to the community. I remember all the emotion we invested in this team, and all the excitement we took from it. It truly has been a labor of love.

I will be forever grateful to you for taking a chance on a young, inexperienced English major from Notre Dame, and for allowing me to play a part in this team's success.

I have been so fortunate to have actually experienced what the poet Robert Browning once wrote, "I do what many dream of, all their lives."

Through all those seasons and their many ups and downs, you have been such an incredible tower of strength, a leader with compassion for the community as well as an exemplary son, husband, father and grandfather.

Your faith, your integrity, your loyalty and your heart define you and all that you've accomplished thus far. I have no doubt that you have much more in store for us. But in the final accounting, yours will be a legacy that very few men will ever match.

Jerry, on behalf of my family... and your entire Phoenix Suns family... please allow me this opportunity to say, "thank you" for the many things that you have done for us, for this franchise, for the NBA and for this community that we all love.

Sincerely,
Tom Ambrose

In closing, I'd like to go back to the very early days of the franchise, when some Suns employees were complaining about the fact that the citizens of Phoenix were not exactly turning out in droves to support their new NBA team. Jerry Colangelo stopped them short and said, "This community owes us nothing. It's up to us to go out and earn their respect!"

And here today, almost forty years later, those are still words for all of us to live by.

> **This community owes us nothing. It's up to us to go out and earn their respect!**
> – Jerry Colangelo

And whether it was on the basketball court or in the community, Jerry, by any measure, you have earned the respect of all of us here and generations of Suns fans everywhere.

Thank you, Jerry, and Godspeed.

ACKNOWLEDGEMENTS

Many thanks to Jerry Colangelo, Bill Shover, Bob Machen, Harvey Shank, Rich Dozer, Janelle Ornelas, Tom Leander, Debra Stevens, Tom Chambers, Gregg Gant, Mike Ambrose, Dick Ambrose, A.J. Sulka, Dan Majerle, Connie Hawkins, Philip Barnett, Wayne Witt, Constance Cardone, Bob Nanberg, Dr. Craig Phelps, Thom Meaker, R. Charles Coffman, Bill King and Ruthie Dryjanski.

I am truly grateful for the assistance of JoAnn Fitzsimmons, Brian Larive, Bob Melka, John Olson, Bill Howard, Joe Proski, Rich Wolfe, Dr. Mike Kates, Julie Fie, D.C. Headley, Vince Kozar, Sherry Reed, Henry Rojas, Steve Koek, Dick Van Arsdale, Steve Rich, Chris Montgomery, Josh Greene, Neal Walk, Shelby Burgus, Pat Poulson, Dr. Paul Steingard, Jeramie McPeek, Dick Todd, Bryan Neddoff, Tom O'Malley, Bob Woolf, Ray Artigue, Vince Watson, Ted Kort, John McLaughlin, Paul Coro, Bob Young, Mike Nikolin and the volunteers at the Phoenix Police Museum.

All were contributors of research, photos, anecdotes, one-liners, inspiration, support or encouragement.

PROCEEDS

Royalties from this book project will support:

Big Brothers and Big Sisters of Central Arizona

The Phoenix Zoo

The Children's Museum of Phoenix

And other Phoenix-area charities.

TOM AMBROSE

ABOUT THE AUTHOR

Tom Ambrose is a public relations professional who spent 37 years (1973-2010) with the National Basketball Association's Phoenix Suns.

He was born and raised in New Rochelle, NY where he attended Iona Prep. He later matriculated at the University of Notre Dame, majoring in English.

He moved to Arizona in 1970 to begin his public relations career with Phoenix Newspapers, Inc. Two years later, he entered the world of sports management as public relations director for the Suns.

On a league level, Ambrose founded the NBA's Public Relations Directors Association (NBAPRDA), authored its code of ethical standards and served as the organization's first president. In 1996, the NBAPRDA honored Tom with its Tribute to Excellence Award for his contributions to the profession.

Throughout his career with the Suns, he managed the team's public relations and community relations efforts. For 20 years, he headed the team's community foundation, Phoenix Suns Charities.

Ambrose has also served as a volunteer board member for many non-profit agencies, including Big Brothers and Big Sisters, the Children's Museum of Phoenix and the Phoenix Zoo.

The Zoo honored Tom with their Oryx Award in 2012 and he was also recognized as Valley Leadership's Man of the Year in 2013 for his community involvement.

Tom lives in Phoenix with his wife, Alice. Their daughter Casey and grandson Logan also reside in the Valley of the Sun.

In 1992, Tom teamed up with Jim Brewer to co-author the commemorative book, **A Silver Anniversary Celebration of Phoenix Suns Basketball**. In 2011, Ambrose wrote and published, **Notes From the WACKO! File**, the prequel to **2 WACKO!**

RONALD LEE THOMAS

ABOUT THE ARTIST

Ronald Lee Thomas has been drawing his entire life and has been an avid Suns fan since the team first arrived in Phoenix in 1968.

A native of Crown Point, Indiana, he attended the University of New Mexico where he played football and majored in art. He honed his artistic talent at the Ray Vogue School of Commercial Art in Chicago and the Visual Arts Center of Phoenix.

Always experimenting with new artistic mediums and materials, Ron has continued his art education through workshops put on by Raleigh Kinney, Judith Spalchasky and Doris Dubose.

In 2002, Ron Thomas was named to the very exclusive fraternity of Ernest Hemingway look-alikes following the annual competition in Key West, Florida.

Ron is a proud member of the Crown Point High School Hall of Fame, Class of 1959.

His drawings and illustrations have been published in numerous books, magazines and newspapers, including *The Arizona Republic*.

He has developed his own unique style of caricatures which he calls "sportratures."

Check out Ron's work at www.sportscartoons.net. Contact him at: **occamsedge@cox.net**.

Notes from the WACKO! File and Tales from the Madhouse on McDowell is one PR man's collection of stories and oddball letters saved over a 37-year career with the NBA's Phoenix Suns. The book covers the author's personal journey and its intersection with the first quarter-century of Suns history (1968-1992). It features behind-the-scenes stories on Jerry Colangelo, Connie Hawkins, Dick Van Arsdale, the Phoenix Suns Gorilla and many others who help shape the early days of the Suns franchise. "The Madhouse on McDowell" was the nickname given to the Arizona Veterans Memorial Coliseum, where the Suns played their first 24 seasons.

WHAT THEY SAID ABOUT TOM AMBROSE'S ***Notes From the WACKO! File and Tales From the Madhouse on McDowell***:

"Notes? I just knew about those notes on the keyboard of my piano... but that was before my eyeballs wrapped around this wonderful book... Notes from the Wacko! File. WOW... what a read! After my 40 years broadcasting SUNS games, this will be under my pillow from now on. Tom... thanks for the memories."

–**Al McCoy**, Voice of the Suns

"Even considering my limited experience with basketball, this book made me smile and, at times, laugh out loud. Tom has a real flare for different levels of humor, including the very difficult genre of subtle touches that pack a punch. I think that Suns fans, who know the history, will enjoy it even more."

–**Hugh Downs**, Author and TV Personality

"WACKO! File definitely lives up to its title. Open it up to any page and you'll leave with a smile. A great read!"

–**Joe Garagiola**, TV and baseball personality

Order books and Kindle versions through:
amazon.com

INDEX OF NAMES

A

Abdul-Jabbar, Kareem... 21, 159
Adams, Alvan... 70, 253, 264
Ainge, Danny... 71,106, 111,112, 131, 138, 139, 203
Albeck, Stan... 264, 265
Alcindor, Lewis... 21, 159, 251
Allen, Lucius... 214
Ambrose, Alice... 28, 149, 150, 254
Ambrose, Casey... 13, 14, 149, 150, 288
Ambrose, Dick... 29-33, 319
Ambrose, Mike... 34, 319
Ambrose, Tom... vii, x, xx, 180, 248, 262, 278-281, 286, 320, 321
Amundson, Lou... 239, 240
Anderson, Kenny... 145
Arizin, Paul... 181
Artigue, Ray... 199, 319
Ashe, Richard... 72
Autry, Gene... 255, 286, 287

B

Bailey, Toby...148
Barber, Leon the... 264, 265
Barkley, Charles... 1, 83, 94, 95, 99, 100-114,117, 133, 134, 136, 137, 154, 182, 185, 266, 267
Barkley, Maureen...100, 113
Barnett, Philip... 319
Barry, Rick...143
Baylor, Elgin... 15, 16, 181
Beauvais, Ed... 62, 65
Bell, Raja...160, 243
Bergamo, Ron... 255
Berra, Yogi... 141
Bettman, Gary... 59
Bevans, George... 91, 92, 133
Bibby, Mike... 216
Bird, Larry... 265
Birns, Bill... 21
Blount, Corie... 201
Bogar, Charles... 255
Bol, Manute... 182, 188
Borgia, John... 20-23
Borgia, Sid... 19, 20, 22, 23
Bradley, Bill... 20
Braet, Jerry... 255
Brenly, Bob... 177
Brewer, Jim... 87
Brown, Chucky... 137, 138

Brown, James...12
Brown, Larry... 266
Browning, Robert... 315
Bruner, Jim...198
Bryant, Kobe...165, 209
Bryant, Mark...137
Burgus, Shelby... 319
Burke, Richard... 59
Bush, President George H.W. ...178, 258, 259
Bush, President George W. ...176-178
Butkus, Dick... 31
Byron, Bill... 257

C

Caan, James... 206, 207
Calhoun, Corky... 247
Caltabiano, Bob... 255
Campbell, Cloves, Jr. ...163
Cardone, Constance... 319
Cassell, Sam... 137, 138
Ceballos, Cedric... 183
Cesmat, Brad... 113, 114
Chamberlain, Wilt... 159
Chambers, Tom... 93, 94, 106, 155-158, 182, 204, 205, 237, 238, 319
Chapman, Rex...185, 201
Clay, Dwight... 190
Clinton, President William Jefferson... 100, 101
Coffman, R. Charles... 319
Colangelo, Bryan...74, 75, 95, 137, 138, 176, 190, 221, 248
Colangelo, Jerry... vii, viii x, 39, 40, 42, 46, 48, 49, 54, 56, 59, 61-63, 65-70, 74, 76, 78-80, 85, 92-94, 111, 122, 123, 129, 130, 133, 134, 137, 138, 149, 157, 158, 160, 168, 176-179, 182, 186, 187, 197-200, 209, 210, 248, 255, 256, 259, 260-262, 264, 269-271, 280, 287, 294-298, 300-305, 307-316, 319
Colangelo, Joan...63, 176
Coleman, Mark... 255
Columbus, Christopher... 122-124
Condon, John... 36
Consoli, Art... 122
Cook, Rosalind... 86
Cooper, Sally... 255
Coro, Paul... 319
Cosby, Bill... 4
Costello, Ron... 122, 124
Counts, Mel... 247
Cousy, Bob... 181
Coviello, Andy... 71
Crow, Michael... 176
Cruise, Tom... 270
Crystal, Billy... 111, 112
Curtis, Mike... 31
Cussler, Clive... 285

D

D'Antoni, Mike... 139, 182, 219-224, 226, 241
Davis, Walter... 157, 189
Dawkins, Darryl... 159, 160
Diaw, Boris... 224, 246
Dillard, Linda... 256
Doneghy, Tim... 208, 209
Downs, Hugh... 325
Dozer, Rich... 40, 63, 80-82, 117, 126, 127, 180, 255, 256, 305, 319
Dragic, Goran... 240
Dryjanski, Ruthie... 319

Dudley, Jared... 240
Duncan, Tim... 246
Dunn, Dan... 237, 238
Duva, Jack... 122

E
Elliot, Win... 35, 36
Embry, Wayne...168
Erickson, Keith... 247
Erving, Julius... 4, 173, 297
Ewing, Patrick... 144, 145

F
Falk, Peter... 299
Fang... 71, 72
Ficker, Robin... 264-267
Fie, Julie... 103, 104, 319
Finnan, Bernie... 24
Fischer, David... 285
Fisher, Greg... 75
Fitzsimmons, Cotton... 74, 99-101, 111-113, 125, 138, 139, 155, 182, 260-262, 268, 269, 280
Fitzsimmons, JoAnn...100, 255, 319
Fratello, Mike...111
Frazier, Jim... 255
Fushek, Fr. Dale... 255

G
Gambino, Joe...157, 158
Gant, Gregg... 319
Garagiola, Joe, Jr. ... 177, 198, 255
Garagiola, Joe... 179, 270, 325
Garcia, Pete... 255
Garner, James...119
Garretson, Darell... 163, 164
Gekko, Gordon... 179, 180

Gentry, Alvin... 240-242
Gilmartin, Joe... 263
Glenn, Kenny... 119
Gluckstern, Steven... 59
Gooding, Gladys... 36
Goodrich Gail... 247, 251, 252
Gordon, Jeff... 119
Gorilla, The... 11-14, 54, 127, 128, 152, 153, 206, 224, 225, 270, 306, 307
Gould, Brad... 279, 281
Goyette, Phil... 35
Grapentine, David... 205
Greeley, Horace... 254
Green, Charles... 255
Greene, Josh... 239, 319
Griffin, Dave... 205
Gugliotta, Tom... 202
Gwynn, Tony... 113, 114

H
Hallmark, Michael... 58, 211, 213
Hardaway, Anfernee... 153, 154
Harris, Rob... 117
Hattrick, Tim... 189
Hawkins, Connie... 11, 157, 165-173, 183, 247, 297, 298, 319
Headley, D.C. ... 319
Heard, Garfield... 53, 253
Hooper, Dana... 215
Hornacek, Jeff... 99, 160, 255
Hornacek, Stacy... 160
Horry, Robert... 137-139, 226, 245
Howard, Bill... 7, 319
Hughes, Mark... 255
Huhn, Bob... 37

Hunter, Lindsey... 242
Hussein, Saddam... 9, 258
Huston, John... 90

J
Jackson, Mark... 182
Jackson, Reggie... 172
Jacobsen, Casey... 202
Jiabao, Wen...178
Johnson, Eddie... 204, 205
Johnson, Frank...108, 109, 154, 289, 291
Johnson, Gus...159
Johnson, Joe... 220
Johnson, Kevin...111, 114, 115, 136, 155, 182, 256, 291
Johnson, Paul... 62, 65, 69
Johnson, Randy... 270
Jones, Sam...181
Joplin, Janis... 243
Jordan, Michael...113, 266, 297, 308
Jude, Saint... 244
Julian, Alexander... 83, 77

K
Kates, Dr. Mike... 319
Kennedy, J. Walter... 252
Kerr, Steve... 107, 234
Kidd, Jason... 185
Killeen, Art "Zip"... 177
King, Bill... 271-273, 319
King, Dr. Martin Luther, Jr. ...153
Kissinger, Henry...178
Kleine, Joe...185, 202-204
Klotz, Marlene... 256
Knight, Phil...112, 113
Koek, Steve... 239, 240, 319
Kolbe, Kathy... 256
Kort, Ted... 319

Kozar, Vince... 319
Krahenbuhl, Sarah... 281

L
Labas, Eric... 76
LaBelle, Patti...189
Lang, Andrew... 99
Lanier, Bob... 7
Larive, Brian... 206, 319
Laurel, Marty...189
Lavidge, Bill... 255
Lavin, Ira... 255
Lawrence, Don... 30
Lawson, Ty... 144
Layden, Frank...128, 129
Leander, Tom... 205, 206, 319
Leonesio, Melissa... 237, 278
Lewis, Huey... 65
Long, Huey... 3
Loon, Willie D. ...189
Lopez, Barry... xv
Lynch, Eddie... 256

M
Machen, Bob... 63, 309, 311, 319
MacLeod, John... 182, 214, 253
Macy, Kyle... 152, 153
Majerle, Dan... 71, 72, 118, 119, 129-131, 182, 280, 288-292, 319
Mallory, Chris... 293
Manning, Danny...185, 217
Manning, Wayne... 256
Marbury, Stephon...154, 289, 291
Marion, Shawn...173-175, 201, 220, 227
Marshall, Penny... 224, 225
Martzke, Rudy...15, 16

Mason, Roger...144
McAvoy, Harold...19
McCoy, Al... 5, 110, 178, 186, 245, 247, 268-270, 286, 325
McIntyre, Brian... 263
McLaughlin, John... 319
McMahon, Pat... 96
McPeek, Jeramie... 319
Meaker, Thom... 87, 173, 260, 319
Melka, Bob... 319
Mickelson, Amy...196
Mickelson, Phil...196-198
Mikan, George...158, 159, 181
Miller, Oliver... 66, 124-128, 202
Miller, Reggie... 266
Mills, Armon... 255, 259
Millsaps, Bill... 29
Milne, Robin... 281
Miranda, Ernesto... 50-53
Mobley, Cuttino... 107
Montgomery, Chris... 319
Moore, Roger... 103
Moore, Sam... 189
Moreno, Arte... 177
Moreno, Ezequiel... 51
Mullen, Margaret... 48-50
Mullins, Gerald... 30

N
Naman, Marvin... 92
Nanberg, Bob... 319
Nance, Larry... 182
Nash, Steve... 104, 138, 205-209, 215, 219, 220, 221, 226, 227, 241, 243-247
Naulls, Willie... 23, 24
Neddoff, Bryan... 216, 319
Nelson, Donnie... 291, 292
Nicholson, Jack...165, 265
Niednagel, Jon...139
Nikolin, Mike... 319
Nordahl, John E. ... 286
Norman, Rolf... 255
Norton, Kelly... 280
Nunez, Tommy... 296

O
O'Brien, Jim... 168
O'Malley, Tom... 96, 210, 225, 319
O'Neal, Shaquille... 104, 160, 231, 232, 234-241, 243
Olajuwan, Hakeem... 182
Olson, Bob... 308
Olson, John... 4, 319
Ornelas, Janelle ... 319
Ostertag, Greg... 185
Ostrom, Lonnie... 256
Outlaw, Bo... 291

P
Parker, Tony... 245
Patrick, Dan... 206, 207
Pavlov, Sasha... 264
Payton, Gary... 145
Peck, Wiley... 214
Perry, Tim... 99
Person, Wesley... 118
Pettit, Bob... 181
Phelps, Dr. Craig... 319
Pitt, Dirk... 286
Podleski, Ted... 3
Porter, Terry... 241
Poulson, Pat... 319
Proski, Joe... 83, 84, 269, 319
Pulos, Mike... 3

R

Rambis, Kurt... 141, 142
Ray, Clifford... 253, 254
Reade, Duane... 214
Reed, Sherry... 319
Reed, Willis... 23, 24
Rich, Steve... 319
Richards, Stan... 13
Richardson, Quentin... 220
Richter, Les... 31
Rivera, Geraldo... 183
Robinson, Cliff... 148
Robinson, David... 112
Robinson, Leonard... 216
Rogers, Rodney... 201
Rogers, Roy... 287
Rojas, Henry... 13, 306, 307, 319
Ronstadt, Linda... 66
Russell, Bill... 159, 181
Russell, Cazzie... 20
Ruth, Babe... 247

S

Sagan, Carl... ix
Salahi, Michaele... 242
Salahi, Tareq... 242
Salazar, Ernesto... 163
Santayana, George... 143
Sarda, Michel... 286
Schayes, Danny... 124
Scott, Alvin... 252, 253
Scott, Charlie... 167
Scott, Ray... 5
Scully, Vin... 263
Selfridge, Andy... 31
Shank, Harvey... 157, 158, 196-198, 310, 319
Sharman, Bill... 181
Shing, Tang... 48, 50
Shirley, Paul... 227, 228

Shover, Bill... 187, 248, 249, 255, 280, 314, 319
Shumate, John... 54
Smyth-Wilson, Dr. Walter... 89
Smyth-Wilson, the Widow... 89
Sokol, Manny... 7
Squires, Joan... 308
Steingard, Dr. Paul... 319
Stern, David... 69, 112, 226
Stevens, Debra... 173, 175, 319
Stires, Sonny... 10, 11
Stotter, Ruth... xv
Stoudemire, Amar'e... 209, 210, 220, 222, 223, 227, 245, 246
Strait, George... 66, 69, 91
Suffolk, Lillian... 256
Sulka, A.J. ... 319
Swiat, Stefan... 239
Switlik, Mark... 54, 55, 61, 67-69
Symington, Fife... 69

T

Tabuse, Yuta... 214, 215
Taggatz, Ryan... 12
Talia, General el Duri... 9
Taszarek, Jim... 255, 259
Tegeler, Dorothy... 286
Thomas, Ronald Lee... 322, 323
Thompson, Charlie... 256
Thornstenson, T.C. ... 72
Tisdale, Wayman... 190
Todd, Dick... 319
Tognoni, George-Ann... 124
Tomjanovich, Rudy... 136
Trout, Dave... 280
Tucker, Alando... 240
Turner, Ted... 242
Twain, Mark... xv, 101, 102

V
Valle, George... 265
Van Arsdale, Dick... 78, 157, 283, 287, 319
Van Arsdale, Tom... 283
Van Gough, Vincent... 283
Vandevier, John... 256
Venjohn, Gary... 256, 257
Vitale, Dick... 23

W
Walk, Neal... 286, 287, 319
Wallace, Ben... 264
Wallace, George... 112, 113
Wallbanger, Harvey... 72, 73
Walton, Bill... 263
Wasch, George... 5
Washington, Pearl... 167
Watson, Vince... 251, 252, 319
Webber, Phil... 210
Welts, Rick... 204
West, Georgia... 291
West, Mark... 141, 142
Westphal, Paul... 118, 119, 124, 133, 139, 182, 189, 256

Westphal. Cindy... 256
White, John... 263
Whitney, Tim... v
Whittier, John Greenleaf... 137, 138
Wilcox, Mary Rose... 92
Williams, John... 288
Winfrey, Oprah... 107, 108
Witt, Wayne... 264, 265, 319
Wolf, David... 171
Wolfe, Rich... 319
Wonka, Willie... 90
Wooden, John... 159
Woodstone, Arthur... 183
Woolf, Bob... 286, 319

Y
Young, Bob... 319

Z
Zhizhi, Wang... 291
Ziegler, John... 56-59
Zinkoff, Dave... 29

Made in the USA
San Bernardino, CA
14 January 2014